Together Forever

Books by Eric Marcus

Together Forever
The Male Couple's Guide
*Making History: The Struggle for Gay and Lesbian
Equal Rights, 1945–1990*
Expect the Worst (You Won't Be Disappointed)
Is It a Choice?
Breaking the Surface (with Greg Louganis)
Why Suicide?
Icebreaker (with Rudy Galindo)

ERIC MARCUS

Together

Forever

Gay and Lesbian Couples
Share Their Secrets
for Lasting Happiness

ANCHOR BOOKS
DOUBLEDAY
New York London Toronto Sydney Auckland

AN ANCHOR BOOK
PUBLISHED BY DOUBLEDAY
a division of Random House, Inc.
1540 Broadway, New York, New York 10036

ANCHOR BOOKS, DOUBLEDAY, and the portrayal of an anchor are
trademarks of Doubleday, a division of Random House, Inc.

The Library of Congress has cataloged the hardcover edition of this book as follows:

Marcus, Eric.
Together forever: gay and lesbian couples share their secrets
for lasting happiness/Eric Marcus.
—1st Anchor Books ed.
p. cm.
1. Same-sex marriage—United States.   2. Gay male couples—United
States.   3. Lesbian couples—United States.   I. Title.
HQ76.3.U5M354   1998
306.84′8—dc21   98-9743
CIP

ISBN 0-385-48876-9
First Anchor Books Trade Paperback Edition: June 1999

1   3   5   7   9   10   8   6   4   2

Please visit my Web site at www.ERICMARCUS.com

To my H.B., for the long term.

To my H.B., for the long term.

Contents

Acknowledgments

This book would not exist without the scores of couples who volunteered to be interviewed. I am grateful to all the gay men and women who responded to my call for long-term couples, and I'm deeply indebted to the forty couples who welcomed me into their homes and their lives. Thank you all.

I am also grateful to Judith S. Wallerstein and Sandra Blakeslee, authors of *The Good Marriage: How and Why Love Lasts,* whose work provided the initial inspiration for *Together Forever.*

Many thanks to my editor, Rob McQuilkin, who came up with the idea for this book and whose enthusiasm has propelled *Together Forever* every step of the way. Thank you also to Siobhan Adcock, my editor's able assistant; and thank you as well to my new editor, Peternelle van Arsdale.

I adore my agent, Joy Harris. I couldn't hope for a better advocate. And thank you to the staff at Joy Harris Literary Agency, especially Kassandra Duane, with whom I also happen to share a birthday.

Thank you also to all the professionals who helped produce *Together Forever,* including copy editor extraordinaire Benjamin

Dreyer, cover designers Mario Pulice and Ashwini Jambotkar, book designer Randall Mize, and production manager Kim Cacho.

When I met Jennifer Finlay, my self-described "research babe," I knew I'd found a gem—but such a gem! (Jennifer was research assistant to the late Randy Shilts.) I treasure Jennifer's hard work, sense of humor, enthusiasm, and friendship. A very special thank you to Kathy Prata and Robert Melton for transcribing the hours and hours of audiotape.

Thank you to Evan Wolfson, Marriage Project Director at Lambda Legal Defense and Education Fund, who helped distribute my call for couples on the Internet.

Thank you as well to Ann Northrop, friend and adviser, for reading the manuscript and offering her sage advice.

Many people called, wrote, and e-mailed me with information about couples they thought I should interview. I'm grateful to all of you, including Linda Alband, Olivia Blumer, George Brown, Adele Franzblau, Jim Hannawalt, Richie Holland, Andrew Knox, Anne MacKay, Anita Manning, Michael Shernoff, Dave Rompa, and Lavi Soloway.

Thanks also to my friends, who never fail me when it comes to offering support, advice, or a shoulder when I need one. These include Sally Bourrie, Elinor Burkett, Dr. Stephen Frommer, Robert Getlan, Richard Hersh, Dulce Konzen, Daniel Levy, Harry Lynch, Brian McNaught, Stephen Milioti, Brett Morrow, Barbara Moulton, Phil and Debra Roselin, and Stuart Schear.

A special thank you to my family, including May Marcus, Cecilia Marcus, Elliot Stern, my beloved significant other, Barney Karpfinger, and Rachel, Ryan, and Evan, who give me much hope for the future.

INTRODUCTION

An Adventure Begins

Together Forever follows in the path of a not so long line of pioneering books that have taken an intimate look at gay couple relationships. For example, Mary Mendola wrote about this topic in *The Mendola Report: A New Look at Gay Couples,* which was published in 1980. Mendola compiled surveys from more than four hundred couples. In *American Couples,* an extensive study of several thousand couple relationships published in 1983, Philip Blumstein and Pepper Schwartz included homosexual couples along with heterosexual couples. David McWhirter and Andrew Mattison published *The Male Couple: How Relationships Develop,* their study of 156 male couples, in 1984. And in the years that followed, there have been several "how to" books published on gay and lesbian couple relationships, including my own, *The Male Couple's Guide,* and two excellent books by Betty Berzon, *Permanent Partners* and *The Intimacy Dance.*

Together Forever is, however, the first book that looks in depth at happy, long-lasting gay and lesbian couples. It was inspired by a book called *The Good Marriage: How and Why Love Lasts,* by Judith S. Wallerstein and Sandra Blakeslee, which is about happy, long-term heterosexual married couples. But unlike *The Good Marriage* and the surveys of gay relationships, *Together Forever* is not a study or a book of advice. It's an anecdotal look at how the people I interviewed live as partners in happy, long-lasting relationships, and as couples in a world that often makes them feel less than welcome.

I was drawn to this subject in no small part because I grew up in an era when enduring gay relationships were thought to be impossible. And as the veteran of a nine-year relationship that ended badly, and now a few years into a new relationship, I wanted for very personal reasons to know how it was done.

I was also interested in this subject because of the ongoing gay-marriage debate, which has led to often bitter conflict in all quarters of American society, from the political realm to the dinner table. On one side of the divide are those who believe that granting gay and lesbian people the legal right to marry will somehow destroy family life, undermining the very foundation on which families are built. On the other side are those who, like me, believe that legal marriage for same-gender couples is a constitutional right and completely irrelevant to the success of the heterosexual marriage and family. Whatever the outcome of this debate, no one has predicted that the resolution will be quick or easy.

Whether or not gay people are ultimately granted the legal right to marry, the fact remains that many gay and lesbian people are already in successful committed relationships. As I discovered, there is much to be learned from the experience of these couples, for those of us who are currently in relationships and those of us who would like to be.

In order to create a realistic portrait of relationship life, I spoke with forty self-described happy couples who have been together for at least nine years. I decided on forty couples—twenty male and twenty female—because this seemed like a large enough group from which to draw the big picture. Yet it was small enough to be manageable within the constraints of the time and space allotted.

I chose the nine-year minimum for three reasons. I thought it was important for couples to be well past the legendary seven-year itch. I also thought that if couples were still happy after nine years, the odds were they'd be happy for a long time to come. And I was influenced by Judith Wallerstein and Sandra Blakeslee, who chose nine years as the cutoff for the married heterosexual couples they interviewed.

To find the couples I needed, I first talked with friends and acquaintances. From my gay and lesbian contemporaries, the comments were almost uniformly cynical: "That'll be a short book"; *"Reader's Digest* won't need to condense it"; "A blank book?"; "You're writing a pamphlet?" I'd like to believe that these comments say more about disappointments than about hopes. From my heterosexual friends and acquaintances and from a few gay people, the response was: "Sounds interesting. I know a couple you should talk to."

Gathering the diverse group of couples I needed meant going well beyond my own limited contact network. The Internet proved the most efficient way to broadcast a request for volunteers. I posted a message that made its way across the Internet to various bulletin boards and mailboxes. The response was an avalanche of e-mails from couples volunteering to be interviewed and from people who knew of couples they thought I should meet.

In choosing which couples to interview, I kept in mind my desire for a mix of people who could tell a good story. I planned to use plenty of dialogue in the book, so good storytelling ability counted for a lot. The couples I ultimately selected have been together for nine to fifty years, with most falling in the fifteen- to thirty-year range. The eighty individuals range in age from thirty-one to eighty-six, with more than half in their thirties and forties. They come from fourteen states, including California, Connecticut, Delaware, Florida, Massachusetts, New Jersey, New York, North Carolina, Ohio, Oregon, Tennessee, Utah, Vermont, and Wisconsin. Most live in metropolitan areas—both cities and suburbs—though some live in small towns and rural areas. Most of the couples fall into the broad category of middle-class, although a handful are working-class or affluent. Thirty-four of the couples are white, two couples are black, and four are mixed-race.

One thing that all the couples seemed to have in common was their motivation for volunteering to be interviewed. They wanted to offer their stories as an example to the next generation of gay and lesbian people, to offer themselves as the kinds of role models they themselves never had. Also, they were very proud of what they'd accomplished, and they were eager to show the world, as one person put it, "what it's really like to be gay—that we live life like most people do."

I conducted all the interviews in person, with both partners at the same time, and recorded them on tape. The setting was usually the couple's living room or kitchen table, and the interviews lasted from one and a half to four hours. I almost always began by asking the partners how they met, and almost invariably ended with two questions: "What is a happy relationship?" and "Is there a secret to a happy relationship?" In between I asked a range of questions from how the partners courted each other and how they live their everyday lives to what kinds of relationships they have with their families and how they've planned for the future.

I chose to organize the book in much the same way as I conducted the interviews. I begin with how the couples first met and then proceed more or less chronologically and thematically through the life of a relationship. I end with a chapter in which the couples talk about what they consider to be a happy relationship and in which they share their not so secret secrets of what it takes to have a happy and long life together.

Not all of the forty couples I interviewed are specifically introduced and quoted in *Together Forever*. I've included quotes from thirty-one of the couples, ranging from two sentences to a dozen or more pages. And of those thirty-one couples, I've chosen to focus most closely on about a dozen couples whose experiences, it seems to me, best cover the broad range of issues I wanted to address. Still, given how much material I gathered, having to leave out so much was an enormous frustration.

The couples are identified by their first names only. Making this decision was not easy, especially since several of the couples wanted me to use their full names. They see no reason to hide who they are, and they feel that by using only their first names they'll give the impression that they're not out and proud. But the majority of the couples were uncomfortable using their full names, not because they're gay but because the information they shared about their relationships is of a very personal nature. So for the sake of consistency and because of my own concerns about any unforeseeable fallout from using full names, I have chosen to use first names only.

Eight of the couples asked me to change their names. For most of those couples, that decision was based on their concern that revealing their sexual orientation could cost them their jobs, complicate family relationships, or risk a challenge to a pending adoption.

As I traveled the country and spoke with the couples, there were, of course, many things that surprised me. This was my first opportunity to talk to a broad range of happy, long-lasting couples living in places I'd never visited, so there were bound to be surprises about the kinds of relationships these people have and how they live.

One surprise that I suppose should not have been surprising was that the internal lives the couples described were not very different from what Mary Mendola wrote about nearly two decades ago. Attitudes toward relationships in general have changed, as have attitudes toward gay people, but the kinds of everyday relationship issues the couples I interviewed have had to face are very much the same as those faced by any couple, mixed-gender or same-gender, today or twenty years ago.

But what sets these forty couples apart from many of the couples we've read about before is their success in coping with challenges and building relationships that are both satisfying and enduring. Their lives together, whether they've been a couple for one decade or five, also reflect the changing expectations gay people have about themselves and the changing attitudes of society toward homosexuality and same-gender relationships.

I've had the good fortune to travel on an adventure into the lives of forty gay and lesbian couples who have led lives both extraordinary and ordinary. I hope you enjoy the journey as much as I did.

Together Forever

ONE

Meeting

MY HEAD is filled with the remarkably engaging "how we met" stories of the forty couples I interviewed, and I wish I could tell them all: Stewart and Stanley, two nice middle-aged men who met at a bathhouse in Queens, New York. Anyda and Muriel, a lawyer and a legal secretary, who met at work in the late 1940s. Dayna and Alison, who passed each other on the street going to work for nine months before finally meeting at a Gay Pride march in Boston. Patsy and Lucy, who met while Lucy was in the seventh year of an open relationship with another woman. Nate and Danny,* who met in 1980 when Danny moved into Nate's group house outside Boston. Marjorie and Marian, dairy farmers in Vermont, who met at an Equal Rights Amendment meeting in the 1970s and fell in love at first sight. Lee and Catherine, who picked each other up at a women's bar, simply hoping for a night of hot sex. Brian and Curt,* an upper-middle-class young man from Long Island and a leather-jacket-clad East Villager, who met at a safer-sex workshop in Manhattan. Jim and Martin, who met at beauty school in Detroit in 1946 and then went off to work in Japan for the U.S.

* Not their real names.

military. Ruth and Zenobia, who met in jail, where they worked as Correction Officers, were friends for fourteen years, and then fell in love.

I loved asking the couples how they met because of what the question did to them. Whether it had been one decade or five, talking about how they met transported the couples back in time. Their memories were vivid, warm, and filled with excitement. People blushed, giggled, and laughed. They also disagreed, struggling to put together a joint picture of something for which they had very personal—and inevitably different—memories.

As I listened to their stories and, later, read through the hundreds of pages of interview transcripts, I looked for patterns, for clues. I'm still not sure I knew what I was looking for, but I asked myself: Was there anything I could learn from these couples' experiences? Was there insight to be gained as to why their serendipitous encounters led to successful relationships, while other chance meetings led to brief affairs or nothing? Do these people know something that most people don't?

Before I began the interviews, there were things about the couples that I was pretty sure I already knew. I supposed that most of them met in places other than bars, clubs, or bathhouses. After all, it's common sense—you're more likely to meet someone you can spend your life with in a setting where you share something more than a mutual physical attraction. Plus, I remembered the kind of advice I'd read in "Dear Abby" columns and heard from Dr. Ruth Westheimer on her radio show back in the early 1980s. "Join a club," Dr. Ruth would advise in her signature accent. "Do something you're interested in. That's how you'll meet a nice man or woman who's right for you!" So it was no surprise to find that most of the couples had met at work, in school, through friends, at organization meetings, in church or synagogue. However, I *was* surprised to discover that six of the couples (two female, four male) met at bars, clubs, or the baths. Apparently, it's not nearly as unlikely to meet a potential long-term partner in that kind of setting as I'd thought.

When I joined Anyda and Muriel on the cool, screened-in porch of their modest beach house, I didn't know the circumstances of their meeting. Still, I was sure their story would be captivating—because they first met during the prehistoric days of gay life, nearly a half century ago. At eighty-six and eighty-three, they were the two oldest people I spoke with. Both had been in ill health, but they graciously allowed me to probe their keen memories and consume a few precious hours of a late-summer afternoon.

ANYDA: It was just after the Second World War, in 1948, and that was a very special world. You're too young to remember it, but for people like us, who lived through the war years, it was a very chaotic period—which meant, of course, that there were exceptional opportunities, especially for women. I had just returned from Brazil, where I'd spent two years as a lawyer with the Canadian power company, and was hired by a senior partner at Covington and Burling—Dean Acheson's firm in Washington, D.C. The partner needed somebody with my knowledge of Latin America. Muriel had already been senior legal secretary in that firm since 1941.

MURIEL: Normally I would not have had any contact with Anyda, because she worked in another section. But she was one of only four women attorneys out of seventy-five, and I was involved with one of the other women lawyers.

ANYDA: I stepped into a very closely knit circle.

Their first meeting—a casual introduction in the company of a larger group of people—was uneventful, and neither has a clear memory of it, other than to recall that there were no sparks. But the second time Anyda saw Muriel, something clicked.

ANYDA: I have a very vivid recollection of standing at the window on the seventh floor, looking down. Muriel was crossing the street.

MURIEL: She's much more romantic than I am.

ANYDA: I said to myself, "That's it." I don't know what "it" was, but there was just something that was apparent to me right then— really, what Muriel has always been to me since. It was a feeling that I recognized, because more than twenty years earlier, when I was in my teens, I had had a very strong crush on a girl who was a year or so younger than I. She turned out to be a very devout Catholic, so that put an end to that. In later years I wasn't nearly sophisticated enough to go looking for someone else, but I knew something lived there inside me that needed an answer. When I saw Muriel from the window, it was just a very deep sense of recognition that something was there that you had looked for all your life. And it was there when you least expected it.

A relationship with Anyda, however, was the last thing on Muriel's mind. In addition to the relationship she was having with one of the other female lawyers, Muriel was unenthusiastically dating a man. Besides which, it wasn't yet clear to either Anyda or Muriel that the other was gay.

Martin and Jim met around the same time Anyda and Muriel did, but although they worked at the same factory, their paths didn't cross until they had both quit and returned to school. The two men are now in their mid-seventies and live in a lovingly decorated one-bedroom apartment a couple of blocks from Fort Lauderdale's white-sand beach. The former sun-worshipers used to spend every day at the ocean, but both have had bouts of skin cancer and now do their best to cover up and stay in the shade.

MARTIN: We were out of the service for about a year, living in Detroit and working on the line for the Hudson Motor Car Company. We wanted to get out of that, because it was difficult, and decided independently that we'd become beauticians. So we started to go to school, and that's where we met, in December of 1946.

JIM: Well, the first time I ever saw him, I thought he was just fantastic. He had dark brown curly hair, and he was thin. And, oh boy, to me he was simply beautiful. I'd never felt like that about anybody in my whole life. Not that I'd had much experience. I'd only been with a man once before. But I thought I would never be able to have a relationship with Marty, that it would be impossible for me to be that fortunate.

MARTIN: Of course, in those days, we did look different. He was very skinny. He weighed ninety-eight pounds. And I can't say I felt the same way about him at first. Unknowingly, though, I think I was looking for somebody to be with. I'd had affairs before, but affairs are different than being with somebody full-time. So it started out just like a straight couple would—

JIM: Friends.

MARTIN: We were friends, and we had lunch together.

JIM: I just couldn't wait to get to school to see him the next day. Always, the next day. That's the way it was. And it's been that way ever since. Only it cools down.

MARTIN: I liked him, very much. That's all I can say about it.

When Martin and Jim first met, neither was consciously looking for someone to be with for the rest of his life; this was the case with nearly all the people I interviewed. Anyda had hoped, but didn't dare imagine she would ever find someone; Muriel was otherwise, although unhappily, engaged. There is apparently a lot of truth to the old wisdom that you're most likely to meet someone when you're not looking. Still, I was surprised to find the experience to be nearly universal among the forty couples.

Stewart and Stanley *were* looking, but what they were looking for was a quick liaison. Both men had recently extricated themselves from painful relationships and were out for an evening of recreation at a neighborhood bathhouse. Stewart is now forty-four, and Stanley is fifty-three. Both are of average height and carry a little extra weight around the middle. Stanley wears glasses and has thinning hair. Stewart, except for his beard, has virtually no hair.

Stewart told his parents that he and Stanley met at New York's gay synagogue. He wasn't comfortable sharing with them the true story.

STANLEY: It was in April 1982, on a Sunday during Passover.

STEWART: I had just ended a disastrous relationship a few months before, and my mother was warning me, "You're just getting over this. Don't go out, don't go rebounding again." I'd gotten into the disastrous relationship in the first place because I was on the rebound from *another* bad relationship. And that's when I met Stanley. I wasn't out looking for a long-term relationship. It wasn't even a thought.

STANLEY: I was just getting out of a horrendous five-year relationship, so while I knew I wanted to be in another relationship—I'm not the kind of person who likes to live alone—I wasn't looking that night. I had spent the day with my son, who was seven at the time, and I dropped him off at my ex-wife's house around six-thirty. When I left there, I decided, Well, let's get on the bus and go to the sauna, because that's really the only place in the area that was even safe to go to meet anybody. I'm not a bar person. I never was, and I don't think I ever will be. So I'm in there and I'm walking around, wearing my towel, and I see Stewart sitting in one of these little booths.

STEWART: I didn't know who was standing there in the doorway, because I didn't have my contacts in or my glasses on. But we wound up spending the next hour and a half together, and then I drove him home.

STANLEY: I was really taken with Stewart's wit, his warmth. He had a lot of love to share, and I saw that and I felt that.

STEWART: My expectations were different at that moment than Stanley's. I didn't see this instantly as a relationship. But here was somebody who was willing to give me a name, stayed with me for quite a long time, then asked for a ride home and gave me a real telephone number.

STANLEY: Stewart walked me to my door, but I couldn't invite him in. I was renting a bedroom in someone else's apartment, and I'd promised this man that I wouldn't bring anybody home. I told Stewart that if he wanted to see me he could call me at work—I didn't have a home phone—or come to my apartment building and ring the buzzer and I'd come down and meet him. This was Sunday. Monday night at around nine P.M., the buzzer rings. "Who is it?" "Stewart."

STEWART: I don't know. Something felt right about seeing him again.

There were only a couple of people among those I interviewed who were indeed looking for long-term relationships at the time they met their current partners. Alison was one of them. She is in her early thirties, college-educated, attractive but not someone who would stand out in a crowd. She's relatively shy, also anxious and hyperorganized. She plays the violin, can't stand football, can't cook, and has a warm and very comfortably honest relationship with her parents, who are divorced. She and Dayna, her partner of nearly ten years, live in a modest condominium apartment in a middle-class neighborhood outside Boston.

ALISON: I just really wanted to be in a relationship. It was my first year out of college. I would go out dancing a lot with my friends, and I was definitely looking. I don't know if there were certain character-istics I was looking for other than a woman who was smart, and cute, and fun, but I really wanted to be with someone. Of course, people always say that it doesn't happen when you're looking.

Just because Alison was looking didn't necessarily mean she would recognize that special woman—not even if she passed her on the street. Dayna is a black version of Alison. Her flawless complex-ion is as richly dark as Alison's clear skin is light. They are both athletically slim and of average height. And Dayna, like Alison, is more likely to blend into a crowd than be the focus of attention. At the time they met, Dayna was twenty-five—four years older than Alison—and in the midst of a lukewarm affair when she did indeed pass Alison on the street.

DAYNA: I was seeing this woman on weekends, so I wasn't really looking at all when I first became aware of Alison. I passed her on the opposite side of the street a few days a week on my way to work. I was the only person walking in my direction. Everybody else at that time of the morning was walking the other way, to the subway station. Alison happened to be one of those people. It definitely took me a while to notice her, but I didn't really think anything of it, because you never think you're going to meet the people you pass on the street.

ALISON: I don't think I ever thought, Wow, this is someone I want to be with. Dayna was just someone I noticed. I remember wondering why she was going in the wrong direction, because the only thing at that end of the street is a large park. I didn't realize that the hospital she worked for was in the same direction. I also remember that Dayna walked with a lilt in her step. She just seemed to always be in a good mood, and she always had a smile on her face.

One day, fate intervened. Dayna had an appointment downtown and crossed paths with Alison on the subway platform.

ALISON: We definitely did a double take.

DAYNA: Something registered, but we didn't say anything. It never crossed my mind that we'd wind up together. All my other relationships were with people that I'd been friends with already or had met at college, at work, or through other friends. So the stranger-on-the-train-platform scenario just seemed too far-fetched. I never thought about it.

ALISON: And I used to have to get dressed up for my job at that time. I wore dresses a lot, so Dayna thought I was straight because of that. I also played the violin, so once a week I would carry a violin with me to work because I'd go to rehearsal afterwards. For some reason, Dayna thought that gay people don't play the violin.

DAYNA: I don't know if it was that so much. There was just something about the way Alison looked that didn't say "lesbian" to me.

Nine months after they first began noticing each other, three months after Dayna started walking to work on the same side of the street as Alison and saying hello to her each morning as they passed, fate intervened again.

ALISON: We ran into each other at Gay Pride in Boston. It was June of 1988, when everyone still used to gather in City Hall Plaza before the parade would start. I was with a friend from college, and we were milling around with thirty thousand other people, trying to figure out who we wanted to march with. And I saw Dayna. I told my friend that I needed to say hi to this person. So we walked over to Dayna, and I said, "Aren't you the person I pass on the way to work every morning?" Brilliant line.

DAYNA: I was sort of shocked, and said, "Oh, I guess so." Something equally stupid. We exchanged names, and I took off to find the friend I was supposed to meet.

ALISON: That started a period of time during which we said, "Good morning, Alison," "Good morning, Dayna." We were really making progress.

Not everyone takes nine months to exchange names with their eventual lifelong partner, but Dayna and Alison's experience of failing to instantly recognize their potential bond was typical.

Chris and Sherri were among the bare handful of couples I interviewed—two, to be exact—for whom it *was* mutual love at first sight. The forty-seven-year-old stay-at-home mom and the thirty-three-year-old registered nurse live in a high-desert community with a bucolic name that served only to intensify the overall desolation of the place once I got a firsthand look. I'd pictured a verdant oasis surrounded by soaring peaks, and there were indeed lots of mountains, but instead of the oasis I found a broad, windswept, barren valley where the only green as far as the eye could see was the small patches of continuously watered grass bordering the parking areas of gas stations and fast-food restaurants.

Chris greeted me in the driveway of her and Sherri's nondescript, low-slung, single-story house. Chris is big, masculine, and, when she doesn't smile, rather stern-looking. Her close-cropped blond hair and small blue eyes did not help soften my somewhat intimidated first impression. I quickly reminded myself that Chris and I had engaged in a very warm e-mail correspondence and that, despite appearances, this was the very same Chris from those letters. Fortunately, Chris's angelic two-year-old son, Taylor, appeared at her side, and she smiled at him. Ah, *now* I recognized Chris.

Sherri joined us outside for a tour of Taylor's personal playground, which the two women and their friends built. The bridge and castle and sand pit all made me wish I was two again. Sherri, in contrast to Chris, is not at all scary-looking. She is short and stocky, with dark brown eyes and black hair that shows a hint of silver. Chris and Sherri were introduced at a local gay bar by a mutual friend in 1983.

SHERRI: I'm really not a bar person, because I don't drink. But my date canceled on me and I didn't want to go home. I was living with my parents at the time, so I went to the bar. I didn't have anything else to do.

CHRIS: I'm not a bar person, either, but I had gone with some friends who had dragged me there. I didn't want to go, but they kept bothering me, so to shut them up I said I'd go.

SHERRI: A mutual friend introduced us. And as soon as I saw her eyes I was like a basket case. They were the most beautiful blue eyes I'd ever seen in my life. And I was definitely—

CHRIS: Taken. We were both taken, immediately. She was just somebody that I knew I wanted to spend a whole lot more time with, and get to know really well. I saw her as a potential future lover, immediately.

SHERRI: I was the same way. I'd been casually dating this woman—the one who stood me up—off and on, for about three months. And I'm the kind of person that if I'm dating somebody, I'm really monogamous. I don't float around. So I knew this was different because it was like: *Forget that one.*

CHRIS: And I was the same way. I had been dating someone casually, too. I forgot her. I was completely taken with Sherri. She was very cute, and she could carry on an intelligent conversation, which was something that I really wanted. Still, I don't remember a word we said.

SHERRI: All I can remember is that she kept harping on the age thing, that she didn't want to date anyone young again, and then she asked me how old I was. I was twenty and she was thirty-four.

CHRIS: Oh man! I couldn't believe it! Here was this really cool person, and she was *so young.* It wasn't even legal for her to be in the bar.

Sherri had no problem with Chris's age, and she figured she could convince Chris not to make an issue of the fourteen years between them. And though Sherri's age *was* initially a stumbling block for Chris, it didn't keep her from talking with Sherri well into the night.

CHRIS: We closed the bar. I've never done that, ever. And then I asked her for her phone number. She told me I could have it but I couldn't call her.

SHERRI: I didn't particularly want her calling the house and having my mother answer, because I figured that my mother would totally put her off. So she gave me *her* number and said that she was having a party the next night.

CHRIS: She told me she couldn't come, because she had another commitment. I figured it was the usual line. You know, give me the phone number, but don't call me, and I know you're having a party, but I can't be there.

SHERRI: Well, I had a date with the girlfriend I'd been seeing, but I canceled it.

CHRIS: She was one of the first people who showed up. I was shocked. Pleasantly so. She stayed until three o'clock in the morning, and I didn't introduce her to anybody. I was not going to introduce her to anybody and have them take her away before I had a chance. And so, even though people would come up to me and say, "Who's this?," I said, "Go away. I'm not telling." So we sat and chatted by ourselves the entire evening.

SHERRI: That was fine with me. I didn't want to know anybody else there. You see, the night before, at the bar, there had been another woman who was really flirting with me, a lot. And I was, like, *Go away,* because I wasn't interested. It was really amazing. People say they don't believe in love at first sight. And I do. And so does Chris. It happened. It was the thunderbolts, the cymbals, and—

CHRIS: Immediate, for both of us. Immediate.

As I said, Chris and Sherri were the exceptions. More typically, a relatively uneventful initial meeting was followed by an unfolding awareness that something special was afoot. For most of the couples I spoke to, that unfolding awareness took days or weeks, or—as in the case of Brian and Curt—several hours. The two twentysomething young professionals—Brian worked in a family business and Curt was a psychologist just starting out in private practice—met in 1987 at a safer-sex workshop sponsored by Gay Men's Health Crisis in New York City. They quickly discovered that though they both lived on the same island, they came from very different worlds.

BRIAN: We joked at the time that I got one box with *this* gay kit in it, and he had another box with *that* gay kit in it.

CURT: Mine came with Doc Marten's, a leather jacket, poppers, and Bain de Soleil suntan lotion.

BRIAN: Yeah, and my box had, like, Clinique. Mine was the pseudopreppy, perky, high-spirited gay kit. You know: nice.

Even though their paths crossed one Saturday afternoon at the same safer-sex workshop, Brian and Curt found themselves there for very different reasons.

CURT: I'd been single for about a year, following a two-year relationship. I'd been dating, and I was struggling with safer sex. I was *having* safer sex, but I was so angry at the whole thing. A friend of mine had just gone to a workshop the month before, and he said I had to go. It wasn't anything pornographic. It was just a program of exercises designed to help people talk about and have safer sex.

At the time he and Brian met, Curt was open to the possibility of a new relationship. Brian, on the other hand, assumed that long-term, committed relationships were for other people. At twenty-five, he'd dated a few men in the years since he'd come out after college and had had one four-month relationship.

BRIAN: I was not looking for a boyfriend. I just thought I'd be solo my entire life. I figured I'd go out and date people, but it wouldn't lead to anything serious because I didn't think I could ever sustain a relationship in terms of sexual intimacy. I wanted a relationship—you know, the whole fantasy of connecting with someone, sharing a life, experiencing things together, having someone to be a companion, supporting each other emotionally, financially, and physically, but I couldn't envision it for myself. When I saw gay couples walking down the street, I always thought to myself, I'll never have what they have.

My whole purpose in going to the safer-sex workshop was so I could do volunteer work for Gay Men's Health Crisis. It was a way of getting more involved with doing things in New York. So I'd gone to the GMHC office two weeks before to volunteer, and at the interview they asked me what I wanted to do. I thought education sounded good, so they told me I'd have to go to one of their workshops to see what they do. I thought I was just going to observe, but when I got there they handed me a packet of information and assigned me to a homeroom, and that's when I realized this was some kind of experimental and participatory thing.

CURT: There was a morning session with about three hundred people, and then we broke up into these homerooms of ten people each. Brian and I were in the same homeroom.

BRIAN: I didn't really notice Curt until I heard him speak. He was so young and angry, but I thought he sounded so old and wise and funny and interesting, talking about safer sex and unsafe sex. Most of the people in the room were older and they didn't seem to get me, so I didn't connect with anyone—except Curt.

CURT: Brian made some references to things from *The New York Times,* but nobody understood what he meant, because nobody read the paper. But I thought he was funny and smart. I admired his willingness to say what he was thinking and his determination to get the words out and to ask questions. I also thought he was adorable.

When that part of the workshop was over, we had to go to the gymnasium, to another exercise—this was all taking place at a high school building. And I made a calculated decision to walk next to Brian, because I wanted to talk to him.

BRIAN: We laughed a lot. That was the initial attraction for me. And he got my sense of humor immediately. It was rare for me to meet someone who understood my reference points and to connect with them on that level immediately. So from that walk to the gym, I thought, Oh, maybe I could be in a relationship.

CURT: Throughout the rest of the day, we touched base with each other during the breaks. And then at the end of the day, we stood in the lobby and talked.

BRIAN: I was trying to help clean up. They'd asked for volunteers and I volunteered, which was the reason I'd gone to GMHC in the first place.

CURT: And I probably made Brian stop helping. I know I asked him for his number.

BRIAN: I gave him my business card.

CURT: I still have it.

BRIAN: Then Curt gave me his card with his home phone number. It wasn't until we exchanged numbers that I noticed his dimples and his eyes. I thought they were cute and very handsome and sexy.

CURT: Brian had to go to a dinner party and I was going to meet some friends, so we walked together from Chelsea to the East Village. We just talked about stuff. I asked Brian about college and found out that he'd gone to Vassar. I'd always wanted to go there, but Vassar scared me, so I wound up at a small school in Indiana. I liked that he'd gone to Vassar. The whole thing was immediately comfortable; it wasn't any work. It was a sense of really being at home with someone, and I'd never had that kind of experience before. I loved it.

BRIAN: I have no recollection of what we talked about, but I also remember the sense of ease I felt when we talked—this whole synchronicity of a really nice rapport. I never had to start thinking about what I was going to say next. Even though we came from different worlds—Curt from psychotherapy and me from business— we connected immediately with a similarity of interests.

CURT: We stood on the corner of Lafayette Street and talked for a little bit more.

BRIAN: And then Curt kissed me goodbye on the cheek. I thought I was going to drop dead. A man is kissing me in public! God forbid! People are going to see that I am a homosexual and just die! But I kind of liked it, and I liked that he didn't seem to care what people thought.

CURT: I knew he was a little shy, but at the time I had no idea he reacted that way.

BRIAN: Then we went our separate ways. And as soon as I got to the dinner party, I told my friend Carol that I'd just met someone, and I was really excited, and we'd exchanged telephone numbers, and there was this possibility.

CURT: I went home and told my roommate that I'd met the person I was going to marry.

Brian and Curt were completely free to let their fantasies about a relationship together carry them away. Both were single, and neither labored in the shadow of a recently dissolved relationship. But in nearly half the couples I interviewed—four of the male couples and fourteen of the female couples—one or both of the partners were already involved in other relationships at the time they met. One man was married to a woman the first three years he was involved with the man he's now been with for more than thirty years. Ruth and Zenobia, the Correction Officers, both had boyfriends when they first fell in love. And another woman was still unhappily married to her husband when she left him to live with her new girlfriend, just a few weeks after meeting her.

Sometimes the previous attachments were casual, as was the case for Chris and Sherri, who both dropped their girlfriends within days of falling in love with each other at first sight. But others were not. At the time she met Patsy, Lucy had been with her lover for seven years and had no plans to make any major changes. What she had in mind was a roll in the hay, but the last thing Patsy wanted in the spring of 1978 was an affair with a married woman. Patsy had recently been "all but deserted" by her lover of seven years, who had left her for another woman.

PATSY: To my utter astonishment and disgust, my girlfriend went off and had an affair with somebody else. I was forty years old, and I thought this was the relationship that was going to last. I told her that having an affair was not acceptable to me, that either she had to end it or our relationship was over. About three years later, we finally stopped seeing each other. So it was a long and unpleasant time. I felt battered. I had no feelings at all about having another relationship. And that was around the time I went to City Island to see a friend and met Lucy.

LUCY: Patsy's friend lived in the attic of the house I shared with my honey, Dixie.* We had been together seven years. Seven years seems to be some sort of a magic number around here. Seven nonmonogamous years. I was famous for being—

PATSY: Your honey was monogamous. You weren't.

LUCY: Well, she always said that she didn't care what I did as long as she didn't find out about it. So that was the deal, and it was a great deal. I had so much fun, just as I'd had since I was a kid.

So Patsy's friend, who lived in the attic, who was obviously also our friend, brought this waif into my kitchen and said, "Lucy, I think you should know this woman, because she's a composer." I was a professor of music at Brooklyn College, where I'd also been head of the Voice Department for many years. And I was going to sing in the first program of music by women composers at Carnegie Recital Hall, the first time this had ever been done in New York City.

Well, I have to tell you that when Patsy came into my kitchen, she weighed 106 pounds. She was adorable, but she looked like she'd come out of a concentration camp. Too thin! I couldn't stand it. She was really very sad.

PATSY: My first impression of Lucy was that she was highly volatile, and quite noisy. When she's in a room, the room is full, which is nice, especially for a little wallflower like me. Lucy also struck me as extremely intelligent. And married.

* Not her real name.

LUCY: Patsy is hardly a wallflower. She's a lot quieter than I am, but she makes her own kind of noise. And, yes, I was married, but at that time any attractive woman who came into my life was somebody I would think of going to bed with, if the opportunity presented itself. And I thought Patsy was a very good possibility.

Sitting side by side on an overstuffed sofa in the bright and cozy living room of their nineteenth-century house, Lucy and Patsy are telling their story in very different ways. Lucy, who is a very attractive, white-haired sixty-eight-year-old, speaks with great enthusiasm, her eyes dancing, as she unfolds the tale. Patsy, who is Lucy's junior by nine years, seems more tolerantly bemused than enthusiastic, but it doesn't take much for Lucy to draw her in.

PATSY: I thought Lucy was very attractive, but I only thought of her as a potential friend. I was very interested in what she was doing musically. And, by the way, just to find somebody who was interested in classical music, *and* who was a lesbian, was in itself a miracle. We had a lot to talk about.

LUCY: After that first time, Patsy would come visiting. Sometimes she even came visiting with her former girlfriend, and—

PATSY: Excuse me. Although we were no longer sleeping together or anything, we were very emotionally entangled, and it took a long time to get rid of that. So—

LUCY: *And,* in the meantime, I knew that there was a little hanky-panky going on up in the attic, which gave me hope that Patsy wasn't quite the disinterested person that she pretended to be. She wasn't so heartbroken that she couldn't carry on a little bit, up in the attic. True?

Patsy was cornered. A smile spread across her face. "True," she answered, as the smile turned into a big grin. "Part of the recovery process."

Over and over again, I was impressed by the serendipity of the couples' meetings. Often, the couples themselves spoke of the role chance played in bringing them together. Of course, there are all kinds of factors that go into a happy, long-term relationship—enough to fill this book and plenty of others—but if you don't meet the potential long-term partner in the first place, there's nothing much to talk about.

Of all the couples, it was Nate and Danny whose meeting seemed the most fortuitous. It started with an advertisement.

NATE: It was January 1980, a year after I graduated from college, and I was living in a house near Cambridge, with two other gay men. We needed a fourth roommate, and we placed an ad in the *Gay Community News,* the local Boston gay paper.

DANNY: I was living in the Twin Cities, and I was looking to move to Boston. Well, I was looking to get away more than anything. I had come out to my parents the summer before, and it was abysmal. I come from an Orthodox Jewish background, and my mother didn't know what I was talking about. I explained, in very concrete terms, that this meant that I would probably never get married. I would probably never have children. It meant that I was attracted to men, not women, and that if I wound up with anyone in a relationship it would be a man. The whole concept was totally foreign to Mother. And the first words out of my father's mouth were "In the Bible, people like you used to be stoned to death." On the heels of that he said, "Don't tell your brothers. Don't tell anybody." And I said—I must have been pretty snappy then—that I'd taken out an ad in *The New York Times* to announce it.

So it was a very emotional time. I realized that either I would live their lives or I would live mine. I had to get out.

NATE: Danny had been living in the Twin Cities for twenty-six years. He needed some distance.

DANNY: I'd been to Boston and Cape Cod the summer before, and it seemed like a good place to move. So I placed an ad in the *Gay Community News* looking to share a place in the Boston area.

NATE: Our ad was on top of his ad.

DANNY: I don't remember top or bottom, but one was on top of the other.

NATE: I don't know why, but we didn't think to call Danny. He called us, and he talked to one of my roommates and asked about the house and what the living arrangements were. Then he talked to my other roommate, asking a lot of questions, and then both my roommates wanted me to talk to Danny, but I didn't want to because I don't like talking to strangers on the phone.

DANNY: Since he didn't get on the phone, I asked his roommate what Nate's name was. From his name I knew he was Jewish, which I found appealing. I actually wrote in my journal before I moved east that I thought it would be nice to have this roommate who was Jewish.

NATE: He wanted to take the room, sight unseen. And my roommates asked me what I thought we should do. From the way they described him, he sounded nice. I liked the fact that he was a vegetarian; the house was semi-veg at the time. So I told them, "If this guy's dumb enough to send us money, without looking at this place and without knowing us, fine, let him move in."

A few weeks later, Danny arrived in Boston. But he didn't go directly to Nate's house. He decided instead to stay for a few days with an old friend who lived in the area, and to meet his new roommates over dinner before moving in.

NATE: He brought a quiche, which was a good thing, because it was a pretty sad state of affairs around our house. I think we had some rice and beans.

DANNY: I needed to shape the place up.

NATE: And his clothes! These were the days when we all wore T-shirts and ripped-up jeans. Danny was wearing these very nice jeans with a little stripe and a top that kind of coordinated. He was a little too . . .

DANNY: . . . coordinated, with a nice hot quiche in my hands. I was presentable. The jeans weren't anything special. They were basically solid, but they had a little red-and-blue-stripe trim on the pocket that I picked up in the top, which was a horizontally ribbed turtleneck with dark red and dark blue horizontal stripes. In those days, I could wear horizontal stripes.

NATE: Despite the clothes, I thought he was cute. He had this sweet face and a cute butt.

DANNY: All the roommates were friendly to me, but Nate was sort of quiet. He was cute and he had a lot of brown curly hair. They called it his "Disco Dan 'do."

NATE: Because I had that hair-in-the-back thing going.

Nate is sitting in a plush chair in the toy-strewn family room of the house he and Danny—and their two-year-old daughter—share outside San Francisco. The "hair-in-the-back thing" is long gone, although Nate still has more than enough brown—and gray—curly hair to cover his head. And there is no hint of Danny's former far-from-the-cutting-edge, midwestern wardrobe. He and Danny are dressed casually—Nate in khakis and a light blue polo shirt, Danny in a long-sleeve button-down white cotton shirt and black jeans. "All of my original clothes are gone since Nate has taken over," Danny explains. "But last night one of our old roommates was visiting, and he and Nate were teasing me about my clothes, which they always did, and I said, 'Okay, guys, wait a second.' I went upstairs and brought down that turtleneck I wore the night we all met."

NATE: There was plenty to tease Danny about back then besides the turtleneck.
DANNY: They thought I was nerdy. All right, I'll tell. I had jeans with the faces of the presidents on them. You know, subtle. I had lots of clothes like that.
NATE: They've all been burned.
DANNY: But he didn't get the turtleneck.

Back at that first group dinner in 1980, Danny had no idea what fate lay ahead for his wardrobe. And Nate and his roommates had no idea what plans Danny was formulating for getting their free-wheeling house into shape. "It was a dump," Danny recalls. Nate can only shrug his shoulders in agreement. And while both can look back now and see that there was chemistry between the two of them from that first dinner, it would be a couple of months before they broke the cardinal house rule forbidding fraternization between roommates.

TWO

Courtship

THERE'S A PHRASE my grandmother uses to describe the years between when she first met my grandfather, in 1922, and when they married, in 1926. They were "keeping company." It was the very important time during which they got to know each other, made introductions to their parents, met each other's friends, went to Coney Island dance clubs, and attended the annual Knights of Pythias dinner at the Astor Hotel in Times Square. There was the gift of a friendship ring at six months, an engagement ring later. My grandfather, the perfect gentleman, never tried to steal more than a good-night peck on the cheek. My grandmother, I suspect, wouldn't have minded a little more passion, but she, too, knew the rules of courtship. There were girls who did "it" under the Coney Island boardwalk with boys they clearly weren't going to marry, but my grandmother wasn't that kind of girl and my grandfather wasn't a cad.

Courtship, like everything else, has been transformed in the decades since. But for most heterosexuals, at least, there's still a period of getting to know each other that precedes engagement and marriage. Sex, living together, and parenthood may possibly precede marriage, but there's no way to skip the essential period during which you get to know each other well enough to be sure that what you're involved in is more than a friendship or a casual affair, that your relationship is something special enough to take to the next, more formal, stage.

For the gay and lesbian couples I met, though there was still the essential need to get to know each other, there was never a well-defined period of courtship or as clear an end point as engagement and marriage. There were all the universal joys of courting a new love, plus the usual challenges of getting to know someone and beginning a relationship. But there were additional hurdles as well. The older couples lacked gay and lesbian role models and had to keep their relationships secret. Some of the men and women struggled with negative feelings about their sexual orientation. And others had to deal with parents who rejected both their children's homosexuality *and* their new partners.

For many of the gay and lesbian couples, there wasn't even the *expectation* of a long-term relationship. Nor was there much understanding of the rules that could help a relationship thrive. Of course, I'm not sure that the absence of expectations or rules was such a bad thing. An absence of expectations and rules is often unsettling and occasionally terrifying, but on the plus side there's a lot of freedom in having to find your own way of doing things. No two people are the same, individually or in combination, which means there's no one way of doing things that suits everyone. Not having to squeeze yourself into a predesigned box can be a relief.

Without a set road map or clear expectations—their own, or those of their friends, family, and society—the couples I spoke with were free to do what they wanted and to make their own discoveries. But certainly, those who never imagined that gay people could even have relationships would have benefited from the knowledge that it is indeed possible. And a general road map to relationship life might have helped more than a few of the couples avoid some of the early problems they faced—although with sound instincts and a healthy dose of resilience, they got through their courtships with a clearer understanding of their partners and of the kind of life they wanted together.

After hearing how each of the couples met, I was terribly curious to know how they journeyed from an initial meeting to life as a newly minted couple. More than one of the couples whose stories I've introduced had considerable challenges to overcome as they began their courtships.

Anyda, who at thirty-eight had never had an intimate relationship with anyone, didn't even know if Muriel was a lesbian. Muriel had both a girlfriend and a boyfriend, and neither she nor Anyda knew of other lesbians who were in marriagelike relationships.

ANYDA: I'm of a generation where this was not discussed with anyone, except perhaps with one or two of your extremely close friends. You didn't foresee a life in which you could really settle down with another woman. Or, at least in my background, that was not possible, so I didn't look for that, but I wished for it. There's a difference. I was old enough to be rather skeptical about it coming about, but nevertheless I wanted it.

Anyda is sitting beside Muriel on the sofa that faces out from their screened-in porch as she explains that she knew clearly from her teens that she preferred women to men. As she speaks in her light southern accent, with a dignity and stature that remind me more of Eleanor Roosevelt than of anyone else, Anyda has her feet planted firmly on the ground, her back straight against the cushions, and her hands in her lap. Her hair is casually tied back in a loose chignon, and she looks out from behind glasses that hardly blunt her well-focused gaze.

ANYDA: Women always meant more to me. You know what Virginia Woolf said: "Only women stir my imagination." That's exactly the point. Of course I knew the famous characters in history who had been lesbians, and I knew that this was a phenomenon that existed. But we didn't talk about being lesbians; that was not a word we used, and I certainly never went to clubs or bars. It was not within my social background.

Muriel had far more experience with lesbian life than Anyda did. She had been in a relationship with Anyda's lawyer colleague for six years, but although Muriel was quite attached to her, the lawyer didn't think that a committed love relationship could exist between two women. In fact, she maintained relationships with several other women and encouraged Muriel to date men.

MURIEL: I suppose that for this woman, my friendship with her wasn't something terribly important one way or the other. It was just there. And I don't suppose she even really accepted the fact of lesbianism. Such a thing would have been anathema to her, so perhaps I shouldn't have been surprised when she suggested I have a relationship with a man, which is what you were supposed to do.

I haven't thought about any of this in years. But looking back, it had to have been very disillusioning to have this person I loved and who I thought loved me suggest that I go out and sleep with a man—or any other person, for that matter.

ANYDA: Muriel is a person who is wholeheartedly devoted to whatever or whoever she is involved with.

MURIEL: Nonetheless, I went along with what my friend had proposed. She got a diaphragm for me and showed me how to use it. This was sort of a trial run, to see how I liked it. I had experiences with two males, both very unsatisfactory, although I continued dating one of them.

Though Muriel felt betrayed by her girlfriend for being pushed to sleep with men, she still felt committed. And because of that commitment, it took Muriel several months to allow herself romantic thoughts about Anyda.

At this point in the interview, I found myself struggling to get Muriel and Anyda to divulge something specific about their growing feelings for each other; it was difficult even to get them to describe what they'd first found attractive about each other. Muriel acknowledged that she'd found Anyda to be "very articulate and becoming." And I learned that the two of them had frequently lunched together. Both were clearly private people, but with some effort, they elaborated.

MURIEL: It was obvious to me that Anyda was becoming very fond of me.

ANYDA: Muriel has always been very attractive to a lot of different people, so for her to see that I was attracted to her was not something unusual.

MURIEL: It was a very gradual thing that I became aware of over several months. Anyda was a sort of stalwart, a pillar, during this period when I had my girlfriend and boyfriend. I was very much confused, and Anyda was a great source of strength. There was still nothing really personal or physical between us, but the nature of Anyda's interest had become clear.

ANYDA: I'm sure I made myself clear, except that then more than now, I had a reserved attitude toward these things.

By this point it was clear to me that Anyda and Muriel weren't going to share too much more of this story. I managed to learn that the relationship reached a critical moment over Thanksgiving weekend in 1948. Anyda was living in a fancy boarding house, and Muriel had gone there to share a meal with her.

MURIEL: There were people passing up and down the corridor, and there was no privacy. I knew we could find privacy at my girlfriend's apartment, and she was traveling out west. So Anyda and I went over there.

I wanted to know what happened next, but I could tell this was not a question either of them was eager to answer. I asked if one of them finally took the other's hand. Anyda's response was firm and final: "I don't know, and I don't think we want to discuss that." But Anyda did offer an additional comment: "It seemed the natural thing."

Muriel quickly ended her relationship with her girlfriend and was suddenly unavailable to see her boyfriend, a lieutenant colonel. For Anyda, the future was clear, and she felt completely secure in her new relationship. She explained: "As far as I was concerned, there was no one in the world then but Muriel."

Not long after that Thanksgiving weekend, Muriel asked Anyda to move into the house she shared with her elderly aunt, whom she looked after. The new couple had no concern of arousing suspicion about their relationship, because it was not at all uncommon in those days for two women to live together, especially given the postwar housing shortage. As Anyda noted: "If anyone was suspicious, they kept it to themselves. This is not a subject that you would talk about in public unless you were somebody's enemy and you wanted to get them into real trouble."

Martin and Jim's half-century relationship also began as a friend-ship. They, too, didn't know of any other committed gay couples and had no role models other than heterosexual couples, but they had a far easier time than Anyda and Muriel in finding their way. It helped that both were single at the time they met. Also, their rela-tive youth, their profession as beauticians, and the greater freedom accorded their gender no doubt contributed to making things eas-ier.

At first, Martin was unaware of Jim's overwhelming crush, but his instincts led him to spend more and more time with Jim, which was how they first discovered their common ground.

MARTIN: We had the same kinds of feelings about things. We both came from very, very poor families, and our education wasn't all that good. We graduated from high school, but that's about it. My father worked in a factory all his life, and we both wanted to get away from that kind of thing. Of course, Jimmy's family was a lot different from mine.

JIM: Very different.

MARTIN: We, at least, had inside plumbing and electricity.

JIM: This was in Upper Michigan, and we had no electricity, no plumbing, a potbelly stove in the living room for heat. But when you're kids, you don't know what you don't have, and we were happy. My dad worked in the mill, in Gladstone, and didn't make much money, but we survived.

MARTIN: We both knew we didn't want to be common laborers, doing the same thing over and over, which is why we both decided to get out of the car factory and go to Virginia Farrell's beauty school.

Jim and Martin knew they weren't the only gay men at the school. They were quite sure that most of their male classmates were gay, too. But as they—and Anyda and Muriel—explained to me, in those days people didn't talk about being gay except with their very closest friends.

In the weeks after they first met in December 1946, Martin and

Jim began having lunch together more frequently; occasionally they went out to dinner. I asked if these were casual dinners or dates.

MARTIN: Oh yeah, we thought of it as dating.

JIM: Sure. That's how I knew Marty liked me. He must have, or else he wouldn't be wasting all of his time going out and always meeting me.

MARTIN: I don't know. I just wanted to be with him. Maybe that's what falling in love is. So eventually it came to a point where we really wanted to go further with it, but we didn't consummate the whole deal until April. It had been in the back of my mind for a few months by then.

JIM: Normally, I was afraid of everything, because I didn't know anything about gay life. I didn't even know there were clubs until I met Marty, and he told me about them. So we went out on April fourth, and I wouldn't go out to the clubs, so I asked Marty to come back with me to spend the night at the YMCA, which is where I was living. He was living at home. I don't know what got into me, but I was brazen. I couldn't wait any longer.

Martin had been rather subdued in his comments up to this point, and his face revealed very little. But when I asked him if he stayed over at the YMCA that night, his eyes lit up with the memory.

MARTIN: Yes, of course I did. I'll never forget it. It was a very special night.

JIM: Oh yes, it was. I'd found somebody who loved me. But unfortunately, being raised a Catholic, I had some reservations. It's what I wanted, but it took a few months for those negative feelings to go away. It wasn't easy, but it didn't take me that long to know that I was doing the right thing.

About a week after Martin stayed overnight at the Y, he brought Jim home to meet his mother. Looking back, he thinks his mother probably guessed the nature of his relationship with Jim, but it certainly wasn't something he could discuss. Nonetheless, Martin suggested to his mother that Jim come to live with them.

MARTIN: I just told her that I had a friend who lived at the Y, and that he would really like to live somewhere else. And I suggested he come and live with us. Something like that, something silly, you know? And she agreed to it.

JIM: She was a wonderful woman. We got along beautifully. Anybody could get along with her. We had a good relationship.

MARTIN: It was a small house and we shared the same room, which no one would think twice about in those days.

JIM: There was only one bed in the room.

MARTIN: One. But you know, it wasn't long after, maybe a year later, that we got twin beds. We could never sleep together, because we wouldn't leave each other alone. So there was no sleep, you know?

JIM: It was wonderful, but when you have to get up to go to work every morning, you can't be horsing around all night.

MARTIN: And so we decided that the only solution was twin beds. If we were going to have sex, we'd just get into one bed. And it's always been that way ever since.

JIM: We still have twin beds.

As it was with all the couples I interviewed, Jim and Martin's courtship did not end with their first night together, and it wasn't a flawless, happily-ever-after experience. As I was to learn, it never is. Getting used to another human being and his or her nature, needs, habits, and ways of doing things has proven to be a universal challenge across the decades. For Jim and Martin, their first big hurdle after Jim's Catholic-inspired guilt was his possessiveness.

JIM: I was very jealous of Marty in the beginning. I wanted to be with him all the time, always.

MARTIN: He didn't want me to be too close to anybody else; he was afraid I would run away with them or something. Well, I could never understand that. I couldn't understand jealousy.

JIM: I didn't want to lose him.

MARTIN: I just let him get over it, himself. I didn't try to reassure him. And he got over it, because there was no reason for him to be jealous. We never went anywhere or did anything separately— maybe if somebody died in the family and one of us had to travel to a funeral up north, but that would be our only separation.

Nearly four decades later, Chris and Sherri found themselves in a very different world than Jim and Martin or Anyda and Muriel. Though they lived in a relatively remote area, out gay and lesbian people were nothing unusual in their community, and plenty of them were coupled—both happily and unhappily. Nor was it at all unusual in this time to tell your parents that you were gay. Both Chris and Sherri had had relationship experience, and their courtship moved rather quickly once they got over their own insecurities and figured out how to work around Sherri's disapproving parents.

CHRIS: We're basically insecure people, so neither of us wanted to make the first move, and so that took forever.

SHERRI: Well, not really, because the day after the party was the first time we—

CHRIS: It was the third time we saw each other that we—

SHERRI: I went home from the party about three in the morning and came back the next day.

CHRIS: And I can't tell you anything about it, because I don't remember it, except that we stayed in bed all day.

SHERRI: But how we got there—

CHRIS: And what we did—

SHERRI: I haven't a clue how it happened, because we were both too afraid and insecure to make the first move. It must have been one of those mutual moment things, and we just carried on from there.

CHRIS: From then on we tried to see each other every day. Sherri was still going to nursing school, five days a week. And I was busy starting a day-care business.

Sherri tried to keep her new relationship with Chris a secret from her parents who she knew would not approve, so she saw Chris only briefly in the morning before school and for a short time in the afternoon before going home. When Sherri's mother found out about her daughter's previous relationship with a woman, Sherri was put under "house arrest."

SHERRI: My parents felt like they were major failures and did the whole foot-stomping, What-did-we-do-wrong?, You-need-to-see-a-psychiatrist! routine. That whole thing. I told them that this was the way it was, but I kept a low profile for a while, which let them think things had changed. When my mother found out from someone in the neighborhood that I was dating Chris, then she did that whole I-thought-you'd-outgrown-that! routine.

CHRIS: She was especially upset when she found out that Sherri was dating, to quote her, "an old, fat, poor person." I was not a happy camper about that remark. She was probably the most negative influence on the relationship, and it got worse before it got better.

SHERRI: When my mother confronted me, I said, "Yes, I'm dating Chris, and it's serious." My parents didn't talk about it a whole lot after that, but I was forbidden to stay out overnight, and they put my car on restriction.

CHRIS: She could come over, but the car couldn't come with her. They assumed that because I was "the poor person," I would eventually get tired of her, because I had to pick her up all the time.

Because of the limitations imposed by Sherri's parents and Sherri's desire to keep the peace at home, she and Chris didn't get to spend a lot of time with each other during the first several months of their relationship. But they talked a lot on the phone, which proved to be an ideal way to get better acquainted.

SHERRI: We started out talking about how we found each other interesting and that we were falling in love. I told Chris that I'd always wanted to be in a long-term relationship, that I'd always looked for the kind of person I could live with for the rest of my life. I'd been burned a couple of times in the past, but that didn't stop me from wanting it.

CHRIS: We talked about everything. You know how you sometimes talk better on the phone than you do face-to-face because the emotions don't enter into it? Well, that's how it was for us.

SHERRI: Both of us had been in relationships where we'd been taken advantage of financially.

CHRIS: I'd been in a five-year relationship with a woman who took me for everything, where I ended up with nothing but the clothes on my back. And so we were both really determined that we would get all these issues out into the air before we made a commitment. Neither of us wanted any surprises. So because of the restrictions on Sherri, we got the chance to talk it all out on the phone over several months. We talked about everything, from who would earn more money to who would clean what.

SHERRI: We set it all up before we even considered moving in together. For example, any job that smelled bad was mine. I have the stronger stomach and nose.

By the time Sherri's parents relaxed their restrictions and the two women could truly begin spending time together, they had gotten to know each other very well by discussing their wants and needs and working out the parameters of their relationship, as well as their individual responsibilities within it.

Chris and Sherri were one of the few couples I interviewed who went about their courtship in such a decidedly conscious way. They were also one of the few couples who had to labor under restricted visitation rights, which contributed in no small way to their unusual manner of building a relationship.

Stewart and Stanley were more typical, in that their courtship unfolded, moving from an unexpectedly intimate sexual encounter at a bathhouse to a live-in relationship in a matter of months. One of the hallmarks of their courtship was that they didn't talk much about what they were doing. Things sort of just happened.

STANLEY: After a while, I was spending more time here than in my own apartment. Before we knew it, I went from sleeping over a couple of times a week to three or four times a week.

STEWART: So it was only a few weeks before we had a key made. We didn't say anything. There was no discussion. It was just more convenient to give him a key, or at least I thought it was.

In that early stage of the relationship, one day after work I decided not to go home. I went into Manhattan, or whatever. So I come home really late and he's furious at me, because he's here waiting for me to come home. But we hadn't arranged anything. But I had given him a key, so I should have realized.

STANLEY: I was concerned. I had a feeling . . . knowing that he got through with work at four o'clock, or whatever, and he came home at eleven-thirty, or whatever. I realized that he was out carousing, or whatever. So when he walked in I asked him where he'd been.

STEWART: I was angry. There was no phone call to say he was going to be here. But I don't think it lasted that long, and we went from there.

It was only a couple of months into the relationship that Stewart's family noticed that something was different. They didn't know about Stanley, but something, clearly, had changed.

STEWART: I went to my brother's graduation from law school down in Florida. The only thing they noticed was that everything was nicely folded in my luggage and that I couldn't refold it when it was time to leave.

STANLEY: I'm thirty-five years in men's retail. So I not only packed, but I picked out everything he wore.

STEWART: My mother couldn't figure out how everything got into the luggage and nothing would go back in. I can tell you that it was very easy getting used to having someone pick out my clothes and pack for me, but in Florida I was on my own.

STANLEY: I stayed with Stewart's cat while he was in Florida, and when he came back, we decided to make it official and move in. The discussion was limited to Stewart saying to me at one point, "You give them a hundred dollars a week and you're not staying there most nights and you're not happy there. Move in with me and give me x dollars . . ."

STEWART: He was spending so much time here anyway. And we were obviously comfortable with each other and compatible enough, despite our differences, to take the big leap.

STANLEY: It seemed right. I felt so comfortable with him. I trusted him. I knew that he loved me.

STEWART: I sure didn't say it. I'm not good at that.

STANLEY: The word "love" doesn't come out too often, but I could sense his warmth, his caring. It's very hard to explain, but I've always been a very good judge of character.

Stanley's official move-in day was set for August 1, just four months after he and Stewart first met. The only real complication was that Stewart hadn't let his parents know about Stanley. They lived only a few blocks away; Stewart saw them frequently, and he wanted Stanley to be able to answer the phone.

You could say that Stanley and Stewart's courtship just *happened,* that it unfolded without their active and conscious involvement. And this would be true to a certain extent, as it was for several of the couples. They didn't consciously think that they were going through a dating/courting ritual; what they had was a physical relationship with a strong, unspoken emotional component that compelled them to want to spend more time together. Before long, they found themselves in a committed love relationship without knowing how it had happened.

For a number of the couples, including Nate and Danny and Patsy and Lucy, the courtship was an even less conscious process than that. Shared time led to a friendship, which led to a surprisingly passionate and emotional physical experience, which awakened a deep love. Pretty heady stuff, but not always so easy to handle, as Nate and Danny were to discover in the months following Danny's move from the Twin Cities to Boston.

NATE: As soon as Danny moved in, he was busy fixing up the house. None of us were housekeepers at that time. We weren't that interested in those things. So Danny got things organized and sort of took over that part of things. I thought he was a nice person and we got along well, but I really didn't have the sense that Danny was someone I was going to be in love with, I don't think. But maybe I did and just wasn't aware of it.

Neither Nate nor Danny could quite explain what happened during Danny's first two and a half months in the house, other than Danny's concerted housekeeping and the usual interaction between two roommates. Never at a loss for words on any other subject during our conversation, both struggled to explain what was brewing in those early days but managed only a few words before their faces were overtaken by expressions of puzzlement. They *did* convey their retrospective sense that some sort of chemistry was involved from the beginning; still, neither could have predicted what would happen after a party they threw in March 1980.

DANNY: The Ides of March.
NATE: We had this big party at our house, and the four of us dressed up

like Diana Ross and the Supremes. We even did a couple of numbers.

DANNY: I wouldn't wear a dress.

NATE: He was the only one of the four of us who wouldn't wear a dress. So he wore these harem pants. We all wore black, except for our friend Michael, who was Diana. He wore the peach dress my friend Lauren wore to her prom. Lauren also did our hair and makeup. We did our own choreography and we sang along with a record. We had about 150 people, and it was a really wild time. I got really, really drunk that night.

DANNY: And I was helping you.

NATE: Right.

DANNY: You looked thirsty.

NATE: Well, see, now as we go back and look at this, he was probably giving me these pretty strong drinks, plying me with alcohol.

DANNY: It was more subtle than that. He was much looser when he drank and, therefore, more fun. I'm not sure I had anything more in mind than that.

NATE: After our party, we went on to another party. Danny and I were in the backseat of our friend's car, and Danny attacked me.

DANNY: We started making out in the back of the car.

NATE: And then we came home and spent the night together. It was very intense. I mean, something must have been going on before that for it to be so intense, even if I wasn't aware of it. But there was a problem.

DANNY: We had a very strict rule about no fraternizing between the roommates. So, for the first month, we were sneaking around.

NATE: There was this long hallway in the apartment, and all the rooms were off this hallway. We were on opposite ends of the house, and I had the bigger room and a bigger bed, so we slept in my room.

DANNY: I had a closet, which is what happens when you're the new roommate.

NATE: Danny had these puffy down-filled slippers that he brought from Minnesota, with these scratchy bottoms that would make a scuffing sound on the wooden floors as he came down the hallway at midnight, passing the others' rooms on the way to my room. And then he'd shuffle back around six A.M.

DANNY: We were young and didn't need as much sleep.

NATE: And we were in love. So we would sleep together every night and get together outside of the house for dates, thinking that we were fooling our roommates, which of course we weren't.

When Nate and Danny called a house meeting and explained what was going on, their two roommates didn't object outright, though they did express concern that the relationship would change the dynamic of the house—which, of course, it did.

Danny was very excited by his new relationship with Nate. It was the icing on the cake in a year that had already brought dramatic change to his life: a new city, a new home, a new job. At twenty-six, he felt ready for an intense, committed love relationship with another man, and he thought Nate was the one.

DANNY: He was attractive, intelligent, and Jewish, which was very important to me. My previous boyfriend wasn't Jewish, and it was difficult. It was such an important part of my upbringing that it was really hard to think about being with someone who wasn't Jewish. I'm the child of Holocaust survivors. We grew up Orthodox, speaking Yiddish, went to synagogue, kept kosher. These were all things that Nate knew about, so it was easier for me.

NATE: That part wasn't as important to me, but I was very attracted to Danny. We had a lot of fun. We got along. He was—and still is—so sweet and very giving. Back then I was the more selfish one in the relationship. I wanted what I wanted, when I wanted it. I was very young and he catered to me.

DANNY: I was not a very assertive person back then—not that I'm Mr. Assertive now—but I took on the role that I learned from my mother, which was to be a nurturer and to take care of people. I was giving, in part, out of a sincere desire to take care of Nate, but part of it was also not being in touch with my own needs and not knowing how to set limits.

NATE: So we would do what I wanted to do, go where I wanted to go, and my changing moods dictated what was going on in the relationship.

DANNY: I tended to go more with the flow. None of it really mattered to me. I was just so happy to be in a relationship with Nate.

As happy as Danny was, Nate very quickly felt scared and boxed in. He had never before been in a serious relationship, and he had been out of the closet only a few months at the time of the dress-up party.

NATE: I was very young. I hadn't had a lot of experience. I thought I was going to be having fun for a lot longer.

Danny's face looked as if it would crumble and fall to the floor. He seemed crushed at the suggestion that the start of their relationship had meant the end of youthful fun for Nate.

NATE: I didn't mean it that way. *I didn't mean it.* You know what I mean. I mean, that I was going to be footloose and fancy free, leading a single guy's life.

DANNY: He was four years younger and at a different point in his life. I know that now, but I didn't recognize that until Nate made it quite plain to me and we broke up.

NATE: I was very ambivalent. I knew I really cared about Danny, and I thought I loved him, but I was very scared and just not ready in my mind. We didn't really have the opportunity to date in a traditional way. We were living in the same house, so we spent every night together, and it was a lot of pressure.

DANNY: It was very charged and very intense. Most of that intensity was wonderful, especially the sexual energy.

NATE: This is so complicated. When I moved to Boston after college, I had certain images of what my life was going to be like and who I was going to be with. I was going to be very political and out there, and if I was involved with someone, we would share those interests. Danny was much more interested in having a home life. He was a nester. And he represented things that I was running from, especially the traditional Jewish background. I could relate to what went on in his family, because it was like he was raised by my grandmother. I didn't want that. So two months after Danny and I started sleeping together, I went off and had this fling. I went to Seabrook, New Hampshire, for one of the demonstrations against the building of a nuclear power plant there, and I got involved in a relationship with this man in my affinity group, and it continued after we got home.

Nate and Danny had never discussed whether or not they were going to be monogamous, but both had assumed they were. Nate knew he was breaking the rules of the relationship, that he was doing something illicit. Once he returned from New Hampshire, he started sneaking around.

DANNY: I could tell that something was up when he started pulling back from me. I would ask him what was going on, but at first he didn't say. Then he told me he was going to a men's conference with this man. I don't remember the specifics, but it was really devastating. Nate was someone I really cared for, and he hurt me, badly. I was a wreck. It was a really bad situation, because we were living in the same house. We stopped talking to each other, and within a few weeks I moved out.

NATE: So not only did I destroy this relationship, but I destroyed the house, too. It was a terrible mess, but I went off to the conference with this man and it was not a good trip. I knew almost right away that this new relationship wasn't going to work. And I kept thinking about Danny. It was mid-August by now, and when I got home, I called Danny and he agreed to meet me at a bar in Cambridge. I told him I was sorry, that I loved him, and I asked him for another chance.

DANNY: I told him how much he hurt me, but I didn't want to lose him again, so I basically told him what I needed from him if we were going to have a relationship. I said, "This is either with me or not, and if you ever do this again, I'm out of here. I don't care what other people do, but I can't function emotionally with someone who is partially committed or having a relationship with somebody else."

NATE: I wasn't as clear as Danny about monogamy back then, but I was in no position to negotiate. He was taking me back, and I was willing to do what he wanted to have a relationship with him.

Once they got back together, Nate and Danny maintained separate households. They spent almost every night together at one or the other's house, but some nights they spent on their own. Without the pressure of living together and courting at the same time, they were better able to get to know each other. A year later, they were sure enough of their love to consider moving together to another city when Nate was accepted to graduate school in Philadelphia.

Lucy and Patsy's relationship unfolded in a way similar to Nate and Danny's, but the complications were different. Lucy lived with her lover, from whom she didn't seem likely to detach herself, and Patsy had no intention of becoming involved with a married woman, no matter how much she and Lucy connected over their shared interest in music. So it's no surprise that things moved a little more slowly for them.

Lucy and Patsy spent the better part of two years getting to know each other. About a year into their friendship, Lucy went public with her feelings for Patsy.

LUCY: We were having my fiftieth birthday party. Dixie, my honey, did the party and cooked all southern food, which I'd requested. I had all my special friends there, about twenty in all, and Patsy came.

PATSY: I was very flattered to be included among Lucy's special friends.

LUCY: Dixie and I had recently been to California, and we'd brought back a rehearsal tape of Holly Near's forthcoming album, *Imagine My Surprise*. During the party, several of us were upstairs in Dixie's study, and I decided to play the tape for them. Dixie was probably down in the basement, smoking. By this time, we were all well oiled. We had eaten and we had drunk, and we found the music very moving, because Holly Near was right out there with being a lesbian.

PATSY: Most of us were not that out in 1979, beyond a small group of friends.

LUCY: Well, there was Patsy in this room full of people, and I took a good, long, hard look at her, and I just told Patsy that I had a terrific crush on her.

PATSY: You told everybody.

LUCY: I did, indeed.

PATSY: You didn't even address it to me. I was very embarrassed, of course. In the first place, up until Lucy made this announcement, I didn't know she *had* a crush on me. In the second place, I thought it would be very hurtful to Dixie. And in the third place, I didn't know what in the hell I was going to do about it, because we had a great time together and I had great admiration for what Lucy was doing with her music.

LUCY: I didn't mean to embarrass Patsy, but I had a crush. First of all, I loved her music, which was the common denominator. That was the magnet, the basic pull between us. We had already decided that she was going to do a song cycle for me as part of my women composers concert. So I was really excited about this woman who made the kind of music that I was just terribly turned on by. And she was a lesbian, and she was cute as a button. Now, we're talking twenty years ago, when I didn't have gray hair and wrinkles and Patsy was just adorable. So, there we are.

Do you remember the first time I sang to you?

PATSY: Of course. You were sitting on the piano bench next to me as we went through the new song I had written for you, set to the poetry of Adrienne Rich. Lucy sang a high B-flat in my ear and it just blew me away.

LUCY: My best weapon: my high notes.

PATSY: I mean, to find a singer who was actually interested in the music I was setting to the text of lesbian poets, somebody who was going to perform this music, someone who wanted me to write more, that in itself was an incredible thing, even apart from the sexual aspect. And she *was* attractive. And I had a crush on *her*. I wasn't about to say it, but I'd rather be there with her than anywhere else.

In my tight little world of WASPdom, it would never have occurred to me that Lucy would be interested in me, because she was in a relationship with somebody else. I also thought she was happy in her relationship, and although I knew by reputation that she had affairs with people, that didn't include me.

LUCY: And Patsy had so much integrity about women's relationships. I knew that. And I knew that she had made a friendship with Dixie, and Patsy made sure there was a barrier that wouldn't be crossed with too much intimacy, because that would jeopardize what she had with both of us.

PATSY: That's why I was embarrassed and confused when Lucy made her announcement, because it crossed that barrier.

LUCY: I was more blatant than I usually am, but I was not able to reel this woman in. She was a tough fish. She really was very principled, much more principled than I was.

PATSY: Well, I had this recent, desperate hurt, and I wasn't about to turn around and do that to somebody else.

Months passed. Patsy and Lucy continued to get together as friends and colleagues as Lucy prepared for her concert. During that time, not another word was spoken of the crush. It was forbidden territory. The turning point came on International Women's Day.

LUCY: The National Congress on Women In Music was having a string quartet conference, which I wanted to go to. And it turned out that Patsy was going, too. Dixie wasn't going many places with me at that point, especially on the weekends, which is when she liked to work on the house. So I told Patsy that we'd see each other at the conference, which turned out to be a dud. So we decided to go out for dinner to a Chinese restaurant on West Ninety-first Street and Broadway. And Patsy invited me back to her apartment.

PATSY: Well, three martinis later, for God's sake. And it's not like I asked her to come back to my place. I remember that we kept talking about the choices we had as far as going back to the conference and hearing different performances. And Lucy said she wanted to hear some tapes of my music at my apartment. I really thought we were going to listen to my music. That's what an innocent I am.

LUCY: I was three martinis over the loop, and I was hoping for the best. I thought it was a dandy idea, to go to her apartment, and one never knows, does one? But I have to tell you that I had pretty much given up hope. And by this time I knew that Patsy was having an affair with a mutual friend of ours, so it was getting too murky. Too many people's feelings were going to get hurt, so I was going to take my drunken self off and listen to music at Patsy's apartment. So what happened next, dear?

PATSY: We fell into bed for two days and never got out.

LUCY: No, we got up the next afternoon.

PATSY: Well, it felt like two days. But I thought it was quite extraordinary. I expected her to listen to some music and then go home, because after all, Dixie was at home.

LUCY: Poor Dixie. I never called her until later the next day. Usually I didn't stay out overnight without telling her in advance. But this was different, and it didn't take her too long to figure out that this was different than my just having a date or a roll in the hay, because Patsy and I both fell passionately in love. We fell in lust. I think that was what came first.

PATSY: That was in addition to what we already had, which was our shared love of music and a friendship.

LUCY: We have always had, and always will have, a marvelously intimate friendship. On top of this, great sex? My God, I was fifty, and Patsy was just so much fun. We had such a good time in that little bedroom, looking over the Hudson River and the meat market. Just staring out at the river, hearing the meat trucks in the morning and the garbage collectors, and here we were in this wonderful little bedroom that couldn't be cozier. I mean, the building was vibrating. It was hot stuff.

PATSY: We had a lot of sex, and we laughed, and we really had a wonderful time.

LUCY: She found a new way to get me in good vocal shape. We decided that the only way that I could sing really well is if I had all this wonderful lovemaking. My singing teacher had told me that as the concert approached I couldn't possibly have any sex. She said, "Orgasm weakens the vocal cords." About a month before the concert, I told Patsy that we had to stop, and she said it was nonsense. Patsy knew what was good for my voice.

PATSY: So despite my principles, I did exactly what I said I wouldn't. I have no hesitation in saying that it was the martinis that made it possible for me that first evening. And then it became clear to me as we talked that Lucy and Dixie did not have a working relationship.

Both Patsy and Lucy knew that this was different from what either had experienced before and different from what either could possibly have anticipated. So, despite knowing that there would be more than enough hurt feelings to go around, they began spending a couple of nights a week together as well as time on weekends, which was as much as Lucy thought she could manage without arousing Dixie's suspicion. But after several weeks, Dixie asked if Lucy was having an affair with Patsy.

LUCY: I said yes. I had always told her that if she asked me, I would tell the truth. Then she asked what I was going to do about it, and I told her I didn't know, that I was going to see a therapist about it, which was true. Dixie told me I had three months to make up my mind.

Three weeks later, Dixie said she needed an answer, that she couldn't wait any longer. Having talked once with a therapist, Lucy already knew she was going to leave Dixie for Patsy, and that's what she said.

LUCY: She told me to get my things and get out of the house. This was eleven o'clock at night. I asked her if I could have until morning, and she said, "Okay, but as soon as it gets light out, you're out of here."

The first thing Dixie did after that was to take all the heart-shaped stones that I'd collected for her over the nine years we were together and dump them outside the door of my bedroom. Then she played the Mozart Requiem, all night, over and over and over again. It was an old Victorian house. There wasn't any place I could run not to hear it. I thought I'd go mad.

At first light, I took a few of my things and packed my car. Just before I drove off, Dixie came running out of the house, and she said, "You didn't say goodbye to Albert." Our cat. I was absolutely devastated at the sweetness of that moment. I went back in with her and said goodbye to the cat, and she said, "I don't want us to be friends. I don't want to hear from you. I don't want anything. You're out of my life. And that's the way I have to deal with it." And then she took a beautiful Art Deco plate that I'd rescued from a fire in our house, that she knew I loved, handed it to me, and said, "Here, this is for you."

I got into my car and drove to Patsy's apartment, which is where I stayed until I found an apartment of my own. I wanted my own place, because despite how I felt about Patsy, I didn't know exactly how I was going to work out my life.

Some of the couples got through their courtships without nearly so much drama as Lucy and Patsy or Nate and Danny. For example, following their meeting at the 1988 Gay Pride celebration in Boston, Alison and Dayna's courtship was characterized by little more than relatively minor "should I call?, should I not call?" anxiety and anticipation as it moved into a higher—although decidedly not fast—gear.

Like many of the couples, Alison and Dayna had no expectation that their meeting would lead to anything significant. But they differed from many of the older men and women and those who grew up in less gay-friendly circumstances in that they fully expected to one day have a long-term relationship with a same-gender partner. Alison even enjoyed the support of her parents in finding the right woman.

ALISON: Both of my parents were entirely supportive, and I knew that a relationship would be the kind of thing they'd want for me, that I would find the right woman. I remember having a conversation with my mom about this. I was having problems with my roommate and was trying to decide whether to find a studio apartment, which was all I could afford at the time. My mother said, "I know what you really want. You'd like to be able to meet someone and be able to live with that person." I knew she was referring to a woman, so I knew that that was what she hoped would happen for me. It was my assumption that it would happen someday; I just didn't know when.

Even after Alison formally met Dayna and they began greeting each other on the street by name, neither made any effort to take things further. Fortunately for them, fate intervened yet again when they met up at a dance club one July night.

ALISON: I was supposed to be out on a first date, at the movies, but my date canceled at the very last minute, so I called a friend and told her how depressed I was about it, and she said, "Oh, don't just sit at home. Let's go out dancing."

DAYNA: I was out dancing with some friends who were visiting from Chicago, and Alison saw me and we wound up talking.

ALISON: I actually had a very long conversation with Dayna's friend from Chicago. Dayna stood there looking really scared.

DAYNA: I was a generally shy person. I've definitely grown out of it, I think. But even though I was very shy then, Alison and I did get to talking. At that point, I figure, Okay, I'm attracted to her. She was so cute. She seemed like a sane person. She seemed intelligent, like somebody who had a good head on her shoulders. I thought she was older than she was, closer to my age. She's very easy to talk to. It just seemed like we sort of clicked.

Dayna handed Alison an invitation to a performance of a play she'd been developing as part of a writing workshop. The play had been well received by the group, so Dayna had asked three friends to help her stage the play at her apartment.

DAYNA: We'd been rehearsing the play for a couple of months, and I happened to have an invitation with me that I was going to give to somebody else who I expected to see at the club that night. But she never showed up.

ALISON: I was going to be out of town the night of the performance, but Dayna suggested that I come for the dress rehearsal with a group of her friends who also couldn't make the performance. I told her I'd be there.

I'd never met anyone before who had written a play and just produced it with her friends. And I guess at that point I don't know if I consciously thought, Wow, I'm attracted to this person, but there were things that appealed to me about her all along that I now had a chance to see close up: her smile and the fact that she always seemed friendly and in such a good mood.

DAYNA: But I don't think I had got it that Alison was attracted to me.

ALISON: Until I gave her my number.

DAYNA: Before she left the club, she gave me her work number, her home number, and her address, all on this little piece of paper. I guess that means, *Okay, you should call.*

ALISON: Dayna still keeps that piece of paper in her wallet.

DAYNA: It's a little faded, but it's there.

ALISON: So I went to the dress rehearsal in Dayna's apartment with six or seven of her closest friends in the world, and I'm watching this play, and halfway into it one of the characters appears from the park and magically comes into the main character's life—they meet on their way to work in the same place that *we* first met. Whether it was conscious or not, I sat there thinking, Oh my God, I'm in this play! It freaked me out.

DAYNA: Everybody claims that Alison is the basis for this character. Maybe subconsciously it was, but I didn't see it.

ALISON: Despite how freaked out I was, that was the night I really got attracted to Dayna, because she created this amazing thing and actually produced it. And also, she had friends who were willing to help her create this vision, and seven people who were willing to come to the dress rehearsal at her apartment.

After the play, Alison and Dayna chatted for a bit; then Dayna walked Alison home. Alison had nothing to offer Dayna besides a glass of water, and they sat in her kitchen and talked until two in the morning. Alison remembers discussing Dayna's sisters. Dayna remembers talking about Alison's eating habits.

DAYNA: All she ate was cereal, macaroni and cheese, and hot dogs.

ALISON: I was young. I was just out of college, and I was not a cook.

DAYNA: Still not.

ALISON: So Dayna went home, and she called me a day or two later to ask me if I wanted to go out to this local pub. It was the night before I was leaving on vacation to Hawaii, and I get very stressed out before I travel. I have to make lists and pack and prepare. So I told her I couldn't go. She knows that about me now, about how panicked I get, but at that time she thought I was just making a lot of excuses.

DAYNA: I thought she was blowing me off. But then she called me during the party that I gave at my apartment following the performance of the play.

ALISON: This was after Hawaii, and I was at my dad's house in New York. I was there for a wedding, which was why I couldn't be at the play in the first place. So I called, and someone else answered the phone. I could hear her say, "Dayna, it's that Alison woman." So I knew she had told someone about me. I could tell from our conversation that she was very shocked that I'd call long-distance to see how the play had gone. So we talked. And we both knew something was going to happen.

Soon after she got back, Alison invited Dayna to attend a concert she was playing in. It wasn't really a date; several other friends were going to be there, not to mention Alison's mother. As it turned out,

Dayna couldn't make it; she was under the weather following a wisdom-tooth extraction. But once Dayna recovered sufficiently to go back to work, she decided to reveal her feelings to Alison in a profoundly sweet gesture.

ALISON: I was running really late one morning, shortly after the concert. I could always tell how on-time I was for work based on where Dayna and I passed. On this particular day, we passed almost at the subway, so I knew I was really late. Dayna had a rose in her hand, and she gave it to me. I was just speechless.

DAYNA: It was a spur-of-the-moment, romantic kind of thing for me. I tend to be a very romantic kind of person. So I took a chance. I thought, If I see her today, she's got the rose. If I don't see her today, I have a rose on my desk.

ALISON: All of my co-workers at the temp agency were straight, but they'd been following this whole thing with Dayna, and they asked me where I got the rose. I said, "Oh my God, Dayna gave it to me!"

I must have called Dayna later that day, and somehow a first date got arranged. Dayna suggested that we go for a picnic at a park in our neighborhood, which turned out to be very buggy. So we went to her apartment instead and had a picnic on the floor.

DAYNA: And we watched *Kramer vs. Kramer*.

ALISON: Not a good movie to watch on a first date. But after the movie, Dayna walked me home and we sat in my room and had a discussion about where this was going.

DAYNA: No first kiss, yet.

ALISON: Dayna said she was interested in me. And for some reason I got really scared and said that I didn't know if I was ready to be in a relationship, that I'm not good in a relationship, that the one long-term relationship I'd had in college ended very badly. I was afraid of that happening again, so I was cautioning Dayna. I panicked.

DAYNA: We didn't stay on that too long, and we talked some more about our families, and about my mom, who had died three years prior.

ALISON: By now it was three in the morning and we both had to work the next day. Dayna said she had to go. I can't believe now that I let her go.

After a quick good-night kiss at the door, Dayna walked home by herself. Despite her panic, Alison went to work the next day to tell her friends what had happened and how happy she was.

A week later, Alison went to Dayna's apartment for dinner. Both remember the date: August 15, 1988.

ALISON: After dinner we watched a movie a co-worker had suggested, *Come Back to the Five and Dime, Jimmy Dean, Jimmy Dean.*

DAYNA: We both fell asleep.

ALISON: It was such a nice, comfortable thing. I think the reason we could even lie on the couch together and fall asleep was because we just felt so comfortable together. We woke up when the movie was over, and I knew I was going to spend the night.

DAYNA: This was not a casual thing.

ALISON: The next morning we were kind of flipped out, but we both said that we thought we loved each other.

DAYNA: It wasn't the next morning, but it was soon after, maybe a couple of weeks later.

ALISON: Oh yes. I don't know who said it first, but it was something along the lines of "I can't believe I feel this already. How did this happen so fast?" And we both felt it. It's the whole lesbians-on-the-second-date-with-the-U-Haul thing. I just felt like every day when I got home from work, the only thing I wanted to do was to call Dayna and see if I could come over.

DAYNA: And that's what she did.

ALISON: We spent most of the time at Dayna's house because I had a roommate at my house. Dayna had moved to a new apartment and had the place to herself.

DAYNA: Besides, Alison's room was a mess. It was a pit.

I would never have guessed from their very neat, clean, and simply decorated apartment that Alison had been a substandard housekeeper, but both she and Dayna assured me that this was so. We're sitting at the kitchen table enjoying a dinner of grilled chicken breast, brown rice, and salad, all of which Dayna has prepared.

I ask them how they felt about each other and their future together at that early point in their relationship.

ALISON: A friend at work, a gay man, asked me how I knew Dayna was the one I wanted to spend my life with. I told him that I just felt like I was home. That's nothing specific about Dayna, but it just felt so right and so natural that I didn't even think about what specifically I loved about Dayna. I felt complete. I felt home. All those clichés.

DAYNA: I felt the same way. It just felt right.

ALISON: It maybe felt like an old married couple already.

DAYNA: Everything seemed so easy.

ALISON: The beginning of the relationship is supposed to be filled with turmoil and all the sacrifices you have to make. I just never felt any of that.

DAYNA: It's supposed to be nervousness and unsure feelings about everything. It all felt automatic.

ALISON: There's something about our personalities that just works so well together. We've had arguments with friends who say that a relationship has to be work, and ours has never been work. Occasionally one of us will be tired or cranky or hungry, and we'll have a little spat.

DAYNA: It's over in ten minutes, and then we forget what it was even about.

ALISON: And then we laugh about it.

In case you're wondering if Alison and Dayna are typical of the couples in the way their courtship, once begun, moved quickly and relatively seamlessly into a couple relationship that was never work and never erupted into full-scale arguments, rest assured that by comparison, they are exceptional. As you've already learned from some of the other couples, courtship is usually an extremely complicated process. Learning to coexist with and accommodate another human being, no matter how much you love that person, can be a lot of work and may involve plenty of harsh words.

THREE

Difference

I F YOU WANT to get a group of long-term couples into a rau-
cous discussion, try introducing the subject of sleeping habits—
as I did, thoughtlessly, at a dinner party one early fall evening in
Upstate New York. We were four male couples in all, three long-
term—nine years, fourteen years, eighteen years—and one relatively
new couple of three years. The subject of this book had come up,
and I mentioned how surprised I was by how big a subject personal
differences turned out to be for nearly all the couples I interviewed.
One of the guests asked what kinds of things people talked about,
and I said, "Oh, you know, one likes to sleep with the window
open, and the other likes to sleep with the window closed." That
was the match that ignited the room.

For the next half hour, you had to fight hard to be heard over the
furious trading of stories, the laughter, the shock, and the feigned
outrage. And these were not couples who, on the surface, revealed
much in the way of visible difference between the partners. All had
lived together long enough for their wardrobes to blend. But differences there were: One wears flannel pajamas and piles on the blan-
kets. The other sleeps naked and can barely tolerate a sheet. *He* likes
the blinds up. *He* can't sleep unless it's pitch-black. This one tosses

and turns. That one sleeps like a corpse. One likes a soft mattress. The other has a board under his side of the bed. He likes to get up at dawn. He likes to sleep in. Alarm clock. No alarm clock. Socks to bed. Cold feet. Loves to cuddle. Hates to cuddle. And on and on until we were all laughing so hard we could hardly breathe.

Each of us knew what the others were talking about. The differences were varied, but we all recognized the maddening, endearing, and frustrating aspects of this one seemingly small realm of relationship life. And we all also knew one of the great secrets of being a happy couple—or at least being two people who can manage to get a good night's sleep without killing each other. It's not just a matter of finding someone with whom you have common ground—you can have plenty of common ground and still not agree on nighttime room temperature. No, the bigger challenge is coping with the *un*common ground—learning what those myriad differences are, accommodating them, modifying them, occasionally ignoring them, using them to your best advantage, and even learning to laugh about them.

Brian and Curt, who each got a different "gay kit," knew right from the start that they were different—at least on the surface—which proved intriguing for them both. Early in their courtship, each found himself doing things he was unaccustomed to, and doing them with someone who was far different from anyone he'd ever done them with before.

The day after they first met and exchanged telephone numbers at the GMHC safer-sex workshop, Curt called Brian and asked if he'd like to go to the movies. "Dating didn't come in my gay kit," Curt explained, "so just going on a date was new for me. It was all just an experiment, but I needed to meet people in different ways than sexually or in bars. Sex was so easy. I knew how to do that, but it never worked in terms of finding someone for a good relationship." Brian was delighted to hear from Curt, and they made a plan to meet at a downtown theater to see a film version of Lily Tomlin's one-woman show. Brian drove his car from his apartment on the Upper East Side.

CURT: Nobody in Manhattan drives. Brian was like a space creature to me.

BRIAN: And it's not like Curt was the fantasy guy I thought I'd be dating either—or even anything like the person I'd dated before, a doctor from Long Island who was kind of safe. Curt was a little risky. He looked tough to me. He was wearing a leather jacket and black jeans and Doc Marten's. He's so East Villagey, and he lives in Little Italy. I thought, What does he want with this blue-eyed Jew from Long Island? What's the motive here? I was very confused. And I was nervous, but excited.

Ten years later, on a warm weekday summer evening, Brian and Curt are seated on a black leather sofa in the living room of their recently renovated and very beautiful Upper West Side Manhattan apartment. They are visually compatible in the way that couples who have been together for a while often are—variations on a theme, rather than the original compositions they once were. Both are dressed in neutral-colored shorts. Curt is wearing a T-shirt; Brian, a polo shirt. Curt's black hair is cut extremely short, but the effect is more boyish than East Village tough. Brian's overall look is on the preppy side, with a haircut and Top-Siders to match. Curt has a dark complexion, made darker with a little help from the sun. Brian is also tanned, but he's basically blue-eyed and fair. Curt's feet are bare, and one leg is folded underneath him. I ask them about their second date; they share a glance and smile.

BRIAN: We met at Grand Central Terminal for a drink and then went for dinner at a restaurant on Park Avenue South.

CURT: After dinner, we walked around Gramercy Park and just kissed and kissed and kissed.

BRIAN: In public! Obviously, I'd gotten over my fear of kissing in public pretty quickly. That's what I liked about the whole thing, though. He was pushing me. And that dynamic, that connection, has sustained the relationship, each one pushing the other in terms of growth. We challenge each other. On that second date, it wasn't just the making out in public that was different for me. I was staying out on a Tuesday night until eleven-thirty, something I never did, and I took the subway home instead of a taxi.

It was after their fourth date, a couple of weeks after they'd met, that Brian and Curt made plans to spend the night together at Curt's apartment. Curt had raised the subject, deciding that he wanted this to be "conscious experience, instead of just ending up sleeping together."

BRIAN: When he asked if I wanted to stay over, I remember dying. Like, what do I bring? I'm not accustomed to this. Do I bring my contact-lens case? Do I bring my toothbrush and hair products? How am I going to wake up in the morning? So it was just all of those neurotic things that I still do to this day. Then there was all the anticipation. We were going to have sex, and I was really scared. I was going to be in his apartment, and what does his apartment look like? That was really important. It was a whole other thing, seeing how he lived. All this was going through my head.

CURT: I cleaned before Brian came over, but I'm sure I didn't do enough for his concerns. I probably should have put something up on the door to my bedroom. It was a three-bedroom apartment and I had two roommates, but there were no doors on the bedrooms.

BRIAN: And here I am, a prima donna. Well, I'm not that much of a prima donna.

CURT: You had a car.

BRIAN: Please, it was a company car.

CURT: You had a company.

BRIAN: All right, I had a company. So it was like one o'clock in the morning when we got to the apartment and it's pitch-dark. So thank God I didn't see there were no doors and that people walking around in the kitchen could see us. But that was really the least of my worries that night. I didn't know how I was going to survive it emotionally. Like, Oh my God, how am I going to do this? He's going to be disappointed. This is someone who I had heard speaking about sex at this safer-sex forum, so I knew that he had a lot more experience than I did. And here I am, and I won't perform well, and he'll be disappointed, and that will be the end of the relationship.

CURT: I had no sense that I'd be disappointed or that he'd be disappointed with me. I didn't feel any of that. Maybe I should have been scared, but I was excited. It turned out to be a nice experience.

BRIAN: The icing on the cake was after we had sex, after this very lovely experience with Curt, he said, "Do you want milk and cookies?" And I thought, He's like a big girl, you know? And we're sharing vanilla wafers and milk in bed. And I finally got it at that point. That leather coat, the jeans, everything, it was just a fashion statement.

For the next year, as they got to know each other, Curt's apartment and his small bedroom with no door right next to the kitchen became his and Brian's little world. They watched television stretched out on Curt's bed. They cooked meals and ate them, picnic-style, on Curt's bed. And they made love, safely, in Curt's bed. As Brian explained, "It was like a womb, and we got very connected in that space."

As the months unfolded, Brian and Curt began discovering their differences beyond fashion and styles of living.

BRIAN: He had a whole world of knowledge that I knew nothing about, and I enjoyed learning. It was everything: politics, psychotherapy, spirituality, humanity, and a whole level of intimacy that Curt was willing to explore. But whenever we butted up against something, I thought, Oh, there's nothing wrong with me. If there are any problems in this relationship, it's his fault.

CURT: That's a nice setup for the future. But that was the future. In those early months, I got to see that Brian came from a world I knew nothing about. It was like getting off one ship and jumping onto another with a whole different course. It was the whole car thing, but not just the car. It was also the sense of entitlement, the affluence. He went to the theater. I never went to the theater. He was very chatty and loved to talk on the phone. I wasn't accustomed to being that verbal, talking to a man that freely, and not have the relationship just be about sex or some power dynamic. So for it to be that comfortable and verbal was exciting and new. Brian was very comfortable with men. It was very easy. He was a whole other kind of gay man for me. It was fun, and he had a sense of humor about things.

From their very first date, Brian and Curt knew they were different from each other; it was part of the attraction. So exploring and uncovering their differences as they grew closer was an expected part of their courtship and life as a couple. They would be the first to tell you that it's been very difficult at times dealing with their differences, but they'd instantly add that it's never been boring. Over the ten years of their relationship, there's been plenty of fuel for the fire.

While difference was a given for Brian and Curt, it wasn't for many of the couples I interviewed. The often confusing conflicts that arise out of different ways of seeing, reacting, and doing can come as something of a rude intrusion into the romantic realm in the early days and months of a relationship. It's no small shock to discover that the person you thought was your soul mate, the person you felt so at home with, can stare daggers at you for doing something or reacting in a way that is second nature to you but baffling, annoying, or infuriating to him or her.

The intrusion of difference proved especially trying for some of the younger couples I talked to, as well as for the other men and women who had had no prior relationship experience. Those who had been married or coupled before knew that difference was part of the package. They may have fantasized that a new relationship would involve greater compatibility, but they weren't completely shocked to discover that their new partner came with a set of unique differences, perhaps more bearable than an ex-partner's but, still, a whole new set.

Brigid and Jennifer went into their relationship with the security of knowing they had a lot in common, not anticipating that fundamental differences would find their way to the surface like rocks in a New England cornfield.

JENNIFER: It was this whole lesbian relationship thing, thinking we'll get along so much better, we'll understand each other so much better, because we're both women.

BRIGID: Because we're feminist, because we know how to process, because we are studying the same thing, because we share the same core values and beliefs—

JENNIFER: Wrong!

Both women were twenty-three years old when they met at a Susan B. Anthony birthday party—a sort of alternative Presidents Day party—in February 1987. It was given by a mutual friend, a classmate of Jennifer's from the women's studies program she attended at George Washington University in Washington, D.C. Jennifer and Brigid noticed each other and spoke briefly, but they didn't meet again until after Brigid was accepted to the same graduate program and began classes that fall. Jennifer has a vivid memory of her first encounter with Brigid.

JENNIFER: I was at the party, sitting quietly in the back of the room, and Brigid comes into the room and mesmerizes everybody. She was witty and wonderful and I fell in love with her. She was someone I was really interested in. She didn't even notice me.

BRIGID: That's not true. She was sitting in a corner, and I thought she was really cute. I also thought she looked so young, although lo and behold, she's like a month older than I am. I remember she had on high-top sneakers, and her hair was frosted. She was a really cute little dyke.

Neither had any idea that "this was it," but during the school year they did everything they could to be together and told all their friends how they felt.

JENNIFER: This is how goofy we were. Despite the fact that Brigid was very funny and out there, she was kind of shy. We were both so shy that we wouldn't acknowledge we were in pursuit of each other.

By the spring of 1988 they were working together on a softball league and a women's studies newsletter, and they'd put together a panel on lesbian issues. Still, there was no acknowledgment of their growing feelings of mutual attraction.

BRIGID: The night after we did the panel, we were supposed to go out dancing with our friend Susan, and she didn't show up. I was totally freaked, because now I had to spend the evening with Jennifer. I was totally smitten, but I thought she was way too cool for me in terms of class coolness. I thought she was way out of my league.

JENNIFER: I didn't think that at all. I was just too shy to say anything.

BRIGID: I thought, What am I going to do? What am I going to talk about? Suddenly it was pressure. We didn't have the conference to talk about. We didn't have the newsletter to talk about. It wasn't about softball. It was just about us going dancing, so we did and it was fun.

JENNIFER: Except she wouldn't dance with me.

BRIGID: I wouldn't slow-dance. That's true. Dancing could lead to touching.

More weeks passed. Jennifer gave Brigid flowers, awkward moments ensued, and then finally there was a night when a slow dance couldn't be avoided.

BRIGID: I was caught. So we're dancing, and she starts doing this squirmy-face thing all up in mine.

JENNIFER: I nuzzled her neck, and we started kissing.

BRIGID: And then we kissed through the next fast song. And that was it.

JENNIFER: That was the way we revealed our feelings.

BRIGID: No words. It was very nonverbal. It was fine and dandy.

JENNIFER: Of course, we spent the whole time reviewing the whole history, and revealing we had feelings, and I've liked you since—

BRIGID: That was it. We spent that night together, and we've been together ever since.

Brigid is holding Ely, their two-week-old son, who is asleep in her arms. Jennifer is reclining on the sofa next to her, still tired from the rigors of a difficult birth and full-time parenthood. They explain to me that the shock of difference came within a week of their first night together, and that it arrived in the form of a letter from Jennifer. She began by telling Brigid that she loved her—"which blew her mind," Jennifer says. "Then I explained to Brigid how I wanted to sit down and make some rules and say something about our relationship and how we needed to communicate."

BRIGID: Part of it was like "I've made these mistakes before, blah, blah, blah. I don't want us to get too excited about the new terrain and the possibilities, but there aren't a lot of models, so we're going to be doing this on our own."

JENNIFER: The mistakes were with a man, actually, and we were both very bad communicators. So I was really into figuring out ways to be together and to not have this awful falling into bad habits with each other.

BRIGID: I did not have this baggage, and I felt bad because I didn't want to have to deal with all of Jennifer's. Why am I being punished? I'm having fun. We're having fun. We're doing all right, and here you're bringing all this up.

JENNIFER: Which is why I said in the letter that you can't just look at this as a pleasure thing, you can't look at life through rose-colored glasses.

BRIGID: It hadn't even been a month. You deserve some fun time without pressure. She wanted to dive right into it. Our graduate program was nothing but processing. And my feeling was, Okay, we're at home now, we don't have to do that.

Even though Brigid resented Jennifer's need to get serious when Brigid just wanted to have fun and enjoy their new relationship, she came to recognize how important it was to look at the assumptions each had made about their potential life together.

BRIGID: Here we were, white, middle-class women in the same graduate program studying the same thing. We had a lot of assumptions, especially me, like what we believed, what we thought would comfort the other, and how often we should have sex. Of course, it turns out that our assumptions were clearly not the same.

It took Jennifer and Brigid about a year of tension and hurt feelings to discover that in key aspects, what each was doing was the exact opposite of what the other wanted.

JENNIFER: I derive a lot of physical comfort from Brigid that's not sexual. Just to be stroked. And I assumed I could comfort Brigid that way when she was upset.

BRIGID: But stroking does not work for me at all. I don't enjoy being held and soothed. I just don't react well to it. So, I'm, like, *Back off.* And I just assumed she was the same way, so when she got upset, I backed off. But what she really needed was to be held and soothed.

Even something as simple as supporting an acquaintance in the hospital who was recovering from breast-cancer surgery proved fertile ground for exploring how different the two were. Jennifer wanted to send a card. Brigid wanted to visit the woman in the hospital.

BRIGID: I'm like, Okay, she's had her surgery, we need to see her in the hospital, and once she's home we should make dinner for her. And Jen's attitude is, What makes you think she'd want us to come over? I'm thinking, She's sick. Who's going to make dinner for her? So we talked, and there was no way Jennifer would agree—

JENNIFER: —to go visit her in the hospital. My thinking was, We don't want to interrupt her peace at the hospital.

BRIGID: And I'm thinking, When more than now does she need to see people? And it turned out she was very much a community person who was happy to have visitors.

JENNIFER: She had a similar background to Brigid, raised Catholic.

BRIGID: More lower-middle-class than Jen, who is Protestant and probably a little more upper-class. Jen's family would have been much more reserved, maybe sent a card. Thoughtful, but not intrusive. That was totally different from my experience. Why make them ask for help?

JENNIFER: I think that one of the greatest things that I've learned from Brigid is doing more things like that. Especially since Ely was born, I can see that having all these people around is a comfort.

BRIGID: It's a help and it's wonderful.

JENNIFER: Left to my own devices, having my mother come to help would have been the end of the line. But in the past two weeks we've had my mother and father, two of our friends from out of town, and Brigid's mother came. And during the day, every day, we've had someone over here for lunch, and our basketball group has been coming over and doing the potluck thing.

BRIGID: On the other side of that, though, I've learned that everything isn't community-wide. In my family, you thought just about the family and the community, whereas with Jen I've really learned more about one-on-one and how to make that work. That's been hard, being answerable to one person only, but it's worked.

Stewart and Stanley have also learned to make their relationship work despite their differences, many of which Stewart was happy to list for me. Stanley got as far as high school. Stewart has a master's degree. Stanley rarely picks up a newspaper. Stewart's read every book in the house. Stanley, although Jewish, eats ham. Stewart went to a yeshiva. Stanley grew up on Long Island. Stewart grew up in Queens. Stanley's domestic. Stewart's not. Stanley has no head for money. Stewart runs the household finances. Stanley has an ex-wife and a son. Stewart's never been married. Stanley's in his fifties. Stewart's in his forties. "Just about the only thing we have in common," Stewart stated with certainty, "is that we're male."

Stewart's extreme assessment of their differences seemed to me a bit of an exaggeration. After all, they at least share a religious background and grew up on the same island. And from what I could tell, they share a love for their two cats and are both avid collectors. Hundreds of bells, crystal glasses and bowls, and china cats fill every shelf, cabinet, and corner of their compact one-bedroom apartment. They also share the pride they take in the home they've made together. Both are deeply committed to their volunteer work with gay civil rights and AIDS organizations. And above all, they are very obviously devoted to each other.

Still, they *are* different. And in at least two practical ways, they've made accommodations that seem to benefit them both. From the minute Stanley first saw Stewart's apartment—which is the apartment they've now shared for fifteen years—he knew who was going to have to take charge of the domestic realm.

STANLEY: Trust me when I tell you, what you see here was not here fifteen years ago. There was a sofa bed, snack tables for end tables. Hand-me-down lamps, an old television, a couple of bookcases. The bed had no headboard. He had his desk. And for a dining room set there was a bridge table with a couple of chairs.

STEWART: There were a few pictures.

STANLEY: I thought he was ready to redecorate. But that's not to say it wasn't warm. Even though it wasn't as overwhelmingly decorated as it is now, the basic stuff was here, and the refrigerator had enough food for at least one meal. To this day we go into shock when we go into other people's homes and we open the refrigerator and there's nothing in there.

STEWART: Our kitchen looks like we can live through a siege. If Connecticut and New Jersey cut us off from supplies, we'll still have plenty to eat.

Stanley is clearly the one who runs the house, in part because he likes to, but also because he and Stewart have different standards.

STEWART: The first time he complained about how I did laundry, I never did it again.

STANLEY: He left all the shirts and everything in the dryer for half an hour on HOT. Wrinkled wasn't the word for it. And it didn't take much for him not to want to do something, but I was sort of used to it because my ex-wife wasn't that domesticated. So I cook, I clean, I iron.

When it comes to money, Stanley has happily ceded responsibility to Stewart, which makes Stewart crazy to this day.

STEWART: He gave a very mature impression when we met, but little did I know that I'd end up running the household finances. We're always fighting about that. His method of budget is cash the check, spend the money, and when you run out, ask Stewart for more.

Knowing that he has Stewart to keep the books, Stanley doesn't worry about money, just as Stewart never has to worry about finding shirts in his closet or a meal on the table when he gets home from work. Stewart may still wish that Stanley paid more attention to money, and Stanley will probably never understand how Stewart can forget about the laundry in the dryer. Nonetheless, they've found ways to accommodate these differences that allow them to get through life with well-pressed clothes on their backs and money in their pockets.

As you'll no doubt come to see in the chapters that follow, difference infuses every aspect of a relationship. It is an unavoidable and essential part of couple life. That's what I realized in a profound way from my conversations with Jennifer and Brigid, Brian and Curt, and many of the other couples, no matter how alike—or different— the partners seemed. Difference is often painful, annoying, and divisive, especially as the partners struggle to recognize the ways in which they differ and as each learns the hard lesson of looking at things from another's perspective. But difference can also be a source of excitement, a catalyst for positive change, and a practical resource in day-to-day life. At best, each partner brings his or her differences to the relationship in a way that can make life better for the other in every aspect, from the emotional and the physical to the most basic and everyday.

FOUR

Monogamy/ Nonmonogamy

ANOTHER SUBJECT pretty much guaranteed to stir up a conversation is monogamy. I did this unintentionally once ten years ago while at dinner with a friend and his longtime male partner. I was working on a monogamy chapter for my first book, *The Male Couple's Guide,* and I was telling them how challenging it was proving to be. Without thinking, but having made the assumption, I said, "You guys are monogamous, aren't you?" Simultaneously, one said yes and the other said no.

The two men were still deep in discussion by the time I gingerly excused myself on the sidewalk in front of the restaurant and headed home. I was later to learn that the one who'd said they were a monogamous couple had not been himself, and the one who said they weren't monogamous was. Until I asked the question, they had never discussed the issue; each had made his own assumptions and done as he wished. I have never again raised the subject except in formal, private interviews.

Mostly, I wasn't surprised by the choices made by the forty couples I interviewed. I knew from my reading over the years that women were, in general, more likely to be monogamous than men, so I expected that most of the women I interviewed would be in monogamous relationships; in fact, *all* of them are. I had also anticipated that at least some of the men had chosen a nonmonogamous arrangement, and some had. Three of the male couples I spoke with are currently nonmonogamous. Three others were nonmonogamous for many years, but are no longer.

In trying to understand these seemingly one-sided numbers, I considered a few possibilities—other than the fact that my sample group was small and less than random. Perhaps couples are more likely to be happy and long-lasting if the partners choose to be monogamous. Given the inherent challenges of maintaining a nonmonogamous relationship—above and beyond those of maintaining a monogamous relationship—this seems well within the range of possibility. Or maybe nonmonogamous couples were less likely to volunteer to talk to me because they were uncomfortable talking about something they know many people don't approve of.

In the case of male couples, perhaps many of the long-term nonmonogamous pairs had been casualties of the AIDS epidemic. Before gay men knew enough to take precautions, many who had been in nonmonogamous relationships had become infected with HIV through unsafe sex with outside partners or had been infected by their significant others, who had themselves become infected through outside unsafe sex. With so many thousands of men who had been in long-term relationships dead from AIDS, my chances of coming across them were greatly reduced.

Before going any further with this subject, I feel compelled to note that I'm well aware that this is one of those issues that people who oppose gay marriage have latched on to. How can gay people—gay men in particular—expect to win the legal right to marry if they don't make an explicit commitment to be monogamous, as heterosexuals do? What is too often lost in this part of the debate is that heterosexuals don't have to make a commitment to monogamy to get legally married—although many choose to make that commitment, explicitly, as part of a religious marriage ceremony. And their marriage certificates certainly aren't invalidated if they decide as a couple to be nonmonogamous or if they secretly break their commitments.

So my intention isn't to provide any additional ammunition for the antigay crusaders. Nor am I advocating one style of living over another. I know there are those who see monogamy as a prime target for moral debate. I don't. I see this as an opportunity to learn how a relative handful of happy long-term couples have dealt with the issue of monogamy.

Part of the challenge gay and lesbian people have faced in sorting out their choices regarding monogamy is the absence of clear rules about how two people in a same-sex relationship are supposed to conduct themselves. Again, I think this freedom is a good thing, because it gives people the opportunity to decide for themselves what works best. There's no requirement to follow what society or one's church dictates. But, of course, the freedom to choose brings with it other demands, from sorting out one's personal feelings about monogamy to trying to satisfy the sometimes conflicting needs and desires of one's partner.

As I quickly discovered in my conversations, no matter how the couples actually live day to day, everyone had personal feelings about monogamy—for, against, mixed, or ambivalent—and they'd come to those feelings in a variety of ways. They were influenced by personal experience, cultural values, the example of parents or other role models, the political/social climate, or simply gut instinct.

For example, several people said that they simply couldn't cope with the emotional rigors of a nonmonogamous relationship. That's how Danny felt when he told Nate what the rules would have to be if they were to get back together following Nate's affair with another man early in their relationship. "I know the way my psyche works," he said. "So I was clear with Nate that this is what I want and this is what I need." Other people felt equally strongly—and sometimes instinctively—that they wanted to be free to have sex outside their primary relationship.

Three of the couples, one male and two female, told me that their political/ideological beliefs had led them to think they wanted nonmonogamous arrangements—only to find that in practice, their emotions conflicted with their politics. Pam and Lindsy, who are both on the cusp of fifty, were in complete agreement about monogamy when they met in 1977. Lindsy explained: "When we started dating each other, we thought that monogamy was backward. Just as you can have many levels of family and friendship encounters, there should be no reason you can't have different levels of sexual encounters."

Pam and Lindsy's politics fit nicely with some of the prevailing thinking in the 1970s about nonexclusive relationships. But during their early courtship, as Lindsy continued sleeping with men and Pam continued to sleep with her ex-lover, the arrangement, much to both women's surprise and chagrin, didn't work.

LINDSY: It became a problem, real fast.
PAM: We're very jealous. We are evil, jealous people.

I asked Pam if this was something they talked about, and wondered how they resolved the fundamental conflict between what they believed and how they lived. I seemed to have stirred up some old passions, because Pam just about leapt across the table in my direction. As she answered, her face turned bright red, a color that clashed alarmingly with her flaming orange hair.

PAM: *Talked about it?* We had screaming fights on Broadway, where we threw beer at each other.
LINDSY: It took us a while to admit that we were just crass, jealous, politically incorrect bitches, and that this was not gonna change.
PAM: We made a pact of nonideological monogamy, because this was what was going to work for us.
LINDSY: It wasn't that we judged other people, because I really believed in nonmonogamy as an ideal. We just had so many other intense disagreements, about other things that couldn't possibly be avoided, that we decided this was one thing we didn't have to argue about. I still think if we worked really hard on making nonmonogamy work, we could probably do it, but I can probably learn Chinese, too. Look, I'm a vegetarian, but I still have a leather couch. No one's perfect.

Having witnessed Pam and Lindsy battle out lots of different things during our dinner together at an outdoor restaurant in Miami Beach, I could easily understand why they set this issue aside and chose to be monogamous. It was a matter of self- and relationship-preservation.

One of the points Lindsy made, about not judging other people for the choices they've made, came up repeatedly in my interviews. I'd expected to find that some of the couples had strong moral and/ or religious attachments to monogamy and therefore had judgments about those who were not monogamous, but that didn't prove to be the case. Whether they were in monogamous or nonmonogamous relationships, virtually all the people I spoke with said that what they chose to do was no comment on what anyone else did, that they were simply doing what best suited them in their own lives. A few added that while at one time they might have judged other couples, experience had taught them not to.

For most of the couples, monogamy was the first choice of both partners. Each may have chosen monogamy for different reasons, including a need for stability and security, feelings of jealousy, a fear of wrecking the relationship, and a simple lack of desire to be with anyone else other than their chosen partner, but monogamy was a joint given. Sometimes that preference was stated, as it was for Chris and Sherri, who talked about everything by telephone during the months that Sherri's parents made it difficult for them to court in person.

CHRIS: We talked about the fact that we would be monogamous, but if, perchance one of us strayed—

SHERRI: Accidentally, a one-night-stand kind of thing—

CHRIS: You know, sometimes you end up in situations and you just can't predict. But we would tell the other one about it and we would discuss it, and it wouldn't be the undoing of the relationship, because one mistake shouldn't undo it. However, now that we're this far into the relationship—

SHERRI: If you screw around, you're dead meat.

CHRIS: At this point, don't even consider it, because one mistake would be one too many.

SHERRI: I mean, if you want to go and do that, then get out of the relationship. We have so much invested—our love, our time, our energy, our son—that that would be a huge betrayal. It would be like, Just stab me in the heart.

CHRIS: I think that if it were ever to happen, we would still discuss it. It probably wouldn't be the undoing, but the trust issue would really be damaged. We're committed to a monogamous relationship. Period.

SHERRI: And that's it.

Martin and Jim first talked about monogamy in 1948, shortly before they left for a two-year stint in Japan working as civilians for the U.S. military. Honesty has been very important to both of them during their fifty years together—"except for maybe a fib," Jim told me—and that was how they approached the issue of sex with other men.

JIM: Before we went to Japan, we discussed our relationship. And I told Marty, I said, "You know, if ever you find anybody else, and you want to leave, don't let me find out from somebody else. *You* tell me."

MARTIN: I felt the same way about it. I had had lovers before, especially when I was in the service during the war, because I knew I was gay then. But if they lasted a week, it was a long relationship. When I finally met Jimmy, I thought, Oh, this is it. I was happy with that. Just one person.

JIM: We always had that between us. And so far, I don't think he's going to find anybody else.

Sometimes the preference for monogamy was assumed and never discussed. Such a concept is alien to me, and I was taken aback each of the several times I discovered a couple who had never actually talked about the issue. I couldn't imagine not discussing something that looms so large in my own mind, but some of the people I interviewed were nonplussed that I would even question their monogamy. For example, Marjorie and Marian, two dairy farmers from Vermont, looked at me as if I were speaking another language when I asked them if they were monogamous. They said that it had never crossed their minds not to have an exclusive relationship. Monogamy was always a given.

Other of the couples also assumed they were in monogamous relationships. Brian and Curt were totally matter-of-fact about it.

BRIAN: We never talked about it.

CURT: I felt like this was who I was dating and that was that.

Dayna and Alison paused before answering my question, clearly pondering this issue as a couple for the first time.

DAYNA: I think that was really understood.

ALISON: That was very unspoken. We never actually said, "Okay, I promise not to see anyone else." It would never have entered my mind to see anyone else, and I never would have imagined Dayna wanting to see anyone else. That was just the nature of our relationship, and that was a given.

I asked Stewart and Stanley if their relationship meant an end to visiting bathhouses.

STEWART: As far as I know.

STANLEY: Pretty much, yeah.

STEWART: Oh, except when he goes there to do fund-raising for our local Gay Pride parade. Then he stands there and sells chocolate.

STANLEY: I feel that when you're a couple, or an item, to go to a place that's an obvious pick-up joint or whatever, it's just ridiculous. Unless, of course, you're doing fund-raising.

STEWART: I think the assumption from early on was that our relationship was closed. We just never said anything.

Two of the couples who made an assumption early on that their relationship was closed to outside sexual encounters found that they had to deal more explicitly with the issue when one or both partners broke their unspoken agreement. As we know from the story of Nate and Danny's at-home courtship, that's what happened following Nate's affair. Both were forced to talk—well, Danny talked and Nate listened—and Nate heard in no uncertain terms that if he wanted to be in a relationship with Danny, there was no room for outside sexual encounters or relationships.

Monogamy wasn't the first choice for every couple, as we've already heard from Pam and Lindsy. In most of these cases, however, one partner wanted a monogamous relationship and the other was ambivalent, had not had experience with monogamy, or was certain that he or she wanted a nonmonogamous relationship. Among these couples, it was the partner with the stronger preferences who got his or her way. While compromise is an essential part of every happy relationship, this is one issue where it's difficult to find a middle ground where partners of varying beliefs can rest comfortably.

Before Lucy and Patsy became a couple, Lucy had enjoyed a lifetime of nonmonogamy, an experience she had in common with several of the women and men I spoke to. Her first night with Patsy, she was quick to acknowledge, was clearly special, but sleeping with someone other than her live-in beloved was Lucy's standard operating procedure. Patsy knew this, and she also knew that she could never tolerate being in a relationship with a woman who wasn't committed to her exclusively. Patsy and Lucy's first discussion about monogamy took place on the morning after the night before.

PATSY: Right away, I said, "I don't know if this relationship is going anywhere, but I want to tell you that if it is, I just can't ever be in a relationship that's not monogamous. I'm not capable of doing that." And she mumbled something like "Well, I'll try."

LUCY: I didn't say that, yet. It took me a while, because I still had to deal with Dixie. What was I going to do with this mess I had gotten myself into?

PATSY: But you also had to deal with yourself. You were very surprised that you were so smitten. I know that's true.

LUCY: Oh yeah! I don't fall in love easily.

PATSY: But my decision to tell Lucy came out of my principles, I suppose. I wanted her to know right away how I am and what I'm like, and that this was very important to me. I had been really devastated by my previous relationship, and I wasn't going to go through that again.

Despite her initial apprehensions about monogamy, it proved surprisingly easy for Lucy to settle into an exclusive relationship with Patsy. "It wasn't that I didn't find other people attractive," she was careful to note. "After all, I had a roving eye. I should have been a man, right? But I discovered with Patsy that I only wanted to be with her. I only wanted to make love with Patsy."

I wasn't counting on anything close to Patsy and Lucy's easy adjustment to monogamous life when I first started talking with Lee and Catherine. I had a hard time imagining how they were going to reconcile the desires of, on the one hand, a forty-three-year-old divorced mother of six mostly grown children who was a veteran of two two-year live-in relationships with women and, on the other, a thirty-year-old "Slut of the Western World" (her own partner's description, mind you) who joined the Navy after her lover of seven years became a born-again Christian.

I just assumed that it was Catherine—the very sexually active one of the pair—who would want her freedom and Lee, the middle-aged mom, who set the limits, but as usual, I should have kept an open mind. The year was 1982. The city, San Francisco.

CATHERINE: I was a weekender stationed at Moffet Field, where I would do active duty during the week, and then on weekends I would take the little Greyhound bus from the base into San Francisco, and I was a wild woman. I had a rotating-door policy.

LEE: When I took Catherine out of circulation, they lowered all the flags to half-mast.

CATHERINE: My gay brother lived in San Francisco, and one weekend a month he was on the road, so I would stay there. Otherwise I would stay at a local motel.

I asked Catherine if she'd been looking for a long-term relationship at the time she met Lee. Her booming answer made me think she'd missed her calling as a drill sergeant.

CATHERINE: Hell, no! I was looking for fun! I did a lot of one-night stands, and I was right up front. "I'm not looking for a long-term relationship. If you are, this is not the encounter you want." I was raised among gay men, so the one-night stands were the usual thing.

LEE: "Don't tell me your last name. That's too much of a commitment."

CATHERINE: That's it. That's me. So, I'd save up all the energy I needed during the week, and every weekend I would hit the typical haunts. One of my favorites was Amelia's, and I happened to be sitting at the bar with a girl who I was putting the make on. I chitchatted with her for a while, and I didn't even notice Lee sitting on the other side of her. I was talking with this girl about the military, and she couldn't understand how I could be in the Navy and be homosexual at the same time. And Lee jumped in with some comments about how she'd been in the military, too. So we're all chitchatting, and this young girl suggests we go to this other place because Amelia's was getting too noisy. And I was thinking, Ooh, a three-way. No problem!

LEE: Then they stood up, and that was the first time I got a look at Catherine, and I thought, Oh please, God, let her be twenty-one, at least. She was this young, angelic, big-eyed blond person. She looked like a baby, but from the way she was talking I knew she had to be older.

CATHERINE: I had that angelic look. That's how I got all those women. And Lee? Very hot. Very sexy-looking woman. Age made no difference to me.

The young woman who had suggested leaving turned out to have had a prior commitment, so she arranged to meet Lee and Catherine later in the evening at another bar. Lee and Catherine never made it. After dancing together for a short while, Catherine invited Lee back to her motel. "We had sex till dawn," Catherine recalls. But one night turned into something far more enduring.

Knowing even this much about Lee's and Catherine's characters, you can hardly blame me for misreading their views on monogamy. Even Lee was surprised by Catherine's demand. Lee said: "When we decided to be in a committed relationship, here was Ms. Slut of the Western World saying, 'You know what . . .'"

And it's not even as simple as saying that Catherine is for monogamy and Lee is against.

CATHERINE: *I'm* a firm believer in monogamy, and *Lee* is a firm believer in monogamy. That was never a question in the relationship.

LEE: I'm *not* a firm believer in monogamy. I'm a firm believer in *choice.*

CATHERINE: That's right, you get a choice.

LEE: Catherine's way is to say, "I make this commitment to monogamy." And then she stays with it. Mine is, I wake up every day and say, "Do I want to be with this woman?" So I'm not a firm believer in monogamy as a state, and while we made the agreement to be monogamous, I made the agreement to be monogamous because I know what the result of not being monogamous would be: a split in our relationship.

For Catherine, it was important to be in a totally monogamous relationship, without question. For me, I needed to be in a relationship that I could question every single day, to determine whether I wanted to be there or not. And if I made the choice not to be monogamous, I would not be able to do that in secret, to cheat and pretend that I was in a monogamous relationship when I wasn't. And I know what I would get from that. So, even today, I question every single day: "Is this worth it?" And it is.

Andy and Matthew,* who are both in their mid-forties and have been together for a dozen years, were one of two male couples I interviewed who struggled with their conflicting desires and wound up with an ever-evolving nonmonogamous arrangement that now suits them both. When the two first met, Andy had no interest in monogamy; Matthew couldn't imagine having any other kind of relationship.

ANDY: I hadn't been monogamous for years. My ideal back in the 1970s and early 1980s was to go out to the baths with my lover. We used to get there, split up, and then reunite in the early morning and go home together. It really worked.

MATTHEW: My attitude at the time was that if that's the model you want to throw at me, then admit it didn't work because the relationship obviously disintegrated to the point that it wasn't a sexual relationship.

ANDY: What came first, the chicken or the egg?

MATTHEW: It doesn't matter. The point is, where does it end up? At that point, my concept of a relationship was monogamy. That was my expectation.

Very early in their courtship, Andy asked Matthew to accompany him to a male nudist club, and Matthew accepted, not knowing what Andy knew about the organization.

---

* Not their real names. I'd offer more background details on Andy and Matthew, but they have jobs that could be jeopardized if their employers became aware of the intimate aspects of their lives.

ANDY: I knew it was a front for a sex club.

MATTHEW: We went to a daytime party, which was very nonsexual, and I proceeded to lie out for the first time in my life under the sun naked and burn myself to a crisp, right down to my most intimate parts. Then we went to a nighttime party, which was very sexual, and I was freaked out. Andy made it clear he was willing to play around with other people. And I wasn't. I couldn't handle it and told him we were leaving, *right now.* In the car we had words about it, and he could tell I was pissed.

Matthew gave Andy an ultimatum, insisting that if they were going to continue seeing each other, they had to be monogamous.

ANDY: This was a big issue for me. It wasn't what I wanted, but I learned to accept it because of the greater good of being with Matthew. Remember, Matthew came out when AIDS was already a fact of life. I came out in the seventies, when most gay couples were in open relationships.

MATTHEW: I knew what happened with his last relationship, that once they opened it up, the intimacy part of the relationship dis-integrated. I was scared to death that it was like opening a flood-gate. I mean, I had urges and I was attracted to other people, too. I just saw this as being like a crack in the dam. I was afraid for myself, that I was going to like it too much. I wasn't a prude. I wanted the relationship to exist, and I was afraid that if we started playing around, then that's going to dilute it.

ANDY: I didn't agree with Matthew, but I went along and dropped out of the club because I wanted my relationship with him.

MATTHEW: It meant a lot to me that he was willing to do this. Dropping out of that sex club spoke volumes to me. I knew he didn't want to. I knew he was a big slut. I wasn't holding that against him. I was a big slut, too, for a very short amount of time. And I wasn't going to hold that against myself.

A short time after hashing out their feelings and agreeing to be monogamous, Andy and Matthew moved in together. After a half-dozen years of monogamy, Andy decided it was time to start push-ing the envelope.

MATTHEW: There were a couple of things that Andy wanted to do in stages. The first thing was he wanted to participate in a nude spirituality thing.

ANDY: A bunch of guys get together for a weekend, and you learn to give each other an erotic massage.

MATTHEW: He tried to sell me on the idea that it wasn't sexual, that it was spiritual. You do breathing exercises, and you're not supposed to have an orgasm.

ANDY: No ejaculations. Recycle your orgasm through your body and charge your body with erotic energy.

MATTHEW: Bullshit is bullshit, as far as I'm concerned. A bunch of naked, horny gay men getting together. It's like you're legitimizing it by putting all this New Age mumbo jumbo around it. I didn't want anything to do with it, but Andy wanted to do it.

ANDY: When I decide I want to do something, I do it.

MATTHEW: He did it, and I didn't like it. I told him before he went that it really put a strain on our relationship. But I guess in the end I thought this was a hell of a lot better than if he goes out to the tubs. And it wasn't like he said he wanted to go out and pick somebody up. I also knew that it was so important to him to experience this that if I forced it, all I was going to end up doing was forcing him to do something behind my back. At least this was up front and honest. I still didn't like it.

Andy came back from his weekend and told Matthew what it was like. Matthew wasn't impressed, and he was also angry.

MATTHEW: I was upset. I wasn't fuming at the nostrils and going off the wall about it, but I was uncomfortable with it and unhappy with it; I didn't like it, and I said so. But our relationship was never in jeopardy because of it. I've come to realize through time that we can be angry about something and disagree about something without that threatening our relationship, even this. So I accepted it, reluctantly.

Six months later, Andy decided to push the envelope a little further, and without informing Matthew, he joined another nudist club. According to Matthew, "It was still ultimately an opportunity for people to have sex." At first, Matthew wouldn't have anything to do with the club, but after a few months, Andy convinced him to join.

MATTHEW: In the beginning, I was very uncomfortable about either of us playing around with someone else. But I knew that was what Andy wanted, because he talked about it all the time. And he kept saying to me that it was perfectly okay with him if I went out and had an affair with somebody. I hated when he said that, and I refused to do it. Now, I'm not sitting here saying to you that I didn't ever want to do it. I was attracted to all kinds of people that I would have loved to pursue. But I valued our relationship so highly, so strongly above everything else, that I was afraid that if we put a crack in this dam that our fate would be the same as it was for Andy's last relationship. Just roommates. No sex. I used that as a model.

I asked Matthew what it was that finally convinced him it was okay to do what Andy had always wanted. He shrugged his shoulders and answered.

MATTHEW: He nagged me to death. And we started to play around a little bit. A little hugging, kissing, mutual masturbation. He did that with other people, and so did I. I wasn't getting that big a thrill out of it.

ANDY: I sure did.

MATTHEW: Andy always got a big thrill out of it. He comes from a nonmonogamous mind-set, and he didn't seem to think this would have any kind of negative impact.

ANDY: All of the men in my family were nonmonogamous. But they all had thirty- and forty-year-old marriages.

MATTHEW: One thing I can say about Andy is that he was never dishonest. He wasn't sneaking around. He wanted me to do what he did so we could both do it. And I found that I got really erotically turned on to being with Andy in a sexual environment. Andy thinks that being in a public sexual environment means that you're with somebody else. But I would be happy to go to orgies if I was going to do what I was going to do with him, with all these other guys orgying around me. What a great erotic environment for me, if he could be the focus of my attention.

Over time, Andy continued to push Matthew's stated limits. There'd be words, but then Matthew would discover he liked the new limits, so the line would be redrawn. Then Andy would push again. So Matthew and Andy have gone from being at the same sex party having sex only with each other, to being at the same party and having sex with other men, to Andy wanting to go off on a weekend alone to have sex with a man he was interested in. Matthew dug in his heels over that.

MATTHEW: I never said anything like "If you go, don't come back," but obviously I was upset. But he was determined to go.

ANDY: It was important to me.

MATTHEW: For a couple of days we were hardly talking to each other, and as the weekend approached, Andy told me that he had talked to a friend of his about it. . . . This is your story.

ANDY: This is a person I can talk to about my problems with Matthew. And I told him about this, and he said, "What's more important? Spending a couple of days with this man, or being with Matthew for the rest of your life?"

MATTHEW: Andy came back to me and told me about this discussion and said that his friend was absolutely right. He said, "I don't want to do anything that will hurt our relationship. And, of course, I won't go." I melted. I absolutely melted. That was one of the things about him that made me love him in the first place, that he's so ultimately sensitive to everything.

That was a very pivotal point in a certain way. I realized right then and there, I think for the first time, certainly in a profound way, that I didn't believe that our relationship was that fragile. That was my concern all along. And since then we've relaxed our sexual exclusivity. The postscript to this is that we have done three-ways. Occasionally we've had an informal group of naked guys over here.

A part of all this is this: I know that Andy is my one and only, and he's my favorite sex partner. I would do things with him that I wouldn't do with other people, and there's a certain tenderness to that. There still are limits. I would feel very uncomfortable at this point if there was an event that I wasn't able to go to where Andy went without me. Andy has respected this.

Matthew and Andy have reached a point in their relationship where both are comfortable with how they conduct their sexual lives with each other and with other men. If it were up to Andy, the line would be moved further still, but he knows Matthew has reached his limit. For now.

Matthew and Andy spent many years as a monogamous couple and later became nonmonogamous. On the other side, a few male couples I spoke with had nonmonogamous relationships for years before deciding on monogamy. For one couple, the decision came after nearly two decades of maintaining careers that kept them apart for months at a time. For eighteen years, Gordon and Jay had a nonmonogamous relationship, and each kept his liaisons to himself. They have been a couple for thirty-eight years.

JAY: We never really discussed it.

GORDON: I'll tell you, every time that we discussed it we hurt each other, so we decided either separately or together not to talk about it. We had thought the thing to do was confess. And then we realized, Just do it and forget about it.

JAY: It was no more important than that. It was simply a biological need, an urge, and you needed to do that.

GORDON: In other words, let's say I was in Dallas for six weeks. Well, naturally, I wasn't going to sit at home with my hands folded, right?

Gordon and Jay's "don't ask, don't tell" arrangement worked pretty well. Each was generally sensitive to the other's feelings—but not always. Ten years into the relationship, Jay came to visit Gordon in New Orleans, where Gordon had been designing a set for a local opera company.

GORDON: I was having this brief encounter with a hairdresser, and I didn't, shall we say, bother to tell Bob about Jay. And, of course, I hadn't told Jay about Bob. So here we are at a party—

JAY: And this hairdresser was introduced by someone to me as Gordon's lover.

GORDON: You know, "This is Gordon's Bob."

JAY: I started to laugh.

GORDON: I think you were pissed off.
JAY: I wasn't pissed off, Gordon.

In the recounting, Jay seemed pissed off to me, but the moment quickly passed.

After nearly two decades of periodic separation, Gordon and Jay decided to open a business together, which would mean they'd be together every hour of the day. In the years that followed, their extrarelationship liaisons slowed to a trickle, tapering off, by the mid-1980s, to none.

Before I end this chapter, I know there are two related questions I have to answer. And I know I have to answer them because they're the questions I've been asked by some of the couples I interviewed as well as by other people with whom I've discussed this issue. How did I know that the couples were telling me the truth? And didn't I think that some of the self-described monogamous partners cheated on each other?

I *don't* know if everyone was telling me the truth about this or any other subject. I did assume, however, that if a couple told me they had agreed to a monogamous or a nonmonogamous relationship, that in this regard they were speaking honestly. If they had individually broken an agreement to be monogamous or had gone beyond the limits of a nonmonogamous arrangement, it was up to them to tell me or not—and some did tell me. But as far as the couples who chose not to share that information with me or with each other, that was their business, not mine. As all the couples said at one point or another about any number of issues, some things are better left unsaid.

There are many stories I haven't told about how the couples I spoke with came to live the monogamous or nonmonogamous lives they do. And in this chapter I've only begun to explore the complexities of how the nonmonogamous couples manage this aspect of their relationships. As I've learned over the years, and as we know from Matthew and Andy, nonmonogamy doesn't simply mean an utter absence of monogamy. There are limits. But I hope these stories are enough to convey a sense of how significant this area of couple life can be, and how each relationship is a custom-made affair in which two individuals find a way of living that is acceptable, at a minimum, and enriching, at best. Whatever the choice, it's not always so easy.

FIVE

Communication

PAM AND LINDSY were the most expressive, passionate, emphatic, and volatile communicators I interviewed, and I witnessed this firsthand during dinner at an outdoor restaurant on Lincoln Road in Miami Beach. I also learned from the interview that besides their routinely expressive interactions at home, Pam and Lindsy have yelled at each other at a therapist's office, thrown beer at each other on the streets of New York City, and even slugged it out one time in Central Park. They have no problem expressing themselves, in love or in anger, in public or private. Not surprisingly, the incident in Central Park led Pam to communicate her displeasure by not talking to or sleeping with Lindsy for months.

LINDSY: We were having some problems with a book we were writing together, some junior-senior partner-type arguments, and Pam got pissed off at something I said. She just kind of reached out, like a girl, and hit me. We'd been taking martial-arts self-defense classes together, and without thinking I went into a martial-arts stance and kicked her.

PAM: She kicked me! I couldn't believe it.

LINDSY: Right in her mouth. I split her lip, and she was spraying blood.

PAM: I had blood in my mouth, and I spit it out.

LINDSY: She kept saying, "You hit me!" And I kept saying, "You hit me first!"

PAM: I thought she was gonna hit me like a girl, like any decent person would have. It was a little comforting to realize that she could protect herself on the street, but I saw stars and my lip was split open.

LINDSY: I was really appalled at myself. I had to call her doctor and say, "We had this fuckin' battle." I was a batterer.

Pam and Lindsy have been together for nearly twenty years and plan to be together until they die. But I had to wonder during our conversation if death would come from natural causes or passionate communication.

I asked Pam, who is a part-time rock-and-roll bass player and a mostly full-time writer, and Lindsy, a full-time writer and one-time rock-and-roll groupie, how they managed to recover from their Central Park incident.

LINDSY: This is where gay people have that built-in advantage, because we've already had to learn to work through all kinds of things. If we were a straight couple, it's possible that at that point in our relationship, we would have decided to have a kid or something.

PAM: Or a divorce.

LINDSY: But we had already had enough small fights by then to know we could survive this.

PAM: We're really volatile. We're know-it-all bitches. That's what we really are and we're very up front about it.

LINDSY: Sometimes, we scare our friends, because we'll fight in front of them. To us, it's nothing. It's not like we fight every day. But when it comes up, we're not that shy about it.

PAM: Our impulse is always to get it all out, rather than suppress things. The thing is, we did have to learn how to do it in ways that weren't truly destructive. Lindsy has never hit me again. But I think the best thing is to get it all out. It's a horrible thing to try to pretend the problem isn't there and try not to fight, because that's a really fake kind of peace.

As Pam explained how they get it all out, I found myself thinking that a fake kind of peace sounded relatively appealing. What these women were describing did not fit my fantasy image of good communication in a happy marriage. I always liked to think of good communication as calm, reasonable discourse. It was something done over dinner or during a deliciously cozy half hour in bed before starting the day. It led to good feelings, a deeper level of understanding, and a sense of well-being.

As I conducted interviews, discerned the ways in which the couples communicated, and took note of the things they did and didn't say to each other, I was forced to set aside my fantasy. I had to acknowledge that even in a self-defined happy relationship, truly good communication is simply the ability to convey one's thoughts, emotions, wants, and needs to one's partner and, in turn, to listen to what one's partner has to communicate. There is no guarantee that what is said will be said in the glow of candlelight or the calm of daybreak. Nor is there any guarantee that you'll feel good about what you've said or what's been said to you.

In truth, good communication is a complicated, messy, wonderful, terrifying, comforting, disturbing, reassuring, and profoundly individual thing. It can be as simple and sweet as nightly kisses before going to bed or as painful as a recurring argument over a long-past infidelity. Some couples go about it gingerly and with great reserve; others go at it with unbridled passion. Some are adept at it; others have struggled for years to learn how to understand each other. And more than a few have sought the advice of friends, relatives, and, at times, professional therapists.

I expressed to Pam and Lindsy my own congenital reluctance to say what I think, and how damaging that proved to be in my first long-term relationship.

PAM: Well, I guess it helps if you're not afraid of fighting or you don't think that it's absolutely repulsive. But I think you should force yourself to do it anyway, even if it's not your natural impulse. It's important for your relationship.

LINDSY: If you do it and you don't break up, then you know you can survive.

PAM: It makes you stronger, because you have to delve very deeply.

And that's when you find that the shallow thing you're fighting about is something that relates to one of the three core problem issues in your relationship. It almost always turns out to be a much deeper problem—

Lindsy interrupts to make a point, and with a flash of anger, Pam cuts her off. I hold my breath and hope that we're not headed for an eruption. I know they've just told me that arguing means nothing to them, but when I was young and people argued around my house, things got broken. My instinct in this moment is to excuse myself from the table, but I hold on to the seat of my chair with both hands, look up at the palm trees overhead, and wait to see what will happen next.

PAM: Lindsy, not yet, no, okay? Because you're interrupting me. And you always have.

What we have to learn—what Lindsy has had to learn—is to back off a little bit at first. Because even though we're both people who do want to get to the core of the problem, not avoid it, and to do it fast, I need time to calm down after a fight. If I'm not given thirty-five minutes to come crawling back to her humiliated, then I wind up saying all those things that leave me nowhere else to go. And *her* impulse, once the fight starts, is to resolve it immediately. She would just be there, on me, all the time, and she wouldn't even let me step out of the apartment to get a little privacy, to just cool down.

On occasion, over the years, Pam and Lindsy have sought the counsel of a therapist. Saying what's on their minds has obviously never been a problem, but really understanding each other and finding a way to a reasonable resolution has been—and continues to be—a challenge.

All the couples I interviewed communicate. It's a given of being in a relationship with another human being. More than a given, it's an unavoidable must. But as with everything else in a relationship, each partner brings along his or her own family and relationship history and, consequently, his or her own way of communicating. For Brian and Curt, who knew up front that they were different in many ways, that proved simultaneously interesting and distressing.

BRIAN: We were at dinner. This was probably in the first month or two. And Curt looked at me and said, "Okay, so what's your dark side?"

CURT: I was probably talking about it in therapy that week—just kind of wondering, Well, what's up with this guy? He can't actually be this nice. There has to be *something.*

BRIAN: I had not been in therapy, and this was otherworldly to me. This was Curt and his shit. And I said, "What are you talking about? My dark side? I'm not the moon, you know." But I basically told him that I couldn't answer the question because I really didn't know what he was talking about. I knew he wasn't coming at this from a malicious point of view, but I didn't know what he wanted from me.

CURT: I was genuinely curious, and this was the kind of thing I talked about with my friends. I just wanted to know what to anticipate. Do you get mad? Are you mean? Do you hate people? Do you kick dogs?

BRIAN: I genuinely didn't have the language to even understand what he was talking about.

As the months passed, Brian began to understand what Curt was talking about and vice versa, but there were yet other challenges to deal with. Curt was accustomed to expressing himself in a very direct way that proved upsetting to Brian and that led to arguments. In Brian's family, which Curt described as "a totally merged unit," though discussion was passionate, there was still great sensitivity to the feelings of others. Curt's parents, who are now divorced, had a "messy, loud, awful marriage."

BRIAN: Curt was direct, blunt. And I thought of that as being rude and selfish—that he wasn't giving. I remember once in the beginning we were driving to Little Italy, and he said something in a hurtful way that led to this big discussion.

CURT: I vaguely remember.

BRIAN: We parked on Mulberry Street, and I remember having to lay my head on Curt's lap. I was so upset that someone would talk to me that way. *No one* talked to me that way. And I told him, "How dare you talk to me that way."

CURT: There were things that I found irritating, and I must have said something. Brian had this tendency to be rigid, what I perceived at the time as being very uptight. You know, all the bathroom rituals took a long time. He was very particular and had a hard time kind of going with the flow. And then he had this intolerance of conflict. It was the tyranny of niceness. It made me mad all the time.

BRIAN: We'd come up against these things all the time, and we'd talk about them. We were walking in the Village once and Curt said, "I just need to be alone now." I'm like, well, *We're in the middle of a walk.* I walked back to my apartment alone, just furious. I'm sure he was furious, too, and then we'd come back and talk about it later.

I asked Brian and Curt why they didn't just go their separate ways permanently. In the early months of their relationship, it would not have been that complicated to call it quits.

BRIAN: Because it was him. Because there was something that was right about everything. It intuitively felt right in that no matter what shit we were going through, no matter what turmoil, the other side of it was really worthwhile. And we always came out whole afterwards, and more connected.

CURT: I knew intellectually, from my experience as a therapist, what had to be done, that we had to talk about it, had to have the fights— although at that point I wasn't very successful at the arguments.

BRIAN: I remember saying to Curt when we were together for six months, "Oh, don't you wish we were together for a year already? Don't you wish we had a history already?" I just wanted it all to be over. I dreaded the fights. I didn't want there to be any conflict. So I was looking forward to that day. But it never came.

CURT: It's gotten easier to fight—a lot easier—but we still fight.

BRIAN: We used to have these fights. We'd both brood and not talk. Now they're more like, Wait a second, we've done this before. Let's just get through it and have the day, because we only have the weekend to enjoy, and let's not waste it. So instead of taking twenty-four hours to resolve something, we do it in an hour.

CURT: Brian has friends who are in couples who say they never fight.

BRIAN: And I'm, like, Oh, my God, we're constantly back and forth.

Not all the couples I spoke with argue and fight as often and with as much heat and passion as Pam and Lindsy or Brian and Curt. Alison and Dayna, for example, don't really fight. They have spats that generally last ten minutes, and then they laugh about them. But as is the case in all couples, each partner occasionally does something that upsets the other. And like every couple, Alison and Dayna have their own way of letting each other know when they're unhappy.

ALISON: We'd made plans this past June to take some time off for a trip down to D.C. Dayna's two sisters and her dad live just outside the city, and my sister lives right in D.C. We made a decision to spend two nights with Dayna's sister in Silver Spring and two nights with my sister in D.C. Well, being from the family I'm from, I needed to call my sister at least a month in advance to let her know the two days that we were going to be there and get it all arranged. Dayna being Dayna—

DAYNA: I called my sister a couple days before.

ALISON: I kept waiting and waiting for Dayna to make her arrangements. And it's certainly her responsibility to call her sister. And she never called, never called, never called.

DAYNA: My family is very laid back.

ALISON: I need to have everything arranged. So it's about four days before our departure date, and we're out to dinner. We're having this perfectly nice dinner. But these things bubble up to the surface with me, and I said something like "So does your sister know that we're coming?" That first question was nice. And Dayna said, "No." Then sarcastically I said, "Does anyone in your family know we're coming?" So we had a huge fight in the restaurant.

DAYNA: "Huge fight" doesn't mean like yelling and screaming. I say, "I'll call." And Alison says, "Are you sure you're going to call?" And I say, "Sure, I'll call." That's a huge fight for us.

ALISON: Those are kind of harsh words. Like, Of course I'm going to do it, and you don't trust that I'm going to do it. The way I am, I need to know in advance. I don't know how to phrase the question any other way. So we had the kind of fight you have in a restaurant, and then we sat in silence for two minutes. And then Dayna said, "I don't know why you're with me when you hate me so much."

That's usually how our fights resolve. Then we kind of laughed. I told Dayna that I couldn't believe we were still discussing this after nine years. But I need a month to plan, and she needs the same day. So we need to meet somewhere in the middle.

A few of the couples set aside specific time during the day or after work for talking, sharing the day's events, discussing something that's bothering them, or negotiating a major decision. Marjorie and Marian, the Vermont dairy farmers, get together every day for lunch. This is their time to reconnect, assign afternoon chores, and make plans. They have been a couple for twenty years.

MARJORIE: We talk at lunch, and then after lunch, at one o'clock, we sit down in the living room and relax, and that's when we make our best decisions. That time helps us get centered. We focus on what's important, what we need to do, and what we don't need to do.

It's easy to imagine Marjorie and Marian relaxing in the inviting living room of their partly reconstructed eighteenth-century farmhouse. On this cold late-January afternoon, we're sitting at a large wooden table in the dining area, adjacent to the kitchen. The first floor of the house is mostly open; the kitchen and dining area form a large rectangular space running the full length of the back of the house, and the dining area opens onto the south-facing living room. Sun fills the main room, and from where I sit I have a clear view of the rolling fields and a few of Marjorie and Marian's lovingly cared for cows. Colorful bouquets of dried flowers hang from the exposed beam celing. Froggie, a chocolate Lab, one of the couple's two dogs, is curled up at my feet on the worn wood-plank floor.

Lunch this day is homemade pea soup, a big loaf of crusty bread, cheese made from the milk of Marjorie and Marian's cows, and apple cider. At the center of the table is a big jar filled with salt. I'm relieved to discover that I'm not the only salt addict. Between spoonfuls of soup, Marjorie and Marian tell me that even outside their everyday afternoon visits, they are accustomed to talking about everything.

MARIAN: We don't not discuss things.

MARJORIE: No matter what it is, it eventually comes out. For example, yesterday I did not have a good talk with my mother on the phone. She said something that wasn't very nice, so when I got off the phone I came downstairs and was bitching and moaning at Marian. Before I realized what was going on, I'd accused Marian of being in a bad mood. By this time we were down at the barn, and it finally occurred to me that I just hadn't processed what had happened with my mother, so I told Marian about it and we started talking.

As in every relationship, there are times when Marjorie and Marian are mad at each other, but not talking for more than a few hours isn't an option.

MARIAN: Because we have such a cooperative working situation, it's hard to go a whole day without talking. Sometimes when we're having a fight there will be this moment of *I'm leaving.* But we can't. Neither of us would ever leave the other one with chores to do. It would be impossible.

MARJORIE: We've gone to bed mad, and we've woken up mad. It happens, but it's always something stupid, and then we talk about it. As Marian said, we don't not discuss things.

From the very beginning of their relationship, Marjorie and Marian found it relatively easy to talk about everything, good and bad. It was a second-nature skill that they've refined over the years. But communication isn't something that came naturally to all the people I interviewed. Lack of communication was especially distressing to those who liked to talk things out but found themselves in relationships with partners whose first instinct was silence.

In the early years of their relationship, Nate and Danny struggled with Nate's silence and Danny's desire to talk.

NATE: I know I was very difficult back then. I mean, I can still be difficult.

DANNY: He was moody, very moody.

NATE: And I would shut down.

DANNY: He just wouldn't talk. And I tended to want to talk more, so I'd talk too much.

NATE: He would put a lot of energy into trying to figure out what was going on, and that would just get me more upset.

DANNY: And I'd try to make it better.

NATE: For example, I would get very depressed, but I wouldn't want to talk about it. I wouldn't even acknowledge it. So when Danny would question me, I'd say things like "I'm fine. There's nothing wrong with me. Leave me alone." I did a lot of that back then.

DANNY: And I would feel bad. I always assumed it was me, that whatever he was upset about was my fault.

NATE: Eventually, my mood would pass, and usually I'd apologize after the fact and we'd talk about it. I'm better now about acknowledging if I'm in a bad mood and talking about it, but I'm still not great at it. But Danny's also gotten to a healthy point where he's more demanding. He'll say, "Whoa, this is not acceptable. You don't have to say much, but you have to at least tell me that you're not happy and need to be left alone."

DANNY: In the early years of the relationship, if something happened, it might have taken a couple of days before it got talked out. Now it's an hour later or that evening that we'll talk. I also try not to push as much as I did. It's a balance.

It can be painful and disappointing to learn that your beloved is unable to figure out what's going on in your mind without your having to tell her or him. How much easier it would have been if Danny could have known right off the bat that Nate's bad moods had nothing to do with him and had intuited that what Nate needed was to be left alone. In other words, "If you really loved me, you would just know what I want and know what I mean without having to ask and without my having to explain." But that's not how it works, unless, of course, you can read minds.

Even if partners do a good job of communicating, not everything gets talked about. Besides the private realm that almost everyone maintains, myriad day-to-day experiences and interactions are never discussed. Most of the time there's no decision not to talk about something, but sometimes there is. For example, Jim and Martin never discussed Jim's jealousy early in their relationship. Martin chose to ignore it, and Jim eventually felt secure enough in the relationship to get over it.

On numerous occasions I found myself talking with the couples about things they'd never discussed before, as when Nate said that the "youthful fun" phase of his life had come to an end when he and Danny first became involved. More than one person responded to a partner's statement by crowing, "Oh, I want to hear more about *this!*"

I guess I shouldn't have been surprised how often things came up that hadn't been talked about before. Being interviewed about one's relationship isn't something most people do every day. Some of the couples actually discussed before my arrival what would be off-limits and how they would deal with answering questions that touched on subjects in tender, unresolved territory.

Anne and Cassandra* assumed I was going to ask questions about sex, so the morning before our evening appointment, they talked about what they were going to say. It had been about a year since they'd had sex, and while this was something Cassandra had tried to discuss, Anne was reluctant. Just talking about what they were going to say led to an argument. Obviously, I had no idea of any of this when I asked how their sexual relationship had changed during their eighteen years together, and I found myself discussing with them something they'd been unable to discuss with each other.

CASSANDRA: It's something we would argue about, but Anne just shuts down about this issue, so it doesn't become an argument, because I can only argue when she's coming back at me with something. So I just get mad and resentful.

ANNE: It's a live issue.

CASSANDRA: Yes, it is, but we dealt with this issue this morning, because we said, "Now, you know he's gonna ask us this question!"

Both Cassandra and Anne laughed, but I knew they weren't laughing that morning, as Cassandra confirmed.

CASSANDRA: We went to work mad. Mad! And it's not that I don't think this can be dealt with if people want to deal with it, but I don't feel like Anne wants to deal with it.

ANNE: I do want to deal with it, but for some reason I haven't. But I think I'm ready to. I think I should probably start on my own first,

* Not their real names.

with a therapist, to talk about what's going on and why I'm feeling the way I do. I don't know the best way to approach this. I'm not the therapy queen here.

CASSANDRA: Anne would say it's because we're too busy, and we've got too much going on, and we have too much stress. And you know, she's got a million reasons for it. I don't buy any of those reasons. Of course, I think it's directly related to my weight. The fatter I've gotten, the less sex we've had. But she won't confirm that one.

Anne wasn't going to take the bait, and she simply added that this was something they needed to work on. I let it go at that.

What couples do and don't talk about depends, of course, on the couples and the issue. Sex is something that's difficult for Cassandra and Anne to talk about, and it's a rough subject for some of the other couples as well, whether the sticking points are lack of sex in the relationship or specific likes and dislikes. For others, it's monogamy that's left undiscussed, and for others still, talking about past infidelities or current crushes is off limits.

As I quickly discovered, though, one couple's forbidden territory is another's fun. Some of the couples, for example, liked talking about their crushes on other men and women. Alison and Dayna not only like talking about it but believe that discussing attractions is essential.

ALISON: People are surprised that we talk about our crushes. We both think it's really healthy to talk about other people we're attracted to. In a way, it helps dissipate the feeling, because it's out on the table.

DAYNA: It's no big deal. Alison will just say, I have a crush on so and so.

ALISON: I was singing in a choir for a while, and I told Dayna about this woman I had a crush on who had an incredible singing voice. I think I had the crush on her voice more than anything else. But I told Dayna about the crush, and so when I came home from rehearsals she'd say, "Did you see so-and-so tonight?" And occasionally, when we meet a new friend, we sort of get crushed out on that friend. And if either of us is uncomfortable about it, we're able to talk about it.

DAYNA: It definitely has made a big difference. You don't feel guilty about it. Things don't feel secretive. Everything is just right there on the table.

One thing that all the couples communicate verbally or in other ways is their love and appreciation, whether that means saying "I love you" or "Thank you for making dinner." Each of the couples has their own way of doing it. Alison and Dayna, for instance, have a nightly ritual.

DAYNA: She has to tell me every night before she goes to sleep. That's the last thing she says: "I love you" and "Good night." And if I happen to fall asleep watching TV, she'll wake me up just to make sure it's been said.

ALISON: I'm afraid to jinx us if I don't.

DAYNA: I also know she loves me just because she'll put up with my bad moods. You just know. It's, like, coming back from lunch and checking my voicemail and hearing, "Hi, it's me. Call me back."

ALISON: It's the same for me. I just know. There's nothing she has to say. And sometimes I wonder if I'm being too trusting. You hear about people being in a relationship where they think everything's going great and it just blows up. But my instinct tells me that I can trust Dayna implicitly. I feel I can trust her that much, and she tells me everything.

DAYNA: I have to. I can't go to sleep otherwise.

Brian and Curt also tell each other "I love you," if not once a day, then every other day and a couple of times on weekends. But beyond saying it, they show it, in a loving goodbye when leaving for work and in their daily caretaking routines.

BRIAN: Curt's very good about bringing flowers and setting out the vitamins. Maybe it's a weird way to express your love, but it's part of living together and sharing a home. You know: making the coffee, putting out the garbage, emptying the dishwasher.

Besides doing things for each other in a practical sense, Brian said that he and Curt also show their love by listening to and supporting each other.

BRIAN: He's been my sounding board. He was instrumental in supporting me emotionally and believing in me when I left the family business. He really believes in me, and he recognizes potential that I didn't even know I had. It sounds Pollyanna-ish, but it's true.

Chris and Sherri stated their love for each other after their first week of courtship, at a McDonald's on the way back from a day trip to Los Angeles. Although Sherri was hiding her relationship with Chris from her mother, she used the excuse that she was going to Los Angeles to check out the UCLA medical school.

SHERRI: It wasn't even a fib, because I was kind of toying with the idea of going to medical school after I finished nursing school.

CHRIS: So we were sitting in McDonald's and I asked, "Do you think this is going to last?"

SHERRI: I said, "Yeah, I think it is, because I love you."

CHRIS: And then I said, "Oh good, because I love you, too." I was so afraid to say it.

SHERRI: It was one of those spontaneous, feel-good moments.

CHRIS: Now we say it regularly, at least once a day.

SHERRI: Especially if we're going out someplace, before one of us leaves. We're very big believers in "I don't ever want to have any regrets about not saying 'I love you' if something happens."

CHRIS: We're also big on telling each other things like "You know, I really like the way you did this." And once or twice a day it's not unusual for one of us to tell the other one, "You know, I'm really glad we're together" or "I really like our life" or—

SHERRI: Just little things, like "I appreciate you cleaning up my mess. I hadn't had a chance to get back to it."

CHRIS: Yeah, not taking each other for granted, making sure that the other person knows that they're appreciated.

SHERRI: I'm always telling Chris, "I really appreciate the fact that you made me lunch." Because I work night shift, and there's nothing open all night. And she'll make me something special, which makes everybody else envious at work. It's wonderful.

CHRIS: It's not uncommon for me to barbecue her a steak and give her a baked potato, with all of the works, and a salad.

SHERRI: It just pisses everybody off at work. They're eating dull tacos, and I'm having steak and potato.

CHRIS: Or I'll make homemade chicken pot pie. You don't get to be this size without being a good cook. So that's an important factor to us, to make sure that you tell the other person all of the good things. You know, too many people dwell on the negative things. You know, "You've done *this*" and "You've done *that*." And that's not to say we don't do that, too, because we do. But we make sure we do the other stuff, to balance out. Because we don't have a perfect relationship. There are no perfect relationships.

I was curious as to whether telling one's beloved "I love you" was peculiar to the younger couples, who I imagined would be more likely to put into words their love. But with the exception of only a handful of people—like Stanley, for instance, who has trouble verbally expressing his love—it was a virtually universal practice. Even the two people who have been together the longest have no trouble saying it.

JIM: We say it many times. Oh yeah. I can't see staying with somebody and not telling them you love them and not being affectionate. We never display it on the street or when we go to visit. We're not hanging all over each other, the way some people are. We do it in private and we've done it every day, right from the beginning.

MARTIN: Every day, just like any married couple. It's the same with everybody who really loves someone. I'll tell you what we do. Every day when we leave this apartment, we kiss each other. If we leave it fifteen times a day, we kiss each other fifteen times before we leave. That's just a habit, but it's a nice habit.

SIX

Home

Photo: Beth Bischoff

AS MY PLANE made its final approach into Salt Lake City's spic-and-span airport, I struggled to pay attention to the couple seated to my right, who were telling me about their recent vacation to Disneyland. I didn't want to seem rude, but my attention was completely consumed by the extraordinary landscape I could see from my window. The couple's stories were simply no match for the glistening Great Salt Lake spreading out below us across an otherwise barren desert valley and the jagged mountain peaks looming in the distance.

From the pictures I'd seen of Salt Lake City, I'd imagined a metropolis that filled much of a large valley on the edge of an enormous lake. Instead, the city looked tiny, as if it were taking shelter in one very small corner of an indescribably vast valley on a rise of land set against towering, razor-sharp mountains.

The pilot took us into one last turn, which gave me a direct view of the city. I had no trouble picking out the Mormon Temple or the dome of Utah's state capitol. But unlike the Capitol in Washington, D.C., which dominates the surrounding city, Utah's state capitol, despite its size and commanding site above the Great Salt Lake, is utterly dominated and dwarfed by the mountains behind it. This is a place where nature rules.

You might think that going to a place like Salt Lake City, the home of the Mormon Church, an institution not known for embracing homosexuals, I'd be wondering why gay people would choose to live in such a place. And when I first made plans to visit the area, I did think about that. But as the wheels of the 737 touched down on the runway and I had a close-up look at the moonlike landscape outside my window, I wondered why *anyone* would want to live in a place that seemed so remote and, to my eyes, forbidding.

I'd flown to Salt Lake City because it offered me easiest access to the town where Molly and Irene* live. I first met Molly and Irene via e-mail, and I remember how delighted I was to hear from them, especially after I learned that both are Mormon, one of them still actively so. They were proof that, indeed, gay people live everywhere, which is what I'd always responded when asked if gay people lived only in places like New York and San Francisco. But did happy lesbian and gay couples live everywhere?

Before hearing from scores of couples all over the country, from Charlotte to Milwaukee and Miami to Juneau, and visiting forty of the couples in person, I couldn't have confidently answered that question in the affirmative. But now I can. Happy gay and lesbian couples live everywhere, even in places where many of us would least expect to find them. The couples I interviewed live in urban, suburban, and rural areas; working-class, middle-class, and affluent communities; in apartments, in condos, in houses, and on farms. Everywhere.

On the drive out of Salt Lake City toward the small farming community where Molly and Irene live, I knew I was very far from San Francisco, a place I once lived, and Manhattan, the place my partner and I call home. For one thing, the highway speed limit was 75, which meant that just about everyone was driving 85, a ground speed I'd never experienced in the past for more than a few seconds

---

* Not their real names. I'm not giving the name or specific location of Molly and Irene's town, or describing what they look like, because the women fear that if they are identified in any public way as being lesbians, they will be forced out of their jobs. Given where they live, this is a well-founded fear.

at a time. The speed limit on most highways at home is 55, and even though there are some people crazy enough to bait the police and tempt fate, I think it would be suicide to drive 85 anywhere in New York City. But there I was in Utah, keeping up with traffic, watching in my rearview mirror for the police.

In addition to speed, there was, again, that landscape. Expansive valleys, towering mountains, and—once I'd gotten past the strip malls and suburban subdivisions outside Salt Lake City—the vastness of a place without people. Add to that a sudden storm and hail the size of large marbles smashing into my rental car with a terrible pinging sound and covering the highway with lumpy slush—in August!—and I felt as if I were on another planet.

The radio kept me company on the long drive, and I'd tuned it to one of the local Christian radio stations. My significant other thinks I'm crazy for listening to Christian radio, but I find it weirdly fascinating, especially when the subject turns to gay people, which it inevitably did during a syndicated show produced by the decidedly antigay Focus on the Family organization. I still find it hard to believe that the antigay religious folks are talking about people like me, or a hardworking couple like Molly and Irene, when they rail against gay marriage, but I know they are.

The topic of that day's on-air editorial was the Southern Baptist–led boycott of all things Disney because Disney provides domestic-partner benefits to its gay employees and because of the gay-positive television programs and movies that Disney and its subsidiaries occasionally produce. I couldn't help but wonder why the Southern Baptists and the other antigay crusaders were wasting their time on us when there are so many real problems that could use their attention, but rail they did, encouraging Christians everywhere to join the boycott and shun Disney theme parks, companies, and products. I had to chuckle at the thought of thousands of Christian parents wrestling toy Buzz Lightyears and Ariels from the hands of their children. Was there ever any doubt who would win *that* battle?

By the time I got to Molly and Irene's town—which, they'd told me, I could easily miss if I blinked—I was in the ideal frame of mind to meet a couple who have felt less than secure living in a conservative religious community. I made a left onto their broad three-block street and had no trouble finding their house, although it looked much like all the other postwar rectangular ranch houses in the neighborhood, with a large patch of lawn and a concrete stoop.

The only hint that this house was occupied by homosexuals was the small sign next to the stoop. Molly and Irene wanted to be sure I'd find them, so they planted one of their camping stakes, with a pink triangle and a drawing of a small pig mounted in the middle of it, in a place where they were sure I'd see it. The pink triangle, of course, is the relatively universal symbol of gay pride, one that Molly and Irene felt certain their neighbors would not recognize. And the pig . . . Well, Molly and Irene live in farm country, and the pig was simply decorative.

Molly and Irene had several reasons for moving from a large and growing community just outside Salt Lake City to the small town where they now live. Both were unhappy with their teaching jobs, and there were suspicions among their colleagues about their relationship, which they feared could get them fired. They also wanted to get away from the watchful eye of the Mormon Church. So they applied for jobs in a rural part of the state where Molly had taught earlier in her career and where her mother had lived until her death in the mid-1980s. Molly and Irene secured positions in the same school, as it happened, and then set about buying a house. Their first surprise was finding a gay-friendly real estate broker.

IRENE: A gay friend gave us the name of a guy who had a gay sister. He was very easygoing and understood us. One time, he was showing us a house, and he went ahead of us and surprised us when he came out of the closet with a drape wrapped around himself. He wasn't gay, but he knew that we were and he was trying to have a little joke with us. We couldn't have imagined that we'd find a gay-friendly realtor out here.

Even before they started looking for a place to live, Molly and Irene decided that they didn't want to live in the same town where they taught, and didn't want to live in a city.

MOLLY: The one time I lived in the same town where I worked, I found out that I never left school. At the grocery, the kids would look at me and go, "You eat?" That's cute, but I thought it wasn't too cool. I also found that I was having to be really careful at home. I mean,

I'm not going to do anything outrageous, but if I happen to slip and say something pretty silly, I don't want to be doing it around the people I live with and work with every day.

IRENE: I also wanted to be out in the country. I was raised in a little postwar house, where the yards were pretty close and the houses were small. I didn't want to live like that. And I always thought I'd marry a farmer.

MOLLY: Another reason we didn't want to live right in the town where we teach is because it's even more Mormon than Salt Lake, like ninety-five percent Mormon.

IRENE: If we were found out, we would be ostracized. And while they probably know they'd have a hard time firing us because we're gay, they would be looking for other ways to get rid of us.

Why didn't Molly and Irene consider putting even more distance between themselves and a region of the country that's heavily Mormon and not-so-gay-friendly? Both women have deep roots in the region—if not the actual town—where they live, especially Irene, who was born and raised Mormon and retains very strong ties to her religion and the Mormon community. Molly, who converted to Mormonism and no longer practices, has spent much of her teaching career in the region around Salt Lake City and often visits her mother's grave, which is just a short drive from Molly and Irene's home. They also have friends, including a good handful of gay and gay-friendly friends. Irene is president of the local Mormon parents-of-gays support group, and she and Molly socialize with other gay women in the area.

IRENE: We have a group of gay friends—lesbian friends, actually—that we do a video night with. And there's this group of women who get together at a coffeehouse, which is just a short drive from here. They have a coffee group. "Well, why don't you come with us on Thursdays to the coffee group?" I'm thinking to myself, I don't drink coffee, so what am I going to do at a coffee group? I'm sometimes embarrassed by that, because I still have the Mormon standards. I don't drink. I don't smoke. I don't drink coffee. Mostly because I don't want to. But we went anyway.

MOLLY: There are a lot of gay people here. They're just hidden. And the women are hidden even deeper.

Actually, I didn't have to journey nearly as far as Molly and Irene's community of five hundred people to feel as if I'd left the gay-friendly cocoon I live in in Manhattan. All I had to do was take the F train from Twenty-third Street to where Stewart and Stanley live in Queens. There was nothing unfamiliar about the F train or Queens. I grew up not far from Stewart and Stanley and the F was the same train I traveled on as a child with my sister, brother, and mother on our way to see the Christmas tree at Rockefeller Center. What *was* unfamiliar, though, was my feeling of foreboding the night I went to see Stewart and Stanley, as the train slid underneath the East River and passed into Queens, a place I'd left fifteen years before.

There was a moment after college when I considered living in Queens, and I even had an apartment lined up in the lovely 1930s development I grew up in, but instead I chose to take a tiny room in a friend's apartment in Manhattan. Besides the usual pull of the big city, I knew I'd have no trouble living life as an openly gay man in Manhattan. I wasn't sure it would be so easy to do that if I lived someplace where everybody knew me by name. So like many gay and lesbian people all across the country, I left the community I grew up in for the relative anonymity of the city. Now I was heading back to meet Stewart and Stanley, who lived in the same neighborhood where Stewart grew up.

Most of the people I interviewed had left home, usually for a variety of reasons having nothing to do with being gay. But for many, sexual orientation was indeed a factor, as it was for Danny, who needed to put some distance between himself and his less than accepting parents. Stewart, however, was one of the handful of people I spoke with who stayed put. He was in kindergarten when the building he and Stanley now live in was built, and he remembers walking by the construction site. His parents live just a few blocks away.

STEWART: That's where I'm different than a lot of people. I'm still in my own neighborhood. I was raised here, went to school here, came out here, and I work here.

STANLEY: And, as it happens, my sister, who is six years older than me, taught at the yeshiva where Stewart and his brother went.

STEWART: Stanley's brother-in-law is a podiatrist and shares an office with my parents' doctor.

STANLEY: There were so many "Small world!" things going on when we met.

Because he lived so close to his family, Stewart knew right from the start that he couldn't hide his relationship with Stanley from his parents. But hiding wasn't in fact the goal, and shortly after Stanley moved in with Stewart, they made plans to introduce him to Stewart's parents.

For virtually all the couples I interviewed, their reasons for living where they do and choosing the type of housing they have are as simple and/or complex as they are for any two people trying to make a home together. These include what the couple can afford, jobs, climate, good schools, and proximity to family. For some of the gay and lesbian couples, like Molly and Irene, there were additional issues, including how welcome or unwelcome they would be.

Two of the couples, Nate and Danny and Jennifer and Brigid, opted for the San Francisco Bay area because they wanted to live in a place where a gay couple with children would be comfortable. Most of the couples, though, simply chose to live in the places they wanted to live. Judy and Bev* felt pressure from their real estate broker to live in their city's gay neighborhood, a rapidly gentrifying area just outside the business district. He thought they would be more comfortable there, but they wanted a big yard and a house that didn't need extensive renovations.

Most of the couples I interviewed have never had a problem renting or buying the place of their choice. A few did, though not in recent years. In 1983, Cassandra and Anne were moving from a very gay-friendly college town in the Northeast where Cassandra had been an administrator to a small, mid-Atlantic coast city where she'd gotten a new job. While Cassandra stayed behind to recover from an unexpected hysterectomy, Anne went ahead to look for an apartment. Cassandra's new boss offered a staff member to accompany Anne around town and help find a place.

* Not their real names.

ANNE: I found a one-bedroom in this little rental town-house community not far from the school. But they would not rent a one-bedroom to me, because they knew another woman was living with me. And I'm like, "Well, what do you mean?" "You're two single-sex people, and you have to have two bedrooms." I was blown away.

CASSANDRA: We didn't want to pay for it, because we didn't really need it, but we took the two-bedroom.

ANNE: I had only three days to find an apartment, and this seemed to be the best place. So I said, "Okay, fine, we'll take the other room. We're not gonna use that room for anything but guests, but okay."

This is not a happily-ever-after story. The community was occupied mostly by young, relocated corporate couples who were not terribly welcoming.

ANNE: You know, Dad goes off to work. Mommy stays home with the kids. They all meet together at lunchtime. They're all out in the yard, and all the kids played together.

Cassandra and I lived in an end unit, and everybody had to walk past our place to get to the parking lot. No one would speak to us. It was awful! We would talk to them, and some of the men would talk to us. But the women would not speak to us.

CASSANDRA: And they would not let their children come near us. So that was not a very cool thing.

ANNE: I was shocked, because I'm a very friendly person, and it's not like we had big parties. I mean, we were pretty normal people.

CASSANDRA: There was one guy who would come talk to Anne during the day.

ANNE: There was a male truck driver who came around and visited me all the time.

CASSANDRA: She always attracts truck drivers.

ANNE: I don't know, what can I say?

Cassandra and Anne had a one-year lease on their apartment, and as soon as it was up, they moved to a city neighborhood where there were plenty of other gay people.

I expected to hear from Anyda and Muriel and Jim and Martin that they had had trouble finding a place to live together, especially during the early years of their relationships. But though they were out renting and buying apartments and houses long before gay and lesbian couples were as visible as they are today, they never had a problem. One of the other older couples I interviewed, however, did. And in a place where I would not have expected it.

Bill and Phil have been together since they knocked each other down on a street in San Francisco on the night of August 25, 1967. Phil was out "looking for a trick, not a boyfriend," and Bill had run away to San Francisco from Indiana, where he was in college. Once they picked themselves up off the sidewalk, Phil invited Bill to his place for a drink. Bill accepted.

Phil is now sixty-six, and Bill is fifty. Phil is a big, commanding presence, and he enjoys conversation. Bill is slight, intense, a man of few words. They live in a grand post-1906-earthquake apartment house in Pacific Heights, a charming upscale neighborhood on the hill above the Marina district. At the front door of their apartment house I notice that only Phil's name is on the buzzer, and I suspect there's a story here.

When we sit down for the interview in their filled-to-the-rafters den, I ask Phil and Bill what it was like in San Francisco for a gay couple in 1967. To my surprise, Phil says it was difficult. I ask him to explain.

PHIL: Renting an apartment. I lied. I said Bill was my young cousin. I wanted that carriage house.

BILL: As it turns out, it would have been fine.

PHIL: The landlord found out we were a couple, and we ended up being very cozy. She was a psychiatrist.

Phil's fears were not entirely unfounded, however, at least in terms of the overall climate of the times. In the 1960s, Phil was working in the insurance business for a man who he thought was "broad-minded about gay people."

PHIL: I was wrong. A friend of mine who was a very, very major client, who has since died, called me at the office late one afternoon. We weren't talking frivolities, so I don't know what my boss could have heard, but he picked up the phone and apparently listened in on our conversation. After I finished the conversation, my boss asked me to come into his office and he said, "Phil, I want you to tell him to take his business elsewhere." I asked why, and he said, "Because I really don't want to have any fags in this office."

Phil kept his mouth shut, but he didn't tell his client friend to take his business elsewhere. I asked Phil if his boss's comment had an adverse effect on their working relationship.

PHIL: Not really. It just made you a little more sneaky about getting things done. It's like that phrase in *Bonfire of the Vanities.* "If all else fails, lie," which you found yourself doing.

When we moved from the carriage house, after six and a half years, to an apartment on Russian Hill, I lied again. I said I was taking it for myself and that a cousin of mine would occasionally be staying with me. Actually, my mother suggested the cousin thing. Somewhere along the line, when Bill was going around with me at the debutante cotillion and things like that, she said, "Darling, just say he's your cousin. I'll back you up." And she did.

BILL: It was what you had to go through at that point in time. Now, in more and more circumstances, it doesn't make any difference. And I think I came to that realization a little bit before Phil did.

In 1977, Phil and Bill moved to the apartment in which they now live, and again Phil put the lease in his name alone. He was certain the owner would not rent them the apartment if he knew they were gay. The single name on the buzzer still reflects the single name on the lease, but the issue of their homosexuality is now ancient history. The buzzer issue is not.

BILL: We've been here twenty years, and after a certain period of time, they all knew what the story was and they didn't care. So the only thing that annoyed me—

PHIL: Still does. The lease is still in my name.

BILL: No, no, not even that silly little thing. You come in by the elevator and see the list of names of people who live here and you see, "Phillip——," and I think my name should be right next to his.

PHIL: Well, yeah, it's gotta change. It has to. But I don't like rocking the boat. That's the problem. But I should do something about it, and I probably will.

BILL: At some point in time, I would like to be up there.

As the conversation unfolded, I was struck by how the prejudice and fear of another era had carried over into this one. The absence of Bill's name on the buzzer and the lobby resident list is a small but terribly potent reminder of an all-too-recent past when same-sex couples were visible only at their own peril. I wonder if this is the golden age that the Focus on the Family folks yearn for.

Despite the old joke about what lesbians bring on a second date,* only a handful of the couples, female or male, set up house together quite so quickly. Most decided within a few months of meeting that they wanted to live together, and by the end of the first year most were sharing a place. Whether the desire to set up house comes from an ancient genetic code or is something we're socialized to want, the progression from courtship to shared domicile was universal.

For two of the couples, the progression to a permanent shared home was a long one. For Gordon and Jay, both of whom had jobs that kept them on the road for six months out of every year, eighteen years passed before they lived together full-time. And once they decided to take the plunge, Gordon and Jay did it in grand style, buying "The Castle," a grand French-style chateau built in 1912 in Stamford, Connecticut. For Patsy and Lucy, it was thirteen years before they made the move.

After Lucy left Dixie for Patsy, her first big task was finding a place of her own. Lucy wasn't ready to live with Patsy—or anyone else—after the breakup, and she also thought she should have a place where her teenage daughter would feel comfortable visiting during school breaks and holidays. She found an apartment in Greenwich Village, just a half-hour subway ride from her job at Brooklyn College. At around the same time, Patsy bought the house the two women now share on the eastern end of Long Island. For thirteen years, Lucy spent half the week at her apartment in the city and half the week at the house. They've always thought of the house as their joint home; the apartment in the city was Lucy's.

* A U-Haul.

LUCY: I always needed to be in the city. Still do. My ideal life is to have a place in the city and a house out here. But since I retired, I just can't see spending the money to have an apartment in the city and running a house.

PATSY: Lucy is a city person and I'm a country person, so it's always been a compromise.

LUCY: It took a few years to really work it out so that I was comfortable not spending at least half my time in the city.

PATSY: Until Lucy retired, we only spent half the week together. The good thing about that was Lucy could easily do concerts and movies and things that she loves to do, without me having to do them all. I started teaching music at the local school and also teaching privately. Plus I compromised quite a lot in the amount of time I went to the city.

LUCY: Patsy came in every week. We had subscriptions to a million things, but she came in reluctantly. There's always been a division between us. And she had gotten pretty fed up with my constantly packing and coming and going. She used to complain about it. It's one of the reasons why I retired at sixty-two. I felt that I had to finally make the full commitment about us living together all the time. And I was really scared about that, although after thirteen years we knew each other pretty well.

PATSY: You never know each other *that* well. I learned more about Lucy when we started really living together. I also learned more about myself.

Lucy and Patsy had many discussions over the years about their living arrangements, and they talked at length about Lucy's permanent move to the house before she made the decision to retire and give up her city apartment. Talking about living together in advance of actually doing it was typical of the couples. But not everyone did it. For example, Stephanie didn't realize that Lilia had actually moved into her apartment until she noticed that Lilia was having her mail forwarded. Stephanie and Lilia, who are thirty-two and thirty-four respectively, met through friends at a club two years before they began dating. Now a couple for ten years, the two women share a home in Portland, Oregon, with their newborn son. Stephanie explains how Lil came to live with her: "Lil just started spending a lot of time with me, and then she started leaving her clothes. You know, it happened gradually. And then the next thing I know I'm getting her mail. And I said, 'So, I guess you moved in.' That was it, and I didn't have a problem with it.' "

Brian and Curt negotiated a long time before deciding to move in together, about a year after they'd started dating. But among the couples, their decision was exceptional, because it had more to do with fear than with the natural progression of their relationship. Brian and Curt were afraid of missing the chance to live as a couple if they didn't seize the opportunity. In 1988, eleven months after they began seeing each other, Curt tested positive for HIV. At that time, no one talked about AIDS being a manageable disease. People with full-blown AIDS were given, at best, two years to live. Curt hoped for five.

From the time Brian and Curt first started dating, both assumed that Curt was HIV-positive. Curt knew that his sexual experiences in the late 1970s and early 1980s had put him at significant risk, and Brian heard all about it the day they met in the Gay Men's Health Crisis workshop. Like many men in those days, Curt had put off getting tested until it was clear that something could be done to treat AIDS. By 1988, doctors had a clearer understanding of the disease and had begun using antiviral drugs that they hoped would prolong life for those whose immune systems were under attack. Curt decided it was time.

BRIAN: I remember when Curt said he was going to be tested. I was scared, but it was his decision. And there was a part of me that wanted to know. There would be an answer, yes or no. I assumed he was positive, but there was this eternal hope that he would be negative.
CURT: On some functional level I assumed I was positive, but that's a whole different thing from knowing that you are.

On the day he went to get his test results, Curt arranged to take the afternoon off from work. He planned to call Brian as soon as he left the testing center.

CURT: I wound up having lunch and going shopping before I called Brian.

BRIAN: He called me at work, and I took the phone in the other room. I don't remember what he said other than that the results were positive. The blood drained out of me. I went back into the office to say I had to leave. I never left work in the middle of the afternoon.

I drove to my apartment to meet Curt, and all I could think was, Oh my God, I can't believe this is my life. Of course I picked someone who is positive. This is my life: the drama, the tragedy! All of our friends were dying, and now Curt.

CURT: When Brian got home, we got into bed and cried. We spent the whole afternoon crying. It was awful, but Brian was perfect. He cried with me.

BRIAN: It was overwhelming. It changed everything. From that point, everything about the relationship felt pressured. We didn't have time to waste.

Two months after his diagnosis, and after much discussion, Curt moved into Brian's apartment. Seeing the place as it is now—the original apartment has been joined to the studio next door and completely renovated—I simply assumed that their moving in together had been the right move from the start. I asked Curt what it was like, and his answer surprised me: "It was hard and horrible." Everything about their apartment as it is now says the opposite: The soothing colors, the polished floors and small area rugs, the simple furnishings, the artwork, the lighting, the layout, all contribute to a sense of serenity. This is clearly a shared home into which both have invested considerable time, energy, and money. There is no evidence of their early struggles.

For all the couples, moving in together was an adjustment, ranging from smooth and relatively problem-free to wrenching. Without any specific model for setting up house together, the men and women relied on the examples set by the heterosexual couples they knew, common sense, and gut instinct. For Brian and Curt, already coping with the pressure of Curt's HIV diagnosis, Curt's move into Brian's apartment was not what either of them expected. Curt's negative feelings about Brian's apartment and the lack of joint ownership led to conflict.

CURT: I didn't pay attention to my instincts, because I hated the building and I hated the apartment. It was a boxy one-bedroom, just two boxes next to each other. It was just a whole aesthetic thing. I thought it was ugly and claustrophobic. If I'd paid attention to my instincts, I never would have moved here.

And then there was that whole ownership thing, because Brian owned the apartment. There was this assumption that I was coming into his world and what could be wrong? If Brian had been moving into my apartment, I would have made it a point to help him adjust to the new space with things, like doorknobs and light fixtures, that he liked. I just would have changed those things for him.

BRIAN: I was very myopic about the whole thing. When I first moved into the apartment, I didn't change a thing.

CURT: And I'm very aesthetically sensitive. All that stuff makes me crazy. Part of it was my fault, because I never felt ownership enough to say, "We're going to just do this." So it became a source of conflict, because I didn't feel spiritually welcome. I felt emotionally welcome on some level, but not in a larger sense.

BRIAN: It's all so complicated, because there was also the issue of Curt moving in and me doing my will. My father asked who I was leaving the apartment to, and I said, "Curt." And he said, "No, you can't." He wanted me to leave it to my brother or to the family. You know, "Who's this outsider?" And I told my father, "If we were married, this would never be an issue." Of course, Curt knew everything that was going on.

CURT: It didn't feel like my apartment.

BRIAN: It didn't feel like mine, either.

It wasn't until Brian and Curt started decorating the apartment together, a year after Curt moved in, that it began to feel like a shared home. Brian didn't have much in the way of furniture, so they were able to decide on things together. "The decorating has always been good," explained Curt. "We've always decorated together, because we have fun doing that. Even before I moved in, we'd bought the rug for the living room."

Only the completion of their recent renovation made Curt finally feel like an equal partner in his own home, and he and Brian are both justifiably proud of the place. In fact, there wasn't a couple I visited who weren't house-proud. From Stewart and Stanley's tiny one-bedroom rental apartment, hard by the Long Island Expressway, to Marjorie and Marian's renovated Vermont farmhouse, all the couples expressed pride in the homes they'd made together.

From what I saw, you would think that virtually all gay men and lesbians were neat, but on at least two occasions, visiting friends of the couples confessed how much time had been spent preparing for my arrival. Molly and Irene were one of these couples, and once their friend revealed the truth, Irene sheepishly took me down the hall to her office to show me what their house normally looked like.

Another stereotype that got blown out of the water was the one about gay men and cutting-edge design sense. Some of the male couples had great taste—or at least taste that I considered great—and so did some of the lesbian couples. But for the most part, the partners lived modestly, their homes a reflection of their individual and combined likes and dislikes and not a reflection of the latest trend announced in the pages of *Metropolitan Home* or *House & Garden*. And unlike so many of the places pictured in the design magazines, almost all these couples' apartments and houses were homey, not necessarily "beautiful."

One thing I noticed as I toured house after apartment after condo was that in each couple, each partner had a private space of some kind. A few of the couples had separate bedrooms. One of the men had an entire basement workshop and studio to himself. Lucy had built a large music studio for Patsy. But for most of the couples there was at least an office or a corner of the living room or a desk (or a corner of a desk) that each could call his or her own.

Brian and Curt have a small windowless space off their living room that they share as an office, and in that office is a desk, and on that desk each has a separate work area. But there is only one chair, and they joke that one side of the chair is Brian's and the other is Curt's. In truth, they never occupy the one chair at the same time.

Since I had learned that Brian was the more particular of the two, I assumed that his work area would be more organized. And in fact, it looks neater, because his pile of papers, which appeared to be as tall as Curt's, is topped by a paperweight. There was, of course, a story behind the paper-weight (I've discovered that there's always a story). Brian explained that from the living room, you can see the office and, particularly, his side of the desk. Curt objected to the view of Brian's stack of unruly papers. Brian suggested keeping the door closed. Curt wanted the door open and suggested the paperweight. Hence.

For all the couples, their apartment, condo, house, or cottage is a special place they call their own. And, perhaps most important, their home is a place they can be themselves. This is no doubt true of all couples—of all people, for that matter. At home you don't have to worry about what the neighbors will think if you want to watch the evening news in torn underwear, slurp cereal from a bowl, or swing from a chandelier. You can say things and do things you would never consider saying and doing if you were in public.

For the gay and lesbian couples I interviewed—and, I imagine, for most gay and lesbian couples—the safety of home goes way beyond that. Jim and Marty kiss each other only at home. Given the world in which they grew up and lived for so long, it's hardly surprising that they never show their affection in any form outside the private realm of home. Of course, you don't have to be older to censor yourself.

Judy and Bev, who are both on the cusp of forty and live in a modest suburban house with a big backyard, have been together for ten years. They wouldn't think of calling each other "honey" except inside the house, although they slip occasionally because the endearment is so automatic.

BEV: We'll be in the grocery store. "Honey." It gets a little embarrassing when you say "honey" real loud and you don't think about it and somebody is standing there. You get a little paranoid. Heterosexual females call each other "honey," but it's just the fact that we know we're gay.

I asked Judy and Bev what makes them uncomfortable about calling each other "honey" in public.

BEV: Somebody will know we're gay.
JUDY: One concern is being confronted physically. That frightens me. But I don't want to offend somebody if they're uncomfortable with it.

BEV: I'm not in-your-face gay. You know, "I'm gay and I don't care who knows." I'm not that kind.

Whether the threat is real, perceived, or imagined, most of the couples limit in some way their public interactions, whether it's taking their partner's hand, exchanging a kiss in a romantic restaurant, or laying an affectionate arm on a shoulder. It's only at home or in a gay club or at a gay resort where this kind of normal interaction isn't routinely censored.

For some of the couples, modifying their behavior outside of home wasn't enough. Though it's been a long time since they've had to do this, in the early years of their relationship Molly and Irene kept a spare room made up as a second bedroom.

MOLLY: We had the dummy room downstairs.

IRENE: I'd forgotten about this, because we haven't done it for so long. But we set up a bed and I had my stuff downstairs, so when the family came to visit, there's *my* room and here's *Molly's* room. Or if one of my nieces or nephews spent the night, I would sleep down in the basement.

MOLLY: We did that for a long time.

Because of Irene's involvement in the Mormon Church, keeping her and Molly's relationship secret involved more than just having a dummy bedroom. Two women from the church came to visit Irene on a regular basis, so any sign of the relationship had to be removed—including Molly.

IRENE: These were really neat ladies. They were very concerned about me, and I bonded with them. I looked forward to their visits. They treated me nice, because they gave me a schedule of when they were visiting, whereas some would just knock on the door some night. So before they got here, Molly would straighten up the house and put any cards away.

MOLLY: Like cards to each other. You know, "I love you" type things.

IRENE: Getting rid of anything that would look like we were gay—we called it "straightening up."

MOLLY: And I didn't want to be hassled by anybody from the church, so when the ladies came to visit I'd go hide and dink around in another room.

I asked Molly and Irene if "straightening up" had been difficult for them, but they said that it wasn't hard because they'd had plenty of practice.

IRENE: We did it at work. You've got to realize, we were working in the same school and we had to pretend we weren't a couple. So we did our professional thing. It was real hard for me for quite a while. It's like you had to click into your school mode. You'd do your school thing. You'd talk to each other in the hall like "Hi, how are you." I'd eat lunch with her, but generally we'd eat in a group. And then we'd come home and be madly in love. I learned mostly from Molly. She'd had more practice at it than I had.

MOLLY: Just professional survival.

IRENE: Like here's my job self and here's my home self. At home, we get to be ourselves.

Just in case you think this is a thing of the past, it's not. One of the couples I interviewed still "straightens up" the house when family members come to visit. Happily, none of the other couples I interviewed do that any longer or feel the need to maintain a dummy bedroom.

SEVEN

Roles and Gender

O N A FEBRUARY MORNING in 1988, copies of my first book, *The Male Couple's Guide,* arrived on the desks of most of my colleagues at CBS News. I was working as a segment producer for CBS's morning show. Several of my colleagues and I shared a broken-down former conference room as a makeshift office, and that morning, there they all were, thumbing through their own crisp, new copies of my book when I walked in. My publisher had apparently done a very good job of media distribution.

I was excited that *The Male Couple's Guide* was out but a little nervous about my colleagues' reactions. Not only was I brand-new to CBS, I was also the only openly gay person on the editorial side of the show. And while AIDS had already transformed the way news organizations dealt with homosexuality, gay issues and openly gay people in the newsroom were not nearly as routine as they are today.

Several of my office mates, all of whom were women, gathered around my work area and started asking questions. Most of them had gay male friends, but they had never felt comfortable asking their friends the kinds of things they were now asking me. I'm sure we talked about all kinds of topics, but the only question I particularly remember came from a woman named Amy, who happened to be married to a CBS executive. She asked, "Who plays the husband and who plays the wife?"

Amy wasn't the first person to ask me that question, and I had traditionally answered with an involved explanation about how things don't work that way in same-gender relationships. But now, instead, knowing that her marriage was more a coequal partnership than an old-fashioned "Me Tarzan, you Jane" situation, I answered her question with a question. I asked, "Who plays the husband and who plays the wife in your relationship?" There were nods of understanding and smiles all around.

Over the years, the husband and wife question is the one I've been asked by heterosexual people more often than any other. Without the standard husband-wife/boy-girl division of the practical and emotional aspects of a married relationship, how do gay and lesbian couples go about living their lives? Imbedded within that question are lots of smaller questions about how gay couples do everything straight couples do—but without traditional gender roles to follow or rebel against. How do decisions get made? Who takes out the garbage? Who drives the car? Who brings the flowers on Valentine's Day? Who arranges the flowers? Who buys the diamond engagement ring? Who *wears* the diamond engagement ring? Who's the strong one? Who's the primary breadwinner? Who leaves the empty beer cans strewn around the living room? Who initiates sex? Who's the submissive one in bed? Who does the grocery shopping? Who pushes the vacuum? Who decides what color the drapes should be? Who does the comforting? Who takes care of the children? Who keeps the social calendar? Who writes the thank-you notes?

I'm well aware that couple life for many heterosexuals has been transformed in recent decades, which is why my colleagues understood my response to Amy's question even before I offered a full explanation. They knew that heterosexual married life is not as rigidly defined as it was for previous generations. Today, we all know women who work, and most of us know men who have diapered a baby. Men of my generation expect that their wives will have jobs, by choice or necessity, and they know how to turn on the vacuum even if they have to be reminded to use it.

This isn't to say that everything about heterosexual relationships has been transformed. Despite all the social changes of the past few decades, men, more often than women, are the primary breadwinners. Women, far more often than men, run the household and take care of the kids. Men do the driving and take care of the car. Women decorate the house, do the grocery shopping, and prepare the meals. Men bring women flowers and anniversary presents. Women *expect* flowers and anniversary presents. Men are supposed to be strong. Women are supposed to be dependent. In the most traditional couples, men make the decisions and women live with them.

If coequal relationships were the dream of those who rebelled against the kind of traditional marriage where roles were rigidly and stereotypically defined, then the gay and lesbian couples I interviewed are living that dream. Among the people I interviewed, none of the women has felt compelled to assume the role of wife, and none of the men has felt compelled to assume the role of husband. For the most part, there are no roles. There are simply two people in one relationship. Money still needs to be earned, decisions need to be made, hurt feelings need to be soothed, the floors need to be cleaned, the baby needs to be burped, and the telephone needs to be answered. It all gets done, but these same-sex couples can't depend on gender roles to divvy up who does what and who is dependent on whom.

This is not to say that within same-gender relationships there aren't struggles over power and control. For Brian and Curt, the struggle is ongoing.

BRIAN: We're battling the power issue with each other all the time, but it's not a gender-role-playing issue. Neither of us is like "I take care of the dishes and put out the plates, and Curt comes home and the dinner is cooked for him." Whoever likes cooking, cooks.

CURT: I think there's a lot of freedom. You can choose things. You can say yes to things and say no to things. You can reinvent what it means to be a couple. You don't have to just accept any of the assumptions, which I think is great.

The bottom line is that all couples have the same issues to work out, whether those couples are male-female, male-male, or female-

female. The difference is that gay people aren't expected to follow conventions, and heterosexuals are born to theirs. Heterosexuals may choose to follow those conventions, rebel against them, or do a little of both, but they are compelled to deal with them in some way.

The couples I interviewed have had the opportunity to create a new form of relationship that works for both individuals and is based on equality. Whether this evolution came about consciously or not, the result is a far more fluid type of relationship where neither partner is forced to take on the role that is traditionally assumed by his or her gender. Ideally, this means that each partner gets to be himself or herself, and that together, the couple creates a relationship that is uniquely their own.

There was, of course, an old gay relationship stereotype based very much on traditional masculine and feminine roles. The partner who was more feminine took on the woman's role, and the more masculine partner took on the man's role. But this "butch-femme" framework had little relevance to the couples I spoke with. In my interviews, I confirmed what I suspected going in: that you can't make any assumptions about who does what based on who is the more "feminine" or "masculine" of the pair.

But while I knew better than to draw conclusions based on traditional images of masculinity and femininity, I still found myself surprised when the more traditionally masculine man was the emotionally nurturing parent or the more traditionally feminine woman drove the tractor. I may know better, but I'm still a creature of the culture into which I was born, and I found myself making stereotyped assumptions embarrassingly often.

I was sure that Marian drove the tractor. I could picture her strong, farm-toughened, sinewy hands gripping the steering wheel as she hauled hay to the barn or spread manure. In truth, this was about more than just hands. Marian's manner and overall appearance contributed to my thinking that she was the one in the driver's seat. Her brown, silver-flecked hair is close-cropped and indifferently scattered across her forehead. Her lean, boyish figure, the day I met her, is clad in jeans and a plaid flannel shirt over a T-shirt. And in

contrast to Marjorie, who is exuberant and instantly warm, Marian, on first encounter, is cool and reserved.

MARJORIE: Sometimes people are surprised that I'm the tractor driver. I'm not exactly sure why, but they think that maybe Marian's more butch than I am or something. Because she has such short hair.

Marjorie is the more traditionally feminine-looking and feminine-acting of the two. She has long hair, which she keeps loosely pulled back in a braid. Where Marian is angular, Marjorie is round. Her broad, easy smile is complemented by round, ruddy cheeks. She has small, girlish hands that apparently do just fine on the steering wheel of a tractor. I asked them who played the husband and who played the wife, and Marjorie answered: "We are both. We have interchangeable roles."

There was never a time when Marjorie and Marian struggled with who was going to do what on the farm. The responsibilities fell into place along preference lines.

MARIAN: It was never "I want to do that." "No, I want to do that." It was always "You're going to do that, fine. I'm going to do something else." There's great cooperation.

MARJORIE: Like with driving the tractor. If I know that manure needs to be put on the garden, we say, "Okay, today's going to be the day to spread shit." I know it's me and not her.

MARIAN: We noticed that with friends who are straight couples, especially on farms, the responsibilities are really delineated. The men do what you expect the men to do.

MARJORIE: Drive the tractor. Spread the shit.

MARIAN: The women raise the kids. And we always feel sort of frustrated for these women, because the couples aren't working together, really, as a partnership; they're just there at the same time and doing really different things. And some of these women are shunted into roles they didn't want. They might have been out there cropping and stuff like that, but they couldn't, because—

MARJORIE: The kids came, and that's what women are expected to do.

MARIAN: I think that's very frustrating. We got to choose what we wanted to do.

MARJORIE: We go to farming get-togethers, and we want to hang out with the guys, because they're talking farming and the women are talking kids.

MARIAN: It's always the men in those situations who are doing the work that we want to talk about.

I don't mean to suggest by offering the example of Marjorie and Marian that all the couples I interviewed have discovered a conflict-free utopia in which there's a complete balance of power and each partner does what he or she enjoys most. Without the organizing strictures of gender or old-time butch-femme guidelines, plenty of other factors come into play in sorting out roles, including age, experience, income, and personality, as well as ability and preference.

For example, not every couple I interviewed has a partner who particularly likes to clean house or pay bills. Sometimes *no one* liked either chore, and in some cases both did, but with varying levels of enthusiasm. And not everyone who cooks does so because he loves to cook. Sometimes it's more a matter of survival, as it is for Jim and Martin. When we took a lunch break during our interview, Martin headed for the kitchen and Jim set the table, a routine that is a half century old.

MARTIN: I do all of the cooking, but I never touch clothes. Jimmy does the washing and ironing.

JIM: That's my job. I like to do the laundry, and I'm a good ironer. Very good.

At the start of their relationship, Jim did the cooking. I asked them how long it was before Martin decided he couldn't bear to eat what Jim was cooking.

MARTIN: Immediately. That's the truth. Yes.

JIM: I made one dinner. Terrible.

MARTIN: He made a pie. Was it a pie you made?

JIM: Oh, the pie. It was an apple pie, and it was about a half inch thick. It was terrible. Oh, it was bad. But Marty, he's a good cook.

MARTY: Cleaning the house we do together.

JIM: Do it together. And we've always had a nice yard. I took care of the backyard; he took care of the front yard.

With Stewart and Stanley, personal preference, personality type (Stanley is more of a worrier than Stewart), and the fact that Stewart earns more money than Stanley figured into how things would get done around their house. Apparently, this was something they never really discussed until I asked them about it.

STANLEY: Stewart knows how to cook. But I worry that he's not going to eat. So, for example, tomorrow I go to work at two in the afternoon. He has the day off, so I will make sure we both have a big meal at one.

STEWART: But we've never sat down and said, "This is your job; this is my job." The house is Stanley's responsibility, but I think a lot of it happened maybe unconsciously. Stanley knows he doesn't bring in the same salary, so he makes up with taking care of the house and being responsible for the cleaning.

STANLEY: The cleaning, the laundry.

STEWART: So in some ways it balances. It's not like I consider him the servant. He's not the hired help.

STANLEY: And believe me, this is a lot to keep clean. I begin to panic when it's getting close to Passover or a family dinner.

The sorting out of responsibilities is sometimes complicated by the expectations and assumptions people bring with them to their relationships. Before she met Molly, Irene had never had a relationship with another woman. She'd been engaged twice, to men with whom she did her best to fulfill her responsibilities as a future Mormon housewife.

IRENE: One time when we went camping, Molly was getting everything ready and I was sitting in the living room watching TV. And she says, "Come on, we're going camping." I told her that I would put things away when we got back. She said no, that I had to help decide what food to take along. I told her that whatever she made was fine.

MOLLY: I wasn't amused.

IRENE: It was like, *If you decide it, I'll make it.* That's exactly what I'd done in my family. Mom always did everything. She didn't want help, because she wanted it done right. And when we got back from a family trip, it was my job to put things away and clean up. So that's all I knew.

MOLLY: And what I knew was partnership. In my earlier relationships, we would figure out what needed to be done, and some way or other we'd get it all done. But it was funny, because even after Irene and I had lived together for a while, I'd say, "What do you want for dinner?" and she'd go into the "Well, whatever you fix is okay" routine. It took a while for her to realize, *Oh yeah, I get a choice.*

IRENE: I usually like whatever's there, so just whatever was fine with me. But here was Molly: "No, I'm asking you what you want for dinner." It was kind of hard for me for a while, because I'd been the dutiful child for twenty-seven years and nobody asked me my opinion. This was new for me.

MOLLY: In every relationship I'd ever been in, I had been equal. No one had played roles, and whatever happened just got done. So this was real foreign to me.

IRENE: At first, I wanted to sit down and make a weekly menu and write a job list. Let's just organize everything. Molly said she couldn't be that rigid. "We'll just get a bunch of food in the house." But, see, at home we used to divide out the jobs. I never cleaned the bathrooms, because my job was the trash and the dishes. So I do that real well. When Molly and I got together, I couldn't think on my own. She really had to help me to become a partner.

MOLLY: It took me a while to figure out that Irene was probably just trying to be a little Mormon housewife and be agreeable about everything.

IRENE: It's not like I really thought I'd be a Mormon housewife. By the time I met Molly, I already felt like I was going to be a failure as a Mormon housewife, but that was what I was expected to do. You know, the wife does all the cooking, all the cleaning, sewing, does everything for the family while the husband goes out and works. But I innately did not like cooking. I hated sewing and some of those other things. And I knew I was going to work, because I knew I wouldn't be able to sit home all day. That's why I went to college. So I thought, I'm not going to be a very good wife, and I know I'm not the husband, but we'll have to decide what we like best and what we don't like best. It was all very confusing.

MOLLY: So I pretty much took the lead and we worked it out.

In talking with the couples, I found that there was more conscious discussion about roles among the women than the men. I suspect that in part this has to do with the historical butch-femme tradition of lesbian relationships, in which one partner took on the classic male role and the other took on the classic female role, often dressing and grooming themselves accordingly. Catherine remembers a time when the lesbians she knew were limited by the roles they were expected to play.

CATHERINE: It was the early sixties, and some of these women were still behaving as they had in the late fifties, and it was very difficult. The women I saw as I was growing up were always in those roles, and I felt very sorry for them, because they had to stay within the confines in order to be accepted. The baby dykes just sat there at the bar and complained because they could not find the ultimate femme that they needed to have a relationship.

LEE: To me, the advantage of being in a same-sex couple is that we can both be women. We can both define our roles as narrowly or as wide as we want. We don't feel bound in by the gender-defined roles. I think that in heterosexual couples, however liberated an individual or couple can make themselves, they're still operating under the umbrella of what society dictates is their role. Their gender itself defines their actions and their manner of dress. We're free of that.

When Chris and Sherri first met and they talked by phone about how they were going to conduct their relationship, Chris was very conscious of how she'd been pigeonholed by other women in past relationships because of her masculine appearance and demeanor. The last thing she wanted in her new relationship was to have to be something she wasn't, and to take on a role that didn't suit her personality.

CHRIS: I was always in a relationship where people took me as being the breadwinner, the macho one, the one who took care of things.

SHERRI: More butch.

CHRIS: Yeah, and that's always the role that people pegged me in, because of my size and the way I look. And I had decided after spending two years single that I really hated playing a role and I wasn't going to do it anymore. Despite how I look, I'm much more of a housewife, the one that arranges things, the one that cooks and cleans. That's where I'm comfortable.

SHERRI: And I'm absolutely not domestic. I am zero domestic. I've gotten better over the years, but I'm not domestic. I go out. I earn the money. That's my role.

CHRIS: I knew she was going to be a nurse and I was always going to be the artist type. She would always earn more money than I did, so we needed to come to an agreement: "You'll earn more money, but I'll do more of this, and together we'll have a relationship."

For all the couples, taking care of each other has not been a static thing, where one partner is always the caretaker and the other is always taken care of. While each relationship is unique, in general I found that the needs and actions of the individuals in the relationships varied with the situation. At times, one would be dependent on the other for emotional, financial, or physical support. Then the dependence would shift. And sometimes it was a simultaneous combination.

Over the life of a relationship, there are, inevitably, shifts. For example, there can be long periods where one partner is more dependent on the other, and then the dependency gradually reverses. This was the case with Phil and Bill, the couple who met when they knocked each other down on a San Francisco street. Because Bill was twenty when he met Phil, who was thirty-six, it seemed natural for Phil to take the lead. He was well established in San Francisco, with a circle of friends and family. He had a career and earned substantially more than Bill, who was just starting his adult life in a new city. Thirty years later, Bill is a very successful investment banker and earns substantially more than Phil, who is semiretired and slowed by age, and it is Bill who, more often than not, takes care of Phil.

Even when couples start out as equal partners, circumstances can force one partner to become the primary caretaker. The cause can be a pregnancy, a broken leg, a bout of depression, a lost job, the death of a parent, or something as life-altering as a cancer diagnosis.

Amy and Jama were twenty-five and twenty-seven when they met. Neither was the other's sought-after type, but after five months of a very unexpected and magical courtship, they moved in together. About a month later, the two women were in the shower, making love, when Amy discovered a lump on Jama's breast.

The subsequent diagnosis, surgery, and chemotherapy left Jama feeling completely dependent on Amy.

AMY: It changed the dynamics of our relationship, incredibly.

JAMA: Totally.

AMY: Jama and I were very much on equal terms in all areas of our relationship—emotional, physical, spiritual, financial—prior to her getting sick. The dynamic between us was . . .

JAMA: Adult to adult.

AMY: Adult to adult or child to child, depending on what we were doing. And there was a definite shift after that. Jama was, by necessity, dependent on me, for a large majority of her . . .

JAMA: Caretaking.

AMY: Sustenance. For everything. We were not aware at the time what it did to our relationship.

JAMA: Instead of dealing with each other on an adult basis, where both of us were equal, Amy became my parent, and I became a child. I asked Amy for everything. I didn't think I deserved anything, because I didn't bring anything to the relationship anymore. Amy paid the bills. Amy made the money. Amy took me places. Amy did the shopping. Amy, Amy, Amy.

AMY: I made the decisions.

JAMA: Amy became my mother.

AMY: And I wasn't very good at it, but you just do what you have to do to get through it.

Even after Jama recovered, getting back on an even keel was not an easy process. After years of struggling with the fallout from Jama's illness and not being able to find their own way back to a balanced partnership that pleased them both, they sought the help of a professional therapist, who they say has helped them enormously.

In talking with the couples, I discovered, not surprisingly, that I wasn't the only one who had ever been asked the husband and wife question. Stevie and Bill have been together since they were sixteen.

They first met and became best friends when they were thirteen. Both are now forty-two. And neither of them is noticeably more masculine or feminine than the other.

STEVIE: One of our friends asked us who was the man in our relationship.
BILL: And we both pointed to each other and said at the same time:
STEVIE: "He is."

EIGHT

Commitment

TEN YEARS AGO, I traveled to rural North Carolina to interview twenty-nine-year-old Jim and forty-year-old Lane. To me, they were exotics, living in a part of the country far more hospitable to the Ku Klux Klan than to a Vietnam vet and his male lover of seven years. Their house was an old trailer partly enveloped by the shell of a new house. The cramped quarters were home to Jim and Lane and to Lane's fifteen-year-old son, his elderly mother, a bird, a couple of cats, and an impressive collection of African violets.

It's now the summer of 1997, and I'm sitting with Jim and Lane on their screened-in porch, overlooking a broad pasture that's adorned with a towering flagpole flying the rainbow flag. The trailer is nowhere to be seen, having been swallowed up by the spacious house that Jim designed and Lane built around it.

There have been other changes as well. Lane's son no longer lives with them, although he works with Jim and Lane in the family carpet-cleaning and dyeing business. Lane's mother died in 1991. Two grandchildren visit frequently—one each from Lane's son and his daughter. And Jim and Lane both have plenty of gray in their once-blond beards.

We're joined on the porch by Jim and Lane's close friend Lila, a retired lawyer, formerly from New York, who has been my friend since Jim and Lane first introduced me to her in 1987. Then, as now, whenever Jim and Lane are at a loss for words, Lila jumps in to help.

As I did with all the couples, I asked Jim and Lane if they'd exchanged some token or symbol of their commitment, and I listed some examples: rings, watches, and I added jokingly—tattoos. They smiled, exchanged a look, and rolled up their sleeves to reveal matching tattoos. "We got these in Decatur fifteen years ago," Jim explained. Their eagle wing tattoos are adorned with a ribbon design, and on the ribbon is written the word "Harley."

JIM: A little redneck southern. I guess it was a kind of wedding ritual, a permanent mark.

LANE: We got titty rings, too.

I hadn't thought to ask any of the couples if they'd exchanged nipple rings, but since Lane brought it up, I asked if they had one each or two. I found myself nervously playing with my plain platinum wedding band, a hopelessly middle-class symbol of my own committed relationship.

JIM: One each, but he took his out. It didn't do right.

LANE: I didn't have a big enough tit for it to stay in anyway.

JIM: We did that before I had any clue that I was going to wind up being a mother, let alone a grandmother. When we got up here with the kids and all, I eventually took it out. The kids were asking, "What you wear that for?" I decided it wasn't a good impression for these kids. It stayed out for years and years, but I found it a couple of years ago and put it back in, and it still fit. So I'm back to wearing it now that the kids are grown. So we did that. And Lane gave me his Army ring that I wear in place of a wedding ring.

LANE: I gave him my ring when we moved in together. I bought it through one of the military catalogs when I was in Vietnam.

JIM: He said, "I want you to wear this." It was only a couple of weeks after we met. Lane didn't have anything then. He was still on the road driving a truck, he didn't have an apartment of his own, he didn't have a vehicle of his own, his ex-wife had the kids. It was pretty much what you saw was what you got. He took that ring off and gave it to me to wear.

Without the prescribed societal markers of engagement and marriage, Jim and Lane, like all the couples I interviewed, had chosen their own way to express their commitment. For most, the commitment was spoken, as in "I want to spend the rest of my life with you." For others, the commitment was unspoken though marked by the start of a physical relationship, a decision to live together, a commitment to monogamy, or the signing of legal documents to confer on each other some of the rights automatically given to married heterosexual couples.

More than half the couples had exchanged rings, opting for either custom-designed rings or traditional gold bands. A handful had had public commitment ceremonies. One man had taken the last name of his partner. And one couple were legally married in the mid-1970s in Boulder, Colorado, a story that's a book unto itself.

Some couples made a commitment early in their relationship; others waited for several years. Pam and Lindsy have affirmed their relationship several times and in several ways during the nearly two decades they've been together.

PAM: We've been married seven times—to each other—if you count the two ceremonies at the twenty-four-hour Church of Elvis in Portland, Oregon, which we do. Some people just do it for a joke, but I think we took it seriously, which is why we went back a second time, because the first time, Lindsy fucked up one of the questions.

LINDSY: I did. I did. I was too cynical.

PAM: I sort of resented her for answering the question wrong when she knew what the answer should be.

LINDSY: I was being a smartass. But by then, we'd already been married in Notre Dame in Paris. That was our first wedding. It was the first time Pam had ever been to France, and I insisted on taking her. We'd been together for a year, and we got it into our minds that we wanted to do something official.

PAM: All we did, basically, was write our names on little postcards and also write that we were committed to each other and—

LINDSY: We went to Notre Dame and climbed as high as we could go on the tower stairs, which we assumed went as high as heaven. But we were stopped by a locked door and decided to slip one of the cards underneath. Then we posted the other card on the church bulletin board, just like Jeanne-Marie and François and all the other couples who posted their notices.

PAM: We also swore an oath that we considered ourselves married, and we bought special little necklaces.

LINDSY: Then for the next two weeks, at every church we visited, we posted a card announcing the betrothal of Pam and Lindsy.

A year later, Lindsy's two young daughters decided that she and Pam should get married. Pam and Lindsy let the girls plan a ceremony, which they held while they were all house-sitting at Pam's mother's house. Besides Pam and Lindsy and Lindsy's daughters, the guest list included their three cats, the girls' gay godfather, and Pam's mother's cat and two dogs. Lindsy notes, "A good time was had by all, and we have it on videotape."

In addition to these ceremonies, Pam and Lindsy have participated in a couple of group gay weddings, including one at the 1993 March on Washington, and one on the Greek island of Lesbos. I asked them, "Why so many ceremonies?"

PAM: If you can't have quality, why not have quantity.
LINDSY: And it's been fun.

Without having to follow the heterosexual model of marriage, and absent the legal right to marry, Pam and Lindsy have felt free to make their commitment over and over again, in different ways. As always, with the freedom to do what you like, there are advantages and disadvantages.

PAM: Heterosexual couples have paths that they follow, and can always fall back on them. Sometimes, it's really comforting to be able to do that. And while I think it's terrible that we don't have the option to legally marry, there are advantages to having to do it on your own. I really think human beings are mentally lazy and we just don't think unless we have to. By having to think and to figure out how to get there yourself, you'll end up with something that is much more personal and more relevant to your life. So, ideally, it's more solid. That said, if gay marriage becomes legal in Hawaii, we'd be the first couple on the plane.

Chris and Sherri, too, have made commitments on more than one occasion, although they've never been to the Church of Elvis even once. They considered themselves committed to each other from almost the beginning of their relationship, having revealed their mutual love at a McDonald's one week after they'd met. They increased their level of commitment once they finished sorting out every possible aspect of their future lives together and agreed that Sherri would move in. For Sherri, her decision to live with Chris was an especially major step, because leaving the family home meant defying her parents. Her parents retaliated by refusing to allow her to take anything other than her clothes.

Nine years later, at a time when commitment ceremonies were becoming more common, and following their decision to have a child, Chris and Sherri felt the need to make a formal, public statement.

CHRIS: I told Sherri that if we were going to have a child, we had to make it legal. That's exactly what I said.

SHERRI: That was the proposal, and I said, "Okay."

CHRIS: I really believe that you shouldn't have children out of wedlock. I don't believe anybody should have children out of wedlock.

SHERRI: Since we can't legally do it, we did the next best thing.

CHRIS: I'm very conservative in my ideas. And not only that, we kept thinking that if anyone ever tried to take him away, we would have a record of stability.

Once they agreed to have a ceremony, Chris and Sherri had to figure out what kind they wanted. They talked to a few people who had already had ceremonies, as well as to the minister of a local, nondenominational gay church.

SHERRI: We talked to her at great length, and decided on a really conventional ceremony.

CHRIS: It was just your basic, pretty conservative ceremony. We had one person who read a poem.

SHERRI: We had a friend who played the guitar and sang a song. And we each had a best person. We did it in the backyard, and I invited all of the important people from my work.

CHRIS: And I had several students that I was teaching stained glass to, who had become close friends. I invited them and their husbands. I invited one brother, but other than that we didn't consider inviting our families. You can't expect them to do more than they're capable of doing. And we didn't think this was something that was in their realm.

With the ceremony planned and the guest list completed, Chris and Sherri hand-wrote the invitations and mailed them. The next big decision, which proved to be the most difficult, was what to wear.

CHRIS: That was horrible. That was the worst part of the entire thing. We could not decide what to wear.

SHERRI: I mean, neither of us are dress people.

CHRIS: I look like my brother in a dress, like a guy in drag. It does not look good. Sherri's seen me in one and said, "Don't ever do that again." Not pretty.

SHERRI: No, not pretty. So dresses were out. And we didn't want to do traditional tuxes, because that's just, like, so *done.*

CHRIS: And they're too warm. So we ended up buying tux shirts. I made really nice matching vests in a black, teal, and purple material. And we wore white jackets and black shorts.

SHERRI: Black shoes, like wanna-be Doc Marten–kind of shoes.

CHRIS: That was the hardest thing for us to find. Shoes that we both liked in her size and mine.

More than one hundred people attended the ceremony, which was officiated by the minister of the nondenominational gay church. Chris and Sherri said traditional vows, with one exception. Sherri explained, "We left out the 'obey' part." And they exchanged rings made of Black Hills gold, decorated with grape leaves. A potluck barbecue reception followed, featuring a wedding cake topped with two doves. "It was made by one of our gay male friends," Sherri says, adding, "That was before you could get those unisex decorations—you know, two brides, two grooms."

I asked Chris and Sherri if the ceremony had had any impact on their relationship.

CHRIS: It was important to us to do it, but it hasn't had a huge impact on our relationship. If it made any impact, it was to make me a little bit more complacent than I should have become.

SHERRI: I think it did the same thing for me, too. It was kind of like, "Well, now we're married, so . . ."

CHRIS: We've had to go backwards a bit and—

SHERRI: Relearn to appreciate each other again, and not take each other for granted.

CHRIS: The piece of paper didn't mean that much. It's the relationship that means that much.

I was a bit taken aback by Chris and Sherri's response. I thought they made an important point about not using a commitment ceremony as an excuse to take each other for granted. But I'd expected that they would talk about how the ceremony had changed their relationship. When my partner and I had a commitment ceremony, two years after we first met, our ceremony made a difference in two ways: First, we both felt more profoundly committed and secure in the relationship after we'd exchanged vows in front of our families and friends. (On the other hand, I imagine that if we'd been together as long as Chris and Sherri had been at the time of their ceremony, a public statement of our commitment would not have had as much impact.) Second, the ceremony changed how supported we felt in our relationship by our friends and family, who treated us differently after we'd made a public commitment. I think the reason behind the change is that we'd shown them who we were and what we meant to each other. Everyone who attended the ceremony, straight and gay, had the opportunity to see that our love and our commitment were no different than the love and commitment between a man and a woman who marry. There could be no doubt in their minds that we were a dedicated couple. He is no longer my boyfriend, a potentially temporary thing; he is my partner. Now, for example, when we get invitations, they are always addressed to the two of us. Our young nephews and nieces call us "Uncle." Certainly, we could get along without the joint invitations and the endearments from the kids, but it sure feels good.

All the couples I spoke with took great pride in what they had accomplished, and much of what they had accomplished as couples was achieved without the full and explicit support of friends, family, and colleagues. They are rightfully proud of having sustained their relationships without the support that many heterosexual couples enjoy.

Jim and Martin paired up decades before anyone imagined that gay and lesbian couples would be registering at Williams-Sonoma for pots and pans, and cutting cakes adorned by twinned brides or twinned grooms. As was the case for most of the couples I spoke with, when Jim and Martin first got together, a commitment ceremony was not only not an option, it wasn't even a thought. Jim and Martin both recall speaking of their commitment early in the relationship, but neither remembers precisely what he said. They also never exchanged rings. But on their first trip to Europe, twenty-four years after they met, Jim and Martin made a commitment that they both recall.

JIM: That was really exciting, because we were going for five weeks. We saved for it. We went to the Vatican, and they were saying mass. So we stayed for the mass and we just made a commitment to each other. We looked at each other, and we said that we were going to be together for always. I always remember that.

The following year, in honor of Jim and Martin's twenty-fifth anniversary, two close friends gave them a surprise dinner party.

JIM: Ralph and Bill said to us, "Come on, it's your anniversary, so we're going to take you two out for dinner." They picked us up, and on the way to the restaurant we were about to pass their place, and Bill said, "Oh, come in for a minute because I need to get something." We went in, and of course it was so dark. And he said to us, "Go into the dining room." The doors were closed, and he told us to open them. We opened the doors and everyone yelled, "Surprise!" He had twenty or twenty-five people there. My God! The tears! We were all crying!

Twenty-five years later, a few weeks shy of their fiftieth anniversary, Jim and Martin participated in a public commitment ceremony at their local Metropolitan Community Church, a predominantly gay and lesbian church that they attend in Fort Lauderdale. Initially, because they had long since committed to each other, their plan was simply to watch and be supportive.

MARTIN: We weren't going to be part of the ceremony, but we go to that MCC church. It's a nice place to meet people. There were maybe a hundred people in the audience that day, and almost everybody was there to participate in the ceremony.

JIM: Some of the people were dressed in tuxedoes.

MARTIN: We were dressed in our finest, you know. Just black suits.

JIM: We went mostly for the other people, to be supportive, because Martin and I had committed ourselves years ago.

MARTIN: The best way we could, you know.

JIM: But it's nice to see your own kind of people and to know that some of us do stay together.

MARTIN: Well, we weren't going to be part of the ceremony, but the pastor saw us and he asked someone about us and found out that we'd been together for fifty years. So he asked us to come up to the altar for the ceremony itself. And he announced in front of everybody that we'd been together for fifty years. There was an explosion of applause, and it startled the hell out of us! We didn't know what to think of it, because we didn't think it was so great. But evidently they did!

JIM: So there we were at the center of everything, with everyone around us.

MARTIN: I felt embarrassed, you know.

JIM: We're not that kind of people. I could feel my face getting real hot.

Jim and Martin survived the group commitment ceremony as well as the congratulations that followed. But for their actual anniversary, they chose to celebrate on their own at a local gay nightclub.

MARTIN: We go there maybe two or three times a year for dinner, for special occasions. So we went, and of course there was this article written up in *Sage,* which is a publication for gay seniors, and it told about our fifty years together. Some people recognized us, and the owner of the bar sent us over martinis, which we love, you know. And we danced, and it was a nice little evening.

Stewart and Stanley have not had a ceremony, but Stanley would like one. Stewart, like most of the people I spoke with, isn't interested in any ceremony unless marriage between people of the same gender becomes legal. Our conversation regarding commitment began with my asking if they'd talked about having a ceremony.

STANLEY: I've wanted to.

STEWART: That's news to me.

STANLEY: I've said it.

STEWART: Not to me. If there were such a thing as marriage, yes. There would be no question. But if it doesn't change anything at this point, it's just an excuse to get presents from people.

Stewart and Stanley haven't let the lack of legal marriage keep them from being committed to each other, although their commitment is unspoken. Knowing that Stewart and Stanley are not big communicators when it comes to their relationship, I didn't find this surprising.

STEWART: It's assumed. It's like a motto my mother used to say: "Divorce never, homicide often." Just the thought of breaking up this apartment would stop anybody from breaking up.

STANLEY: If he or I ever decided to break up, I wouldn't know where to begin. *That's my figurine, that's your figurine. That's your TV, that's my TV.* We have a magnet on the refrigerator that says: "We're staying together because of the cat."

STEWART: It's something we never really sat down and talked about. There was no prenuptial agreement. I've told Stanley to write a will, if only for the sake of his son. As far as I'm concerned, if anything happens to Stanley, that door gets locked and nothing is going to his son unless Stanley's decided in advance. He's still getting around to it.

Despite the fact that they hadn't talked about their commitment or completed legal documents to protect each other in the event of illness or death—something many of the couples *have* done—Stewart and Stanley did exchange rings three years into their relationship. When they showed them to me, I thought they looked familiar; then I realized they're the same Black Hills gold rings with the grape-leaf design that Chris and Sherri have.

I asked Stewart and Stanley how they decided on their rings.

STEWART: They looked pretty on TV.

STANLEY: They're from Home Shopping Club. When we first saw them, we decided that was the kind of ring we wanted. It doesn't look like a wedding band. It doesn't look like a friendship ring, or whatever. It looks like a unique band ring, and only other gay and lesbian people would realize when we're both wearing them that they were our symbolic commitment rings. Oddly enough, none of our family or friends has ever put two and two together.

Several of the couples talked about choosing rings that weren't traditional wedding bands. Others talked about wearing their rings on their right hands, instead of the traditional left. The reasons all these couples gave were essentially the same: They wanted a traditional symbolic representation of their commitment, but at the same time, they didn't want to give the impression that they were in a heterosexual marriage. For one thing, they're not. And for another, if they wore gold wedding bands on the traditional left ring finger, they'd likely get the kind of casual question or comment that can lead to an unwanted conversation.

The natural question that follows is "Why wear a ring at all?" The people I interviewed grew up in the same society as everyone else and, for the most part, want the same things. Like most happily married heterosexual couples, the couples I spoke with are proud of their relationships, and they enjoy and take pride in wearing a physical symbol of their commitment. If there comes a day when no one bats an eye about same-gender relationships, I'm sure gay and lesbian couples will feel perfectly free to wear whatever ring they like on whatever hand feels comfortable without having to think about what will happen if they disclose the truth about their relationship.

Alison and Dayna, the youngest couple I interviewed, chose to have a very public commitment ceremony in the backyard of Alison's mother's apartment building in Northampton, Massachusetts. Yet when it came to their rings, both chose to wear them on their right hands.

ALISON: I wore mine on the right hand until I jammed this finger in softball, so I can't get my ring on anymore. We went back and forth. What does it mean to wear it on the left or the right?

DAYNA: I think mostly for me, I wear it on the right because of work issues. I work in a program for the elderly, and they ask questions. It's one thing to be out to your co-workers, but it's another thing to be out to your patients and clients.

ALISON: They wouldn't get it.

DAYNA: It's a very frail, elderly population. People are well into their eighties and nineties. With the ring on my right hand, they don't ask questions. The questions I *do* get are "Oh, Dayna, when are you going to get married?" "Oh, someday." I just sort of brush it off. Although, I do have a picture of Alison on my desk, but nobody asks about that.

ALISON: Well, it's a picture of the two of us and Dayna's niece.

DAYNA: When the elderly come into my office, I don't think they can see that far.

Alison and Dayna, who grew up in a time when commitment ceremonies were becoming increasingly common and gay and lesbian couples were freer to be open about their relationships, saw their ceremony as a natural expression of their love.

DAYNA: I think it was really just some sort of romantic idea, that this was something I wanted to do. It's sort of this feeling, like, *Will you marry me?* I knew I really loved Alison, so I thought we should have some kind of public ceremony a year or two into the relationship, have all of our friends there and have a great time. I wanted everybody else to know how I felt.

This was not the case for most of the other couples, who expressed little interest in or negative feelings toward the idea of a public ceremony. When I raised the subject, some of the couples responded almost as if I were suggesting that by not having a public ceremony, their commitment was somehow less valid—which, of course, I wasn't saying at all. I was, however, curious about the origins of their strong feelings. Cassandra and Anne, the couple who were forced to rent a two-bedroom apartment when they wanted a one-bedroom, offered some insight.

Early in their relationship, Cassandra and Anne exchanged rings, but they have not had a ceremony, nor have they made a formal stated commitment of any kind. But during the interview, they said they were pledged to each other forever. They are already eighteen years into forever. When I asked them about having a public commitment ceremony, this is what they told me:

CASSANDRA: I don't think anything would change between us. I don't think that we would feel any more committed than we already do.

ANNE: Although, for straight people, it does seem to make a difference. I just went to my brother's wedding a month ago. He's fifty years old, and it's his first wedding. I was sitting with him and his soon-to-be bride at a restaurant, and a friend of his came in and said, "Well, you know, when you get married, things will be different." And I'm thinking, How can marriage make it different? I don't understand that. And I sort of considered it a slap in the face, like all of a sudden somebody says a few words and your relationship is now somehow different, somehow better. And I'm thinking, Well, so mine can't be as good as yours, because I can't get those few words said?

CASSANDRA: Now, see, we've had young lesbians tell us that. I will never forget what these young women said. Anne and I had been together many, many years at that point, and this couple had been together maybe two years. They said we couldn't possibly understand what they had, because they were married and we weren't. You know, these young ones have come of age in this time where gay and lesbian couples have commitment ceremonies, or whatever they want to call them. Whereas in our day nobody did that. And so, people keep asking why we don't do it. Well, I'm not gonna do it now. What the fuck do I want to do that for? I mean, it doesn't mean anything to me. If I'm gonna do it, I want a piece of paper that says it's legal. That's the only reason to do it at this point.

ANNE: And, of course, you know, that young couple no longer exists.

CASSANDRA: But we would do it because we want legal recognition.

ANNE: It's a political thing for me.

CASSANDRA: And there's something else. You know, even though you know you're not like everybody else, you kind of want to be like everybody else. I don't know if you feel this way or not, but when somebody asks you, and you have to check a little box, "Are you married? Are you single?" I feel like a fucking liar when I check that I'm single! But what am I supposed to check? There's this cognitive dissonance.

ANNE: Or "Who's Cassandra?" The other day, one of my colleagues said to me, "How's your . . . your . . . your . . . your . . ." and I said, "Are you talking about Cassandra?" Because I knew she didn't know what the fuck to call her! If we could get legally married, it'd be, like, "my wife," or whatever we want to call it. So it would simplify things for the world, in many ways.

Recently, Anyda and Muriel faced one of those moments when you've got a questionnaire in front of you asking if you're single or married. In their case, it was a hospital admission form, and it was upsetting to Muriel when Anyda checked the "single" box. They have been a committed couple for the past forty-eight years.

MURIEL: I want her to say I'm a relative, but she's honest, so I'm listed as a close friend.

Muriel and Anyda have prepared legal forms that allow each of them to make decisions for the other in medical crises. So that's less a worry for them than being prevented from seeing each other in the event of an emergency. They don't have that concern at the hospital they go to in Delaware, but in Florida, where they spend the winter, Muriel feels less secure of her status as Anyda's spouse.

MURIEL: For instance, down in Florida, if it was a question of only the next of kin being allowed in the room, I'd be out. This worries me.
ANYDA: If you're the significant other, that's what you are.

Unfortunately, in the eyes of the law, a same-sex significant other is not a legal spouse. Besides causing Muriel and Anyda concern, the absence of a legal marriage option leaves many of the couples without the rights that heterosexual married couples take for granted, whether they've been together five minutes or fifty years. Some of those rights can be approximated by completing legal documents and wills. But others can't. For example, until Chris and Sherri go through the complicated and expensive legal process of second-parent adoption, only Sherri is their son's legal guardian. The process for married heterosexual parents is well-established, relatively uncomplicated, and far less expensive.

Lucy's partner, Patsy, is forbidden by the term's of her father's will from leaving her inheritance to anyone other than family members. Lucy and Lucy's daughter and Lucy's grandchildren—who are also, as far as the couple is concerned, Patsy's grandchildren—don't qualify as family because Lucy and Patsy aren't married. Patsy feels certain that her siblings will let her get around the "family" requirement, but Lucy isn't so sure.

One final example. I asked Jim and Martin if there'd be advantages for them in a legal marriage, and they pointed out an anxiety that no elderly couple should have to face after spending a lifetime together.

MARTIN: I can't have Jimmy's pension when he dies. And if I die first, he can't have mine.

JIM: That's why we have a little nest egg put away, to make sure whoever is left behind has enough to live on. And all of our insurance policies that we have, we've written down that he's the beneficiary or I'm the beneficiary. With a marriage, it's all automatic. They get more benefits than we do, you know. Everybody knows that.

NINE

Work

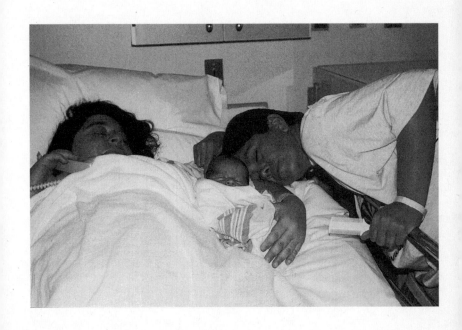

THE GAY MEN AND WOMEN I interviewed have worked and continue to work in a broad variety of professions. I spoke with lawyers, secretaries, civil service employees, engineers, social workers, elementary school teachers, writers, musicians, data entry clerks, carpet cleaners, artists, accountants, nurses, waiters, dancers, college professors, physical therapists, a psychologist, a truck driver, a financial planner, a clothing salesman, a bus driver, a 911 dispatcher, a florist, a restaurant manager, a beauty school instructor, an AIDS educator, and a chemist. That's not everyone, but it certainly demonstrates that even in this not so random group, gay people can be found doing the same jobs as everyone else.

Like the majority of heterosexual couples today, most of the forty couples I interviewed are two-career families, and they face many of the same challenges of balancing their work and personal lives—although most have done it without the added responsibility of children. But if Jim and Martin, Anyda and Muriel, and the other older couples I interviewed are in the least bit representative, then gay and lesbian couples have led the two-career-couple revolution, and they've done it virtually unnoticed. These couples have had to deal with all the familiar issues of balancing two careers, and they did it decades before it was commonplace and in a world that didn't make it easy for them. But they managed.

Jim and Martin finished beauty school in 1947 and both went to work at a salon in Grosse Point, a suburb of Detroit, but between starvation wages and an alcoholic boss, they quit and went back to work on the assembly line, where they remained until 1951. That was the year they set off to Japan for a two-year assignment as civilian employees of the Army.

JIM: We were taking French classes, and became very close to the teacher. She was a great gal. Not gay. And she says, "You know, you guys are always talking about getting out of the factories, and the Army's got ads in the papers. They want people to work for them in Europe and Asia." All you had to know how to do was type.

MARTIN: I had learned how to type when I was in school.

JIM: And I learned when I was in the Army.

Jim and Martin applied and were quickly interviewed, tested, and hired. From the very start of the interviewing process, they explained to Army personnel that they wanted assignments together—although, of course, they never said they were a couple.

JIM: They must have known something.

MARTIN: We were interviewed by women. The women are so much easier to do business with than the men.

JIM: We passed the tests, but there were no openings in Europe. The only places that were available were Japan, Okinawa, and Alaska. So we took Japan.

Jim and Martin were excited about their assignment, although they were sorry they weren't going to get to use their newly acquired French language skills. With their overseas jobs in hand, they gave notice at the factory, packed their things, and boarded a plane for Tokyo.

When Jim and Martin chose Japan, they were assured they'd be assigned to live with the same civilian family. It wasn't until they got to the airport in Tokyo that they discovered the Army planned to send them to different cities.

JIM: I got very upset, and I said to the person who handed out the assignments, "They can't do that. They promised." But no one cared. So we got on the Army bus to leave the airport, and I knew that the gal who drove the bus belonged to the same club I did. She was really butch. Her name was Dusty Roads. So I told her, "You know, they're going to separate Marty and me and they promised they wouldn't do it." She says, "Don't worry about a thing. I'll be right back." She was gone for about five minutes, and she came back and said, "Don't worry, you'll both be staying in Yokohama."

MARTIN: We had the same room together. I don't know what she did, but everything fell into place because of Dusty Roads.

In Japan, Jim and Martin never talked with others about their relationship, but they weren't terribly concerned about being found out.

MARTIN: We weren't afraid, because it was wild. There were so many gays there. Every once in a while the Army would clamp down on the gays, but we were civilian employees and they left us alone.

JIM: Oh, it was wild. There were so many gays there.

MARTIN: They would flaunt it.

JIM: A lot of married ones, too. I was just amazed. We went to a couple of gay clubs in Tokyo, and we went in there and my goodness! I thought the whole Army, Navy, and Marine Corps had left their stations and gone there! It was quite wild.

Anyda and Muriel had to keep their relationship absolutely secret when they worked at the same law firm. They were certain that disclosure would cost them both their jobs. But starting in 1954, when Anyda went to work for the World Bank, she did something that must have been unimaginable at the time. Every third year, when the World Bank's annual meeting was held elsewhere than Washington, Anyda took Muriel along, just as her colleagues brought their spouses.

ANYDA: The bank always arranged it as if she were my spouse. The bank is a very broad-minded institution. The travel people would tell me the dates, and I'd say, "Can you arrange this for Muriel?"

There was, however, a catch. For the married couples, the bank paid the full cost of bringing along a spouse. For Anyda and Muriel, the bank paid only for Anyda's travel costs. Anyda and Muriel had to pay for Muriel's transportation and the difference between a single and a double room. I asked if this made them angry.

ANYDA: No, I thought it was a very fine arrangement, because we were able to travel together.

MURIEL: The accommodations were wonderful. And after the meeting, we'd take a couple of weeks' vacation.

Anyda and Muriel, like virtually everyone I interviewed, were happy with their careers. I realized that this was no accident. Plenty of people talked about having been unhappy in their work at one time or another during the years they'd been a couple. But time and again, the partners had encouraged each other to leave an unfulfilling job, return to school to change professions, or find work they could do and enjoy together. (Surely this was made easier by the fact that most of the couples did not have the added responsibility of children at home.)

The important point here is that the couples saw their relationship as a *partnership,* and if one partner was unhappy in his or her work, then this was a joint problem to be solved, ideally, together. I don't mean to suggest that this was always a neat, loving, and tension-free process, because for a lot of the couples, including Cassandra and Anne, it wasn't.

Cassandra and Anne had a problem. Well, Anne had a problem with her job, and consequently Cassandra had a problem with Anne. At the time, Cassandra was working for a New England college as an administrator, and Anne was working at a local bookstore. (This was before Cassandra changed jobs and they moved to a new city and the two-bedroom apartment they didn't need.) At this point in our interview, the two women were seated in separate chairs opposite me, but while there was physical distance between them, the way they spoke, what they said, and how they related to each other revealed an intimacy that comes only from two decades' worth of shared existence.

CASSANDRA: I gave Anne an ultimatum. I told her to get her shit together or I was leaving. Anne is a very bright woman, and she has a
zillion talents, and in my opinion she was wasting herself working
in a bookstore.

ANNE: I was the assistant manager of a bookstore.

CASSANDRA: And she *hated* working in that bookstore. She liked that
kind of work, but she didn't like the boss, and she didn't like the
owners, and she didn't like this and she didn't like that. I said,
"Honey, you could be doing a lot of different things. There is no
reason for you to work in this damned bookstore." She was upset
about it a lot, and I'm always wanting to look on the bright side, so I
said, "Let's figure out what you can do."

ANNE: So she developed a plan for me. I had been a journalism major
at Indiana University, but I decided that journalism was not for me.
I'm not going to do that everyday deadline that you have to when
you work for a newspaper, thank you very much. So we learned of
a program in technical writing, and I said, "Well, you know, I can
do that." It's taking technical material and writing it for the layper-
son.

CASSANDRA: No, you didn't say that. I came home with this brochure
and said, "Honey, look, this would be interesting."

ANNE: Right, you said, "Why don't you do this?"

CASSANDRA: And you said, "I don't want to do that." That was your
initial response.

ANNE: But I think I came around pretty fast.

CASSANDRA: Yeah, you came around pretty fast.

Despite what Cassandra had said about leaving Anne if she didn't
make a change, her threat, in the recounting, didn't seem serious to
me. So I asked Anne if she thought Cassandra had meant it.

ANNE: I don't know.

CASSANDRA: I don't know that I meant it. But I was frustrated. I was sick
of the complaining, I felt like she was wasting herself, and I was sick
of her not making any money. I mean, money is always an issue,
particularly if you like to live well, which we do. We have always
lived beyond our means and probably always will, and so I was
also sick of her not making any money.

Anne told me she'd been glad to have Cassandra's encouragement and knew that it was a loving push. It also turned out to be just the push she needed.

CASSANDRA: She moved out of the bookstore and started writing commercials for a radio station, which was much more interesting and much more entertaining, and she liked the people she was working with, and she was in a much better mood.

ANNE: The only way I got the job at the radio station was through the bookstore connection.

CASSANDRA: Well, I know.

ANNE: It had nothing to do with the writing program.

CASSANDRA: Oh, I didn't say it did.

ANNE: So, I was writing commercials for AM radio for Madame Sonya's Dress Shop, okay? Now, that was absolutely scintillating! But, you know, it got me back into the writing business.

Anyda and Muriel also changed careers, but it wasn't because they were unhappy with their jobs. Both were unexpectedly forced to retire early.

ANYDA: I was going on sixty-two. Heart trouble. It had been coming on for some time. The doctor told me to go home and retire. And both our doctors told us to go to Florida to get away from the cold weather. We had heart trouble, but Muriel's was complicated by emphysema.

MURIEL: The beginnings of emphysema.

ANYDA: It was pretty difficult. Muriel actually had a breakdown.

MURIEL: My blood pressure was very high.

ANYDA: We had very demanding jobs, both of us. Muriel's was especially so.

I asked if retiring was something they had looked forward to, but it wasn't, they said, at least not so early in life. Despite the demands, both had enjoyed their jobs, and they were not the kind of people who were ready to spend the rest of their lives relaxing on beach chairs. And they didn't.

ANYDA: We were pretty broken down at that point, and that's when we started our own publishing company.

Anyda has been writing under the name Sarah Aldridge, a pseud-
onym, since her first published novel in 1974. The day I arrived to
interview her and Muriel, the first shipment of Anyda's thirteenth
book, *Nina in the Wilderness,* had just arrived. Anyda told me she
had always considered herself a writer, not a lawyer. She had written
her first novel when she was seventeen, but it wound up being the
casualty of a feud between two editors and was never published. At
around that time Anyda was offered a scholarship to law school, so
writing was put on hold for the next forty-five years.

ANYDA: All the time I was practicing law, I wanted to be a writer. Now
that I was retired, I could write. And I found I could write for a very
important reason. What I had been trying to write was, of course,
heterosexual novels. They didn't work. So now that I wasn't working as a lawyer, I could do what I wanted.

What Anyda wanted was to write what she knew, and what she knew
was love between women. But rather than try to get someone to
publish her books, she and Muriel went into the publishing business
themselves.

ANYDA: This is when the small presses came into their own. So I asked
Muriel if she was willing to dump some money into this, the two of
us, and manufacture the book on our own. That was the way *The
Latecomer,* my first novel, was published. That was the first book
for Naiad Press. Then Muriel and I incorporated the company in
1974.

Since the beginning of Anyda's second career, she and Muriel
have worked as partners. I asked them how they've liked working
together.

MURIEL: We don't have any real difficulty working together, and I think
the real reason is that we're outspoken. We say what we think. The
last book, the cover design is by Anyda and I did the typesetting.
The way we work is that Anyda does her draft of her novel, and
then she dictates it to me on the word processor. That's it.

In 1995, Anyda and Muriel, well into their eighties, founded a
new company.

ANYDA: We came to a parting of the ways with the other members of Naiad Press. So we established A&M Books and published *Amantha,* which was my twelfth book. I have quite a reputation. Considering all things, we're doing quite well.

When I got home after the interview, I thumbed through the newly minted copy of Anyda's latest book, which she had autographed for me. The A&M Books logo on the title page caught my eye. It's a sweetly intimate line drawing of two sea nymphs looking out from the page, their heads tilted together, their hair almost touching.

Marian and Marjorie also work together, as they have since the third year of their relationship. Becoming farmers was something they dreamed about from the start, and work has become a central part of their relationship.

MARJORIE: We knew pretty much right away that what we wanted to do was to farm. We thought we wanted to have goats, make cheese, do a garden.

MARIAN: I knew I didn't want to keep doing social work. We wanted to work at home, and everyone was doing that. There was a lot of the back-to-the-land thinking around where we were living, and we'd pick up an idea from this person or that person.

MARJORIE: We heard of people selling parsley to a restaurant, and we said, "Oh, wow. This is great." And that started us on our gardening career.

At the time they met, Marjorie was a classics major at the University of Massachusetts in Amherst. She'd returned to school after working a couple of years as a bank teller. It was through the classics that she became interested in farming.

MARJORIE: The classics are all about seasonal stuff, so that really got me into farming. Then, on the first day of the second year, I met somebody from the school of agriculture. That was it. I came home and told Marian, "Guess what? I just signed up at the agricultural school." I went to a dairy science program for two years. I learned how to make cheese, but I certainly didn't have anything to do with cows. And when I got out, we talked ourselves into a job in Vermont. We saw an ad in this publication called *New England Farmer* for somebody to run a farm, and we went up there and he hired us. We loaded up our U-Haul, our two dogs, and drove there.

MARIAN: It was several hundred acres. It was a beautiful spot, but we knew nothing.

MARJORIE: They had sixty cows.

MARIAN: We had never milked a cow in our lives. And we had to deal with all these adolescent boys who worked on the farm. They hated us because *they* wanted to be in charge.

MARJORIE: And they knew that we didn't know anything. I took a two-day tractor-driving course at the school, and here I was having to back a manure spreader into this tiny little building. We cried almost every day, but we find that stressful periods bring us together. Maybe that's a secret of our relationship.

MARIAN: It was a hard time, but it wasn't a threat to our relationship. The common enemy was the situation we were in.

After six months, Marjorie and Marian's employer decided to shift from dairy to beef cattle, and the women decided to move on. They answered another ad, and on Valentine's Day in 1981 they set eyes on the farm they've called home ever since.

Marjorie and Marian started out with nothing but the belongings they'd brought in their U-Haul. They saved up to buy the farm and their first cow, and went from there. As they introduced me to their cows and took me on a tour of their tidy, well-kept house, barns, greenhouse, and the dairy where they make and store their cheese, it was difficult for me to imagine how hard they've had to work to create the lives they envisioned back in 1977.

Nine of the couples I interviewed have worked together for extended periods. Such a large number could be just a coincidence, but I don't think it is. Working in their own businesses gave these couples the opportunity to spend a lot of time with each other, to do work they enjoyed, and to be themselves. They didn't have to pretend they were straight, hide their relationship, or worry about being fired.

Of course, working together means a whole other set of challenges, especially finding a way to deal with the inevitable tensions and conflicts. Some of the couples are good at expressing differences of opinion without raising their voices. And some, like Gordon and Jay, are good at expressing differences of opinion *and* raising their voices.

Gordon and Jay, who are both now in their sixties, started an antiques and decorating business in 1976 after eighteen years of independent design careers that kept them apart six months out of the year. They gave up their separate careers so they could spend more time together. Both were tired of being on the road and felt that all the travel and time apart weren't good for the relationship. Even so, they argue with gusto, even now.

JAY: We argue constantly. We scream and yell at each other, and everybody that has worked for us has had to realize that the screaming and yelling mean nothing.

GORDON: We argue about colors, fabrics, and things like that.

JAY: Or if I can't find something, it's always Gordon's fault.

GORDON: Well, of course, that's got nothing to do with design talent. It has everything to do with the fact that Jay has the world's messiest desk, and somewhere in it is the thing that he's screaming at me about.

JAY: We had a wonderful woman who worked for us for five years. She explained to the other people who came to work for us that it may sound like the world is coming down and we're going to pull a gun on one another, but it means nothing.

Most of the people I interviewed were either working at income-producing jobs or attending school at the time they met their current partners. Almost all assumed they would work throughout their lives. There were exceptions, of course, including a couple of people of independent means who didn't have to work and one woman who was a married homemaker at the time she met her lover and continued in that role for many years before going to work as a school secretary.

Over time, the men and women who were in school graduated and got jobs. Those who had jobs got promotions or moved on to new positions. Others went back to school and changed careers. For some, there were periods of unemployment, as well as maternity and paternity leaves. And still others left work to retire or, like Anyda and Muriel, were forced to quit because of illness. Two of the women gave up outside jobs to become full-time, stay-at-home parents after the birth of their first child, and one woman, thirty-four-year-old Judy, opted to leave full-time work to become a full-time homemaker, a choice that has raised a few eyebrows among her friends. It's also left Judy feeling a little guilty.

Judy and Bev, who is forty-three, are the couple who avoid calling each other "honey" in public and whose realtor tried steering them to a gay neighborhood. During the ten years they've been a couple, they've moved several times to accommodate Bev's career as a restaurant manager. The first time Bev was transferred, Judy gave up a job she loved with a local children's theater, where she acted and taught art classes. For the next five years she worked as a waitress, and when they moved again, to the city where they've lived for the past couple of years, she became a full-time homemaker who does occasional volunteer work.

JUDY: A lot of people would be bothered that I'm staying at home even though I don't have kids. I'm probably bothered. But I do artwork here and there, and I'm not career-minded.

BEV: Her sister-in-law gives her grief about not working. But if I had my shirts cleaned that would be two dollars; pants, two dollars; hire a maid, fifty dollars a week. She takes care of our home, and I like that she's home when I'm home, despite my irregular work schedule.

JUDY: It's a little weird not working.

BEV: My concern is that Judy feels fulfilled. I feel fulfilled when I come home from work. I'm hoping she works a little bit here and there. She needs that. But I'll be happy to support her for the rest of her life if being at home is what she wants to do.

I haven't offered any descriptive details about Judy and Bev because, unlike most of the younger people I interviewed, Bev has felt the need to keep her sexual orientation—and, consequently, her relationship with Judy—secret from her colleagues. She works for a restaurant chain known best for its down-home cooking and its past hostility toward its gay employees.

Most of the people I interviewed who are currently working are out to their colleagues. (There are a few exceptions, including the lesbian couple who work as elementary school teachers in Utah.) I don't know how representative this candor is of all gay people in happy, long-term relationships, but it is generally true of the couples who volunteered to be interviewed by me. Again, I suspect that the couples who made themselves known to me are more open about being gay.

That Bev feels compelled to hide her sexual orientation has been something of a sore spot between her and Judy, although Judy says that Bev's secrecy is something she's willing to endure.

BEV: Judy wants me to be out and open, but I can't. I was told in my interview that the company doesn't discriminate, that what happened in the past is past. I wouldn't have taken a job there if I wasn't sure of that, but I'm still not comfortable running around telling people I'm gay.

JUDY: Where Bev worked when we first met, I could go in and everybody knew we were together. And here I'm nobody.

BEV: It is hard. People comment on how crisp my shirts look. "Do you iron them?" "Oh, yes." But really, Judy irons them. I can't go in and say that Judy did a great job on my shirt.

JUDY: There's no acknowledgment.

BEV: Judy doesn't exist, and that is hard, and I don't enjoy that. I don't talk about my personal life, and I wouldn't unless I was in a company that was totally gay-friendly.

JUDY: To me it's a sacrifice that I don't get to go to her restaurant and get recognized. I make that sacrifice for her so she can work with the down-home people that she likes to work with. I would much rather she come home happy from work and be fulfilled.

BEV: I love the people who come into our restaurant. They are the nicest people.

I didn't find it at all surprising that the people I interviewed who work in more liberal parts of the country, where gay people are often protected in their jobs by antidiscrimination laws, or in professions where openly gay employees are nothing new, would be out on the job. But I was surprised to interview one couple who are completely open and accepted in their jobs as a city bus driver and a

911 dispatcher. Of course, it helps that the couple live in Portland, Oregon, where they are protected by citywide nondiscrimination laws (and are entitled to domestic partner benefits). Still, I would not have put money on their being accepted at work, particularly Lilia, the bus driver, whose colleagues are mostly men. She says that acceptance is about attitude.

LILIA: I've never hidden it, and I'm not going to hide it. I was out in high school. You're talking 1978, 1979. I didn't give a shit what people thought. I'm grateful for the people that have come ahead of me for what they've done. It's made it possible for my generation to be more out than the previous generation, and we're not going back.

My attitude is, like I told some of the guys at work who were members of this Oregon political organization that's against gay rights, I don't give a shit. We can sit here and talk like two human beings, like we've done many times. But I'm not going to change who I am, and I know you're not going to change who you are. Just don't get in my way and I won't get in yours. I don't have to like you or love you, but at the same time I should be able to respect you for who you are. And that's always been my attitude, and Stephanie's too.

That attitude has apparently paid off, because when Stephanie and Lilia decided to have a baby, their colleagues rallied around them with great enthusiasm.

STEPHANIE: I work with a lot of religious people. I have a lot of friends that are police officers, and a lot of them are Republicans. Still, we had the biggest baby shower I've ever seen ever. Almost fifty people showed up in our backyard. We didn't have to buy Noah anything. And the people from my job that couldn't make it were delivering stuff to my job for me to bring home.

LILIA: The bus drivers would stop right in front of our house, because we're on one of the main routes, and come in and bring flowers. We felt a lot of support.

STEPHANIE: It blew me away.

LILIA: It blew her away. I've always told her that in my job, even if these were religious-right people, they were not antigay. At my job there's about twelve hundred bus drivers. It's like one big, huge family. If we don't take care of one another, who in the hell is going to take care of us? I even had some guys offering to be a male role model for Noah, you know, just hang out and take him to play ball.

Looking at two-and-a-half-week-old Noah asleep on Lilia's chest, I thought it a little soon for him to play ball, but when the time comes there will clearly be no shortage of male volunteers.

Midway through the interview, we took a break for lunch. I helped set out the slices of just-delivered pizza and opened the freezer to get some ice for our drinks. It was packed tight with all kinds of prepared foods. I asked them if their freezer was always so full.

STEPHANIE: No, it's from people helping out.

LILIA: People helping out and just dropping things over.

STEPHANIE: After we came home from the hospital, the women from work brought us dinner because they knew I had had forty-four hours of labor and a C-section and Lil can't cook. So they brought us dinner for a week. The gal at work that organized the dinners had had problems with her last child, and the people from her church did it for her. And she knows that we don't belong to a church here. So she just said, "Let's help Steph out." We're close at work. There's only about a hundred people that work with me. They all pitched in.

LILIA: And most of our friends are straight.

STEPHANIE: I think ten years ago it might not have been the same way. Society's changed. Because people like Melissa Etheridge and k. d. lang and Ellen DeGeneres have come out.

LILIA: And they also see people like us.

STEPHANIE: That's true. I don't know that society is more accepting. They're just more used to us, maybe.

TEN.

Money

MONEY IS A COMPLICATED THING between two people in a committed relationship. I knew that from personal experience, without having to interview a single couple. There was, however, a time in my life when dealing with money in the context of a relationship seemed relatively simple. There were very clear rules back in the mid-1970s, when I went on my first date. I was the boy, so I planned the evening, picked up my date, paid for the theater tickets, paid for dinner, and escorted my date home. We were both fifteen, and that's how it was done. Rules meant we didn't have to think about it.

For gay and lesbian couples, there are no long-standing rules about money. The slate *is* blank. Once again, I don't think the lack of rules is a bad thing: With no right way or wrong way for same-gender couples to handle their finances, and no line of demarcation, like marriage, after which couples are expected to merge their finances, the economic realm of the relationship can evolve organically.

Same-gender couples have the chance to get to know each other's ways of dealing with money, to build trust, and to decide on a system that works best for them. Is this easy to do? For some of the couples it was, but not for most. Is the process conflict-free? For some, but not most. Did these forty happy couples discover the best way to handle money? Well, they discovered ways that suited them personally, but as I was quickly learning, no matter what aspect of a relationship one is talking about, there's no such thing as a universal fit.

The couples fell into two basic categories when it came to dealing with money: those who have merged finances, and those who have maintained separate finances. But it's not nearly as simple as it may sound, because each couple's system was custom-made, and influenced by everything from who made more money to conflicting spending and saving habits. Some couples had joint accounts and joint credit cards, while others had joint accounts in addition to personal checking accounts and individual credit cards. Some had separate accounts and paid for everything fifty-fifty, and others had separate accounts and paid for things proportionately, depending on who earned what. And still others had systems that made no sense to me when they were described during the interviews, and continued to make no sense when I read about them in my transcripts. What mattered, of course, was that the *couples* understood and were comfortable with what they were doing—and apparently they were.

Four fifths of the couples have chosen to merge their finances. Many of these couples, particularly those who were young when they first got together, made this choice early in their relationships. Often there was little to merge, and the combined earnings of the two partners were pooled to pay all the bills. Others maintained independent finances for many years and then decided that conjoined finances would work better for them. Many couples viewed the decision to merge their finances as emblematic of their commitment to the relationship. As one woman noted, "If we say we're in this together for life, why would we have *her* money and *my* money?"

Five male couples and three female couples maintain separate finances, and they've made this choice for a variety of reasons: Some have complicated personal finances that make joint accounts impractical. Others prefer the freedom of keeping their finances independent and paying for joint purchases fifty-fifty or proportionally. And some people had had bad experiences in past relationships with merged finances and didn't want a repeat of the same problems.

Nate and Danny were typical of the couples who have merged finances. They kept their money separate for the first eight years, and have had merged finances for the past ten, an arrangement they are sure would have been a disaster early in their relationship. As it was, their different attitudes toward money led to more than a few conflicts. Fortunately, keeping separate accounts at the start allowed them enough room to avoid violence as they learned to understand and accommodate each other's differences. As an added bonus, controlling his own money allowed Danny to secretly save up for a down payment on his and Nate's first house.

NATE: Danny has always been a saver. Back then, if he made seven thousand dollars, he'd save one thousand. That was just the way he lived, while I was always overextended on my credit cards. We've learned from each other over the years, because now he's a little bit more comfortable about spending money, and I understand that you can't overextend yourself. But in the beginning, we argued a lot about money. I would want to spend it, and he would want to save it. I grew up in a family where you would celebrate a special occasion by going out to a nice restaurant. So going to nice restaurants was not a big deal to me. Danny was, and still is, not that interested in nice restaurants.

DANNY: I was nineteen before I went to my first restaurant. I never went, because my folks kept kosher. Now I go. I enjoy it. But it's not important to me.

NATE: See, we did a lot of that growing up. My father was into spending money on entertainment, on clothes. Danny wanted to save money, which was a good thing. We were able to buy our first house because Danny had this little stash of money that I didn't know about. I think he was afraid to tell me because he thought I would spend it on something we didn't need.

DANNY: I just had a goal, to save. Start the violins. . . . My folks had no money when they came to this country, and my reaction to being raised by people who didn't have much was to live frugally. I was used to not having a lot of clothes and not going out.

NATE: And we were upper-middle-class. We didn't live in luxury, but we had nice things. I was brought up to believe that each generation was supposed to somehow do better than the one before. So Danny and I wound up disagreeing over how we spent money. It would always come down to a compromise.

DANNY: Remember that color TV?

NATE: Yeah, I wanted a color TV. And we also had a big fight about this couch. "Why do we need it?" That was always Danny's argument.

DANNY: I only had one pair of shoes when we met and one pair of tennis shoes. I had one suit and one belt.

NATE: So I bought things for him, but he'd say it was too expensive. "I don't need it. I'm taking it back." He exchanged a lot of things, which hurt me.

DANNY: "I could get six of these. I can't believe you spent that much money." It's better now. I joke about it. A color TV! My goodness!

NATE: I know, he's better now. But back then I'd buy things and say, "This is for me," and slowly, slowly, slowly, he'd be wearing it. At first, it sort of annoyed me, but I've gotten used to it, and now it's fine.

With the exception of one couple, in which each partner had more than enough money to spend on whatever he wanted, nearly all the couples have argued at one time or another over how to spend money. This was as true of the couples who had joint finances as it was of those who had separate finances. The intensity and frequency of the arguments decreased over time, but money proved to be fertile territory for disagreement whether the couples had been together one decade or five.

Part of Danny's motive for insisting on separate finances for as long as he did was to avoid getting into fights over Nate's free spending. In retrospect, Nate is completely understanding of Danny's motives.

NATE: It took Danny a long time to feel comfortable. Out of fairness to him, I wasn't careful with money. I had to get a consolidation loan for my credit cards. They were maxed out. I was just out of graduate

school and making twenty thousand dollars, which seemed like a lot of money to me, and I spent it. I think that worried him and kept him from wanting to totally merge our funds sooner than we did.

For most of the years they've been together, Nate and Danny earned just about the same modest income. Now that Nate earns considerably more than Danny—a very recent occurrence—they've had no problem dealing with the disparity. Both are sure that this wouldn't have been so easy early on.

NATE: We're at a place where it's not really an issue. I think maybe early on, when we were arguing a lot about money, it might have been hard.

DANNY: Now we just share whatever we have, and mostly we spend it on our daughter.

Pam and Lindsy have also had to deal with significantly different incomes. But unlike Nate and Danny, the disparity was something they've had to deal with from the start. When they met, Lindsy was already a well-paid writer, and Pam, who had been playing in a rock-and-roll band, got by on very little income.

PAM: When we first got together, we had this huge emotional compatibility, so it just never occurred to me that this would be a problem. I was used to living in bands. The whole focus was living on very little, and I was proud of that. It never occurred to me that suddenly I was going to be obliged to pay for half of our European vacations, which I had never gone on before in my life. Of course, I loved the vacations, but it wasn't my choice.

LINDSY: Pamela came out of the sixties. She has a strong career impulse, but she has no impulse, per se, to make money. So if that career impulse involved playing music and making nothing, and it made her happy, she would much rather sacrifice her style of life and live in a commune. Over the years, she made really clear to me that a lot of the things that I was demanding that she spend money on were things she would not be spending money on if we were not a couple. It took me years to get that message.

Before I got that message, I would nag her. "Well, you contribute x amount." But I was making a lot more money than Pamela was, so eventually we decided that instead of trying to split everything—and then have one person always being either pissed off or anxious—we would alternate taking each other out. Like, I would take her to Europe, and she would take me to someplace that cost much less. Because it's really not so much where you go. It's just nice to have somebody else plan something for you. Of course, we still wound up fighting about money.

There is still plenty for Pam and Lindsy to fight about. Not only do they have different attitudes toward earning and spending money, they have different ways of dealing with the bills.

PAM: When the bills come, Lindsy has to open them before we get up to the apartment. And as soon as we're home, she gets the checkbook, writes out the checks, and has me mail them an hour later when I go out for groceries. *I* see a bill and it just depresses me, even if I have money in the bank. I've lost many credit cards because I've owed these companies like seven dollars or fifteen dollars, but I get so depressed that I don't want to open it to look at it. So I put them in piles and lose them.

Today, Pam and Lindsy have merged finances—joint everything—but it was many years, many arguments, and more than a few visits to a therapist's office before they understood each other well enough to decide that a merged system, with joint bank accounts and joint credit cards, would work best for them. With their years of experience and insight, they've recently found themselves in the position of giving advice to a younger couple.

LINDSY: We have two friends who are devoted to each other. One of them inherited some money, and it caused a real trauma in the relationship in terms of buying some property. I said to them, "Your brother and sister-in-law inherited the same amount of money. Do you think he and his wife are going through this shit?"

There's a point where you decide you're in it for the long haul, and you just decide that it's your money as a couple. Now, if Pamela went off and bought a Cadillac with our money, most of which *I've* earned, I realize I would probably freak. So I'm sure that there's some unspoken agreements here. On the other hand, I think that having joint credit cards and joint checking accounts has made things so much more pleasant, since we aren't constantly negotiating who's paying for what or looking at who's making what.

Not every couple that has a joint arrangement took years to merge finances. Several of the couples chose right from the start to pool their incomes and to open joint accounts. For a handful of these couples, conjoined finances was a condition one of the partners set for agreeing to a live-in arrangement. Other couples simply couldn't imagine doing it any other way. This was Marian and Marjorie's experience. As Marian noted: "We hear about people with separate accounts and we think, You're not going to last. But when we started out, there wasn't a lot of money. Maybe if we each had fifty-thousand-dollar salaries, we might have thought differently."

Nine years into their relationship, Brian and Curt don't see their separate finances as a threat to their potential longevity as a couple or as a symbol of disunity. In fact, they believe that the system they've devised helps them avoid arguments and makes them feel more connected.

CURT: We've kept our money pretty separate. Very separate. And it has worked just fine.

BRIAN: We have some things together, like the car we own together.

CURT: But in terms of checking accounts and stuff, it's all been separate. We manage money very differently. It's a headache not worth having.

BRIAN: And it's always worked.

CURT: It works fine. I mean, I have the fantasy that we should merge money and have a joint checking account, but it would be so much harder for me, because I have my private practice. I don't have a separate business account, so I'm always depositing these checks . . . I'd hate to subject Brian to all that.

BRIAN: I have a whole other way of handling money, balancing the checkbook. I'm just very controlling, and I didn't like the idea of having someone else involved in doing it.

CURT: It's not about paying bills or any of that stuff. I balance my checkbook to the penny almost every week. It has more to do with the fact that I spend money a lot more freely than Brian, so I don't want him asking, "Well, who took the forty dollars out of the checking account today?" That's a conversation I don't want to have.

BRIAN: I don't want to know what he's doing, and vice versa. We pay our own personal bills, and jointly we know what we have to do.

CURT: Two checks. It has always been two checks. And it works. If the bill is thirty dollars, then we each write a check for fifteen. Sometimes if there are two bills for a hundred dollars, we'll say, "Here, you pay this one and I'll pay that one." Or if I spent extra money on groceries, I'll say, "You pay this bill."

BRIAN: We're both pretty meticulous in that way, so actually it's not work. It's pretty easy. And it's kind of enjoyable, because we connect around it, too. There's a little ritual that we have. I mark the bills on the outside as to who owes what, and Curt comes in and writes a check, usually when I'm not there, and then when I come in to write my checks I see Curt's check shoved in the envelope. He works in the evenings a lot, so when he's not here and I go to pay the bills, it's like, Oh, Curt was here.

CURT: It's true. It's like Brian was here.

BRIAN: It also makes everyone we're sending these checks to see that there are two people living here, a couple.

Several of the couples have lived on a single income at various times during their relationships. Sometimes this has been out of necessity—because of illness or unemployment. Other times it's been by choice—so that one partner could return to school or stay at home with a newborn child. For some of the couples, this arrangement felt perfectly natural, but for others, financial dependence left them feeling uneasy.

Stanley is happy to be out of the loop when it comes to his and Stewart's finances. The subject is just not something that interests him, so Stewart handles all the bills. Stewart works as a speech pathologist at a local hospital, and he has always been the couple's primary breadwinner. His paychecks go into his own checking account, from which he pays all the bills. Stanley cashes his paycheck, and that money goes for their daily household expenses. Stanley and Stewart fell into their merged financial arrangement, with no discussion or grand plan, soon after they began living together.

But despite Stanley's lack of interest in the family finances, contributing to the couple's pooled income is still very important to him.

STANLEY: I'm sorry to say that I'm not the big breadwinner in the family. What I make a year wouldn't keep us in spaghetti. But in any relationship, you have to somehow hold some weight financially.

Shortly before our interview, the men's clothing store Stanley worked for went through a major downsizing, and Stanley found himself out of work for several months, his income reduced to weekly unemployment benefits.

STANLEY: Every two weeks I was getting $222. I would just give the whole thing over to Stewart. It upset me very much that I was contributing so little. It really did.
STEWART: I never said, "You don't bring in enough. You've got to go out and earn more." Whatever he brings in goes to our living expenses. And that's fine with me. My problem is when he overspends whatever it is that he has.

The only time Stewart and Stanley really argue about money is when they've individually or jointly overspent and run up credit-card debt. For all the couples, arguments over money almost invariably arose over the lack of it.

STEWART: So you get into a cycle where suddenly the credit-card bills are high. Recently, we've had to cut back a lot. A lot of the problem was cable-TV shopping.
STANLEY: Seventy-five percent of what you're looking at in this apartment comes from QVC home shopping: the tchotchkes, and the bells, and the throws, and that little rug. We're on a first-name basis with the UPS guys.
STEWART: That's because you think they're cute.
STANLEY: They've started wearing shorts again.
STEWART: So we've had to cut back. My salary is not the highest in the world, but it's a decent salary and I've done some extra work. It's no problem maintaining all the bills when I've had to. He wants to

feel like he's doing something. He doesn't want to sit home and do nothing.

STANLEY: Unless, God forbid, from the diabetes one day I end up losing a foot or something.

Stewart and Stanley have a joint savings account, which they keep for a rainy day. Both hope they never have to use it.

ELEVEN

Sex

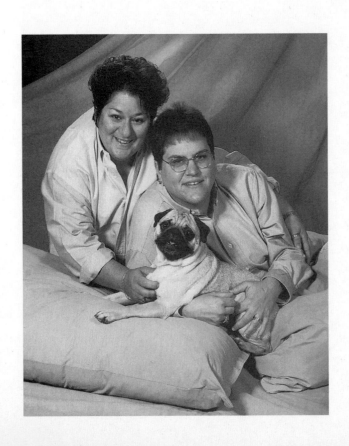

S EVERAL FRIENDS and acquaintances told me that I was lucky
to have the opportunity to ask so many couples about their sex
lives. I didn't feel very lucky during those awkward moments when
a question was rebuffed—as when Anyda let me know that she
didn't think that sex was an appropriate topic for discussion—or
when I found myself in painful territory, as I did with Cassandra and
Anne, who had yet to deal with the fact that they were no longer
having sex.

But in truth, it *was* interesting talking to couples about their sex
lives, and what emerged from the conversations was an overall sense
of the place sex occupies in the lives of those couples who are sexually active. While virtually all the couples said that over time sex
plays a less and less central role in their relationship, it was still
important, and its absence was often a cause of concern.

Nearly all the couples were happy, often eager, to talk about their
early passion. For most, in their first weeks and months, they
couldn't get enough of each other. Sex was hot, spontaneous, fun,
often profound, and exhausting, too. Lovemaking was a time of
shared excitement and discovery, about themselves and each other.

Judy and Bev—the couple who have moved from city to city for

Bev's restaurant career—finished their first unofficial date in the front seat of Bev's car. For Judy, the attraction was instant. Bev required a little warming up, but not much.

JUDY: The first thing I noticed about Bev when I met her was her nails. They were just so gorgeous, so feminine. But her voice sounded so rough. You got the idea that there should be a Harley-Davidson outside. But she had a dress on, and was very soft-featured. She was just stunning.

I asked Judy if her heart was fluttering at the sight of Bev.

JUDY: The heart—or something else—was fluttering. We'll call it a heart.

BEV: She was cute. I loved her smile, and the way her eyes smiled. There was no sexual attraction, but Hey, I thought: Finally maybe here's a female who wants to sleep with me.

Bev had had very little experience with women, having spent several years during her twenties married to a man. At the time she was introduced to Judy, she was dating a couple of different men, but she often found herself thinking about women.

For the next three days after they were introduced, Judy and Bev phoned each other frequently, eventually making a plan to meet up again. The night of their first unofficial date, Bev was scheduled to finish work at midnight, so they arranged to meet at a restaurant at a local strip mall a short time later. Both were smiling, on the verge of giggling, as they told me this part of the story.

JUDY: We thought they'd be open so we could go in and get a beer. But the place was dark, and the parking lot was empty.

BEV: So we sat in my car . . . And I say this as if it were yesterday . . . We've been in the car for ten minutes, and she looks at me and she goes, "Just give me one tiny little kiss." And we kiss, and I guess forty-five minutes later, we're still kissing. I mean, we're just passionate. For both of us, this was the first time we were with a female who wants this and accepts this, and we're going to town and we hear *rap, rap, rap* on the window. It's a security guard. "I see what you girls are doing in there." *How horrible.*

JUDY: As she was buttoning her blouse, Bev says, "I was just consoling her."

At this point, we are all three laughing hard, wiping tears from our eyes. We're sitting at the dining room table of Bev and Judy's trim little house, enjoying a southern barbecue lunch, and I'm sure I'm going to choke on a chunk of spicy pork.

BEV: It was the ultimate embarrassment. So we promptly left that parking lot and went across the street to *another* parking lot.

After more smooching in Bev's car, the two parted and headed home. It was now three in the morning, and Bev had to be back at work at the crack of dawn.

Two days later, Judy and Bev had what they call their first official date. After a quick dinner out, they headed back to Bev's apartment to watch *Harry and the Hendersons,* which Bev had rented in advance of the evening.

BEV: My only VCR was in the bedroom, with my king-size bed. I bet we hadn't watched ten minutes of that movie before all the clothes came off.
JUDY: We were just going at it, and I could hear Bev going "Ahh, ahh, ahh," and I thought, *I'm doing great!*
BEV: I was going "Ahh, ahh, ahh," because I could feel myself falling off the bed. So we both fell onto the floor, and we laughed and laughed. We laugh so much; we always have.

Bev and Judy spent every night together after that, and though at the end of each night one or the other would call for a time-out, the next evening one would show up on the other's doorstep. Judy couldn't get enough of Bev, and Bev, though overwhelmed, didn't stop her.

BEV: We had sex two and three times a night. It was horrible. I don't know what kept me going. It wasn't really horrible, but I'd never seen anybody so sex-starved in my life. But she always laughed. She's a good person, good heart, just happy. I never laughed so much in my life as I did with her. She's very, very quick-witted.

When I talked with Jim and Marty about the early sexual passion in their relationship, they spoke as if fifty years ago were yesterday, recalling how they needed to get separate beds because they couldn't keep their hands off each other.

JIM: Oh, I was horny, all the time!
MARTIN: Unbelievable! I think all young people are like that, though, aren't they?

Certainly, Amy and Jama were like that. The two mid-thirtysomething women met at an AA meeting nine years ago in southern Florida. Their first six months together, prior to Jama's breast cancer diagnosis, were full of sexual passion and very little sleep.

JAMA: We were in bed making love all the time—
AMY: Or in the shower, or—
JAMA: Wherever, because that's what you do when you're infatuated and fall in love. That's how you show your love. And it was *intense*.
AMY: Every day! For three hours at a time. I didn't sleep for the first six months we were together. We might have slept three hours a night. I kid you not. We just hit it off, right away. And we're lucky, because we've never had issues, and I don't think we're ever gonna have issues, about sex. We're sexually compatible—with just one exception: frequency.

As Amy and Jama learned, that early period of passion was also a time of discovering difference. In sex as in all other areas of a relationship, no two people are alike. And just as some like to sleep in a room with the windows wide open and others like the windows shut tight, everyone has different attitudes, histories, expectations, needs, and desires when it comes to sex. As I learned from the couples, some people want sex twice a week, others twice a month. For some, sex is always a deep emotional experience, while for others it's just sex. Lee likes candles and soft music, and Catherine, the former "Slut of the Western World," likes to grope.

LEE: I like romance.
CATHERINE: Oh yeah, the flowers and all that.

Catherine laughed and rolled her eyes as she said this. She and Lee have clearly been over this territory many times during their fifteen years together, and they are good-humored about it. Was it always that way? I wonder.

LEE: Yeah, flowers, the whole thing. Build the fantasy.

CATHERINE: I'm the opposite. She always accuses me of "Oh, you behave just like a man does!" And I always tell Lee that she has to understand, when I was coming up in the homosexual community, I had all gay male friends. So their behavior rubbed off on me, especially the one-night stands and the quick in-and-outs, so the hearts-and-flowers-type stuff was never my forte. But I'm learning.

Lee sent Catherine flowers—a dozen roses in a cut-glass vase—after their first night together.

LEE: You wouldn't believe the teasing she got from her brother.

CATHERINE: He and his lover teased me mercilessly about the red roses. "She must have been a hot one," and all that kind of stuff. I couldn't take the roses back to base with me. I was living in the barracks, and we weren't allowed to have any personal items. So I left the flowers with my brother.

LEE: And Matt loved nice things, so he wanted to keep the cut-glass vase. It was years before we got that vase back.

Catherine has made an effort to be more romantic. And though it's definitely not her first instinct, she knows how much Lee likes that sort of thing. Romance aside, Lee still has problems with Catherine's affectionate groping.

LEE: I don't like being groped, and that's because I lived my entire life, up to a certain point, with men who did that. So sometimes Catherine wants to do something that she considers really affectionate, and I don't see it as being affectionate.

CATHERINE: "Cut it out, you're groping me!" I go, "Okay, fine, but let me finish."

Lee and Catherine spoke about their differences in a very playful way. Whatever pain they may have endured over the issue of romance is long gone, and they deal lightly with their remaining differences. But when Tony* talks about how different he and Carl* were when it came to their sexual needs, it was clear to me that the passage of many years hadn't dulled Tony's memories of feeling rejected by the man with whom he'd fallen in love.

TONY: I remember, twenty-five years ago, going to sleep crying at night because he didn't want to have sex. Shortly after we got together, the physical part started to change. He started pulling back. Where I wanted sex three, four times a day, every day, he didn't. And that would bother me. I tried talking about it, but he would just say, "I don't want it." He'd roll over and go to sleep. And there I was, left alone, and I would be offended by that.

CARL: I think partly it had to do with physical capacity. It wasn't that I didn't want it. I could only do it about once a day, twice a day.

TONY: I've learned to accept that, but when we were young there was lots of insecurity on my part.

The issue of frequency came up with many of the couples, and it proved to be both a difficult subject to talk about and a difficult one to resolve. Jennifer and Brigid had their first fight about this subject within a few months of getting together. Both were surprised, as was the case in many areas of their relationship, by their different expectations.

BRIGID: It wasn't enough for me. And it was very difficult to tell her, especially when you were as inept at communication as I was. I wouldn't talk. I'd go silent for days. She knew something was wrong, but she didn't know what.

JENNIFER: So how could I know what was going on?

BRIGID: This went on for years and years. It was a big one, but we'd eventually talk about it and it would get better for a time. But the discussions were very painful, because they came up only when things got really bad. We never processed it when we were both calm. It came up when a thousand other things had gone wrong.

JENNIFER: This was painful, just painful.

BRIGID: I was really angry. I was having fun with Jennifer. So why not have lots of sex? That's really what's great about a relationship.

* Not their real names.

JENNIFER: I think I was having a lot of stress in my life at that time, so my tendency was to shut down. I was just too vulnerable.

BRIGID: Jennifer was into productive time, and to her, sex didn't seem like productive time. With me, it was, like, It's Saturday morning, let's get up at noon.

JENNIFER: It's Saturday morning and let's get up and do some chores. It was partly a learning process on my part that you just can't leave your partner hanging, and partly it was about relaxing more. I remember it was really bad when we first moved here. We were very poor. Neither of us had a job. It was very tense, and I had no interest.

BRIGID: That was exactly when I wanted it. Sex is a great diversion. It's fun recreation. It's something we can do together without spending big money.

Despite the differences Jennifer and Brigid have over frequency, their sexual relationship has been very important to them. Their lovemaking is a time during which they can relate in an especially intimate way.

BRIGID: When you're having sex, other things come up, new levels of intimacy, you're open, you're freer, exposed, you're vulnerable. You talk about things. It's just a whole variety of opportunities, as well as just a big old orgasm, which I love.

Pam and Lindsy have also valued sex, both as an opportunity to communicate in a special way and for the good times it's provided. But for most of the years they've been together, Lindsy has wanted more sex than Pam. Lindsy's ideal is sex every day, an ideal that isn't ideal for Pam.

LINDSY: Pam is turned off by the whole idea that sex has to take place according to one's horniness schedule. She thinks it should only happen in conjunction with courtship, romance, special couples-y feelings, all that stuff. Your basic bunny versus peacock point of view.

As with many other conflicts they've faced, Pam and Lindsy found themselves going over and over the sex issue without getting anywhere—until they brought their problem to a therapist.

LINDSY: The therapist was great. Everybody should be lucky enough to go to her. We were in a session, talking about the kids and money and whatnot, and I said to the counselor, "And I always want to have sex, and she just doesn't want to have sex as often." And the therapist said, "Well, I have an interesting experiment. How would you feel, Pam, about having sex with Lindsy any time she wanted to for the next month?"

PAM: That would be at least once a day.

LINDSY: And Pam thought about it, and she said, "Well, you know, all right. She's my lover. I'll give it a try." And for the first week, it was, like, *I want to do this all the time!* I was like a kid in a candy store. But then, as the month wore on, I really wanted to read at night. The whole thing was good for me, because I realized that I'd created this false dichotomy. I had this image of myself as the lustful one in the relationship, and it was true, but it was far more dramatic than real life. So we could both kind of relax about it.

Pam and Lindsy could relax about having to have sex every day, but frequency was only one of their differences. Each saw sex as a very different thing. Lindsy sees sex as an opportunity to make everything right when the two of them have been arguing. Pam, decidedly, does not.

LINDSY: I feel like sex is wonderful. Sex is God's gift. And you should use sex to make everything right. Pam's approach is "If the relationship is in trouble, how could you possibly even think about having sex?"

PAM: We would be in the middle of the most horrendous argument, where we've pulled out all the insults, the ones we know will hurt the other person the most, and then it will be bedtime and she'll be "Okay, so let's . . ." And I'll be like, "Are you nuts?" I don't even want to climb into the same room with this person.

LINDSY: But in real life, she would often give in.

Before menopause, Lindsy tells me, she was the one who almost always initiated sex. Hearing this brings me back to the question about who plays the husband and who plays the wife in the bedroom. No one does. While Lindsy is more likely to initiate sex than Pam, this has nothing to do with roles or masculinity and feminin-

ity, and everything to do with the fact that Lindsy wants sex more
often than Pam.

The absence of defined husband/wife roles doesn't mean that in
some couples there isn't one partner who always does the initiating
and one who never initiates, or one partner who always does the
doing and another who always gets done. That has been Bev and
Judy's experience for much of their relationship. Judy, the full-time
homemaker, does the initiating. And for at least the first three
months of Bev and Judy's relationship, Judy wouldn't let Bev do
anything to her in bed.

BEV: Judy is the passionate one when it comes to the bedroom. She is
   the sexiest little thing. During our years together she's been totally
   in control, and I've been one hundred percent submissive in the
   bedroom.

JUDY: I'm just more the giver.

BEV: She gets turned on after she turns me on. I'm very vocal, and then
   she gets very turned on.

JUDY: She let me do anything to her in bed, but I didn't let Bev give me
   an orgasm for a long time.

BEV: It was three months before she let me. She always wanted to
   please me, but she never wanted sex just to please her.

JUDY: I don't think I've ever come up to her and said, "I've got to have
   sex."

BEV: "I need an orgasm. Take care of me."

JUDY: If I needed it, I'd take care of myself.

Amy and Jama told me that in their relationship, there are no
hard and fast rules about sex. I asked which of them is more likely to
initiate.

JAMA: Depends on what month it is, I guess.

AMY: We don't have rules or roles. We make love like two women in
   bed. And that's the way I've always been.

JAMA: We don't do the dominant thing in the bedroom. I mean, we're
   like that in real life. Amy's a real pain-in-the-ass control freak sometimes, and I'm a real bitch if you don't give me what I want. So we
   do enough of that outside the bedroom. We don't need to take that
   into the bedroom.

While Tony is more likely than Carl to initiate sex, when it comes to the act itself, they're pretty fluid about who does what and who is in control during any particular moment.

TONY: We're not into role-playing or anything like that. It's who wants to do what when. Who's in what mood.

CARL: You fuck me. No, *you* fuck *me*. I mean, I'm definitely more . . . I don't want to use the word "aggressive," but if one has to put labels based on the old role-playing thing, I would lean more towards the top. Tony leans toward the bottom. But that's only true of the past ten years. For the first fifteen years, we were clearly equals.

The couples with whom I spoke in some detail about their sexual relationships told me that they engage in a broad range of sexual activity, from oral sex and anal intercourse to using sex toys and sharing fantasies. Of course, not every couple did every thing. Some couples specifically said they didn't use toys or share fantasies; some male couples specifically said they didn't have anal intercourse; some couples said they didn't have sex at all.

The sexual relationship I was most curious to hear about was Brian and Curt's. Because Brian is HIV-negative and Curt is HIV-positive, I wanted to know how they've maintained a sexual relationship—and done it safely. They were not the only couple to discuss sex and HIV. The three male couples I interviewed who engage in sex with men other than their partners were emphatic about their commitment to practicing safe sex. But Brian and Curt were the only sexually active couple I spoke with where one partner was positive and the other negative.

I was surprised to learn that Curt's diagnosis, a year after they met, actually improved their sexual relationship. Until both men got tested, they had been operating under the assumption that Curt was positive and that Brian might also be positive—however unlikely that was, given his limited prior sexual experience.

BRIAN: After we got tested, we started having unprotected oral sex. Well, one of us did. I mean, I wasn't performing unprotected oral sex on him; he was doing it on me.

CURT: I went down on him. I was teaching about AIDS at that time, and there was no evidence of HIV being contracted orally from a positive person to a negative person, with the positive person going down on him.

BRIAN: For our first year, that never got to happen. All that time, we'd never had that basic sexual experience. So after we knew, at least that got to happen and that was really exciting. So, actually, our sex life improved.

CURT: It was liberating in some ways, because we weren't living in fear anymore. We knew exactly what the game was at that point and what the ground rules were.

During the years they've been together, Brian and Curt have found that their sexual relationship has continued to change. Recently, they've started having protected anal intercourse.

CURT: We have protected anal sex where I get to do all the receptive activities. Brian gets to penetrate me. But not the other way around.

BRIAN: Mostly for HIV issues. I mean, we keep talking about doing it the other way around, but we haven't.

CURT: I think it's the next frontier.

BRIAN: Right.

CURT: It's been one of the most freeing things, because we didn't have intercourse for a long, long, long time. It's new. Brian wasn't into it as the receptive partner. And I had a pretty extensive sexual history prior to being in this relationship, and intercourse just put me into a very dark mind-set. I didn't want to evoke whatever spirit that was about. And it took a long time to heal whatever that was about. Now it's actually just so great. Our whole sexual thing these days has been exciting and fun.

BRIAN: It's terrific. And I think there's more territory to explore. Now I'm turning ten shades of red, right?

Besides changing in terms of what specifically they do, Brian and Curt's sexual relationship has changed qualitatively as well.

CURT: It's been really nice, and our experience has taught me a lot about sex.

BRIAN: Right. And me, too.

CURT: To have the feeling of sexual desire not come from an objective form of desire or lust, for it to come from some other completely different part of myself, is just revolutionary. It's definitely love, and it's also this safe connection you have to this other person. It's so safe on an emotional level, and that feeling of safety is so profound. To have sex occur in a really safe, really powerful, passionate way is just big and fun.

BRIAN: And new, too. And the trust. He's never pushed me about the safety issues. It's never been a topic of conflict. We're just going to be safe about this, and we've always respected each other's boundaries. And it's been a real growing experience for me, too. I didn't come into this relationship with a lot of experience. Curt was the one who had much more experience. So I felt like he's the pro and I'm the amateur. And I've learned that I can be just as sexual as he is.

CURT: Even more so.

All the couples talked about how their sexual relationships had changed over the years they've been together. Frequency changed, quality changed, and importance of sex in general and its place in the relationship changed. For the most part, sex became less central to the relationship, less frequent though more intimate, less spontaneous though more adventuresome. Sometimes the changes have been distressing, leading to feelings of insecurity and a sense of loss, but for couples like Brian and Curt, change has been for the good.

Amy and Jama told me that after nine years together, they're no longer having sex every night. But that doesn't mean they don't have a great time together.

AMY: I don't think we're any different than any other couple in that over the course of the years, our sex life has slowed. We certainly don't make love as often as we used to, but I think the sex we have today is incredible! I don't know how else to say it, and I'm not a person who talks about this a lot. But we know each other physically so well. It's stupendous. It's remarkable. I have never been in a relationship where the relationship gets better over time and the sex itself gets better over time. I think when you get those two things, you have a winner. I can honestly say that I love Jama more today than I ever have, and that when we make love, I enjoy it more than ever. She's the basis of my everything. It's remarkable.

JAMA: Oh, blush, blush, blush.

Jama was bright red and fanning herself as Amy spoke of their sexual relationship. The two were opposite me on the gray velvet sofa in their living room, with Amy sitting upright and Jama sprawled like a Rubenesque model, her head on her hand, leaning on a pile of pillows, her feet touching Amy's thigh. Their dog, a pug named Winston, had found a cozy spot between the two of them.

Both Amy and Jama are large women, although Amy is the taller of the two. Amy wears glasses and has short brown hair, and Jama has shoulder-length black hair. Both are dressed in T-shirts and shorts and are barefoot. Jama wears a bracelet on her left ankle and a ring on one toe, and her toenails are painted silver. She also wears a gold necklace, a bracelet, earrings, and a gold commitment ring that matches the one Amy is wearing.

Because both women spoke so enthusiastically and passionately about their sexual relationship, I assumed that they were having lots of sex. I was wrong.

JAMA: Once or twice a month.

AMY: Well, you have to remember you have women involved, who have their period, so the schedule kind of fluctuates and changes. So I would agree that on average it's once or twice a month. And then there'll be the month where all of a sudden: five times. And it rarely goes longer than three weeks. I can't imagine it going longer than three weeks. That would be a long time.

JAMA: Three weeks is the magic number.

AMY: Now, we have sex more often when we're on vacation, because we don't have to get up and go to work, and we have sex more often when we take a week off. Do we have sex most often on the weekends? Absolutely! Because that's when you have the time. You know, sex has to fit inside of conventional life.

JAMA: I think people have a misunderstanding about sex, let alone gay sex. No question that my sex with Amy has been nothing short of magnificent. And I say that proudly. I love to be in bed with her.

AMY: But we're like most people in that we're not doing it on the chandeliers.

JAMA: People think that just because it's different, or it's outside of their norm, that it has to be perverted, and it just isn't.

For any couple that worries they're not having sex as frequently as they're supposed to, I think that what Amy and Jama had to say is comforting, maybe even revolutionary. They've found what works for them, they enjoy each other, and they don't worry about what everybody else is doing.

What most of the couples told me about their sex lives would generally disappoint those people who think that all gay men and women are carnal omnivores. On average, the younger couples were having sex once to eight times a month; the older couples did it less. But the full range ran from a handful of couples who no longer have sex at all to one couple, Carl and Tony, who engage in some sort of sexual activity every night. The two men, both in their late forties, have the most sexually active relationship of all the couples I spoke with. I couldn't help but feel undersexed when they described what they do.

TONY: There are times when we just fuck our brains out all day long.
CARL: Which we did the weekend before last. Four times within twenty-four hours. It's amazing. I couldn't do that when we were twenty-two: four times in twenty-four hours.
TONY: We have films, we have toys. Back then we didn't.
CARL: It was amazing.
TONY: Sex is hotter now than then.
CARL: Yes, much better.
TONY: We are uninhibited. We talk about our fantasies. We play out our fantasies.
CARL: To a certain extent, the most surprising thing is that we share so many of the same fantasies that we never knew we had. We're comfortable being who we are, and we know that it's safe to experiment a bit more than when we were younger.

Pam and Lindsy don't have sex every night. As Lindsy discovered after playing out her therapist's suggestion, even though she thought she wanted sex with Pam every night, she didn't really. And having now been through menopause, she doesn't often feel the urge to have sex at all.

LINDSY: Since I did menopause, I'm not as motivated anymore. Pam has not done menopause yet. I had no other symptoms, but my sex drive definitely went down. And I don't like it. I'm not constantly jumping her bones. When I was, she would be annoyed, but I think she kind of bought it for many years.

PAM: Oh, years. I'm really insulted now.

LINDSY: So we're trying to figure out how to artificially get that back.

Age and health problems—from the natural aging process, including menopause, to prostate trouble, cancer, diabetes, and AIDS—have had a significant impact on the sex lives of many of the couples.

Stanley and Stewart both have diabetes, although Stanley has had it longer and his symptoms have made sex increasingly difficult.

STANLEY: In the beginning, it's maybe four times a week; and then after a couple of years, it's maybe twice a week, and now it's on an anniversary. It's not that bad, but it's not as frequent.

STEWART: A lot of it is because of his diabetes, and we both have high blood pressure.

STANLEY: I hate to admit this, but erections are not that easy to come by, and orgasms are not that easy to come by.

I asked Stanley and Stewart if Stanley's limitations had changed their relationship.

STEWART: No. I don't think so.

STANLEY: I've never been a selfish person. I am just as happy to know that he's been gratified even if I haven't been. It's really not fair to cut things out entirely.

STEWART: But the amount, it's totally random. We could do it two or three times in a row, and then we can go for two weeks without. We're still in the same bed. We'll just hold each other or whatever. There is no plan.

Recently, Stewart underwent surgery for a cancerous tumor, so the last thing on their minds is sex. Both are focused on Stewart's recovery.

Kevin and Paul no longer have sex. For the first seven years of the nineteen they've been together, Kevin, by his own description, was wildly promiscuous. It was something Paul tolerated, hoping it would eventually run its course—which it did—but by then Kevin had contracted HIV. Even before he and Paul knew that Kevin was HIV-positive, even before there was a test for HIV, they modified their sexual behavior to avoid passing anything on to each other in the event that either of them was already infected.

KEVIN: We made a game out of it. At a restaurant we'd go to the men's room and pick out which condom we wanted from the vending machine—you know, a French tickler this time. We went through the different types. But after we found out in 1989 for sure that I was sick, we eliminated just about everything. We had films and that type of thing, but as far as being physical like we used to, the last thing in the world I ever wanted was for him to become positive.

Except for the fact that Kevin is very, very pale, I would not have known that he'd been terribly ill a number of times and that he'd been conserving his strength for several days in anticipation of our conversation. Kevin is tall, very gregarious, and bald. What little hair he has on his head and his mustache is gray, with a hint of blond. He has a very easy, broad smile and a hearty laugh. Paul is of average height, thickly built, and tanned. He also has a mustache, more brown than gray, but his smile is reserved and he doesn't say a lot. During our discussion about Kevin's illness, Paul's eyes fill with tears several times. Kevin and Paul's emotions seem always to be right at the surface; given how much they obviously love each other, and how close Kevin has come to dying, this is hardly surprising.

For a short while, after Kevin's diagnosis but before he became very ill, they watched porn films together on their wide-screen television.

PAUL: We'd watch the films and have mutual masturbation. But Kevin doesn't have the energy for that anymore.

KEVIN: Just to ejaculate wipes me out. It takes so much energy, and I didn't realize how much energy sex takes. I've done much better since I've been on all the new drugs. But before then, forget it. Now he'll be down here watching his films, and I'll be up on the computer because I can't handle it physically. And I can't stand straight films.

PAUL: I watch primarily all-straight films. He doesn't like that nasty stuff. It doesn't bother me.

I asked Kevin and Paul why they were still a couple if they were no longer having sex.

PAUL: Because we love each other.

KEVIN: Sex has nothing to do with it. In fact, it's interesting: Sex, especially when you're younger, is very important. And we had a very healthy sex life. I'm not talking about my extracurricular activities. Between us, we had sex often, and in unusual places, and we did all the fun things.

PAUL: I remember wondering whether I would become bitter. Would I become angry? Would I feel something was taken away from me? I always waited for those emotions, believing that someday I would experience that, but they never came. We just grew closer and closer.

KEVIN: Sometimes for me . . . I'm a different personality than Paul.

PAUL: He gets angry about it.

KEVIN: I do. I get very angry about it, because I feel like my honey is having to live without something that we both enjoyed very much and that was part of our relationship. I know how he feels, and he's always assured me, but it still makes me angry. So I want to do other things for him. So when I feel up to it, I make sure that I get up at four-thirty in the morning when he gets up for work, and we have coffee together.

PAUL: Just about every morning.

KEVIN: I go down and get the coffee. I do things that I can, little things. "I love you, I'm going downstairs to get your coffee." I may not have the energy to do other things, but I have the energy to do *these* things.

I ask Kevin if he's ever told Paul to go out and have sex with other men. Paul's eyes fill with tears.

KEVIN: No.

PAUL: It's never been discussed.

KEVIN: If I tried saying anything, he'd tell me to shut my face.

Not all the couples who have stopped having sex or are having difficulties with their sexual relationship could point to health issues or changes brought on by the aging process as the cause. Over the past three years, Bev and Judy have grown anxious as their sexual relationship has dwindled, and they're not sure what to do.

JUDY: I'm a little concerned that we don't have sex like we used to. I know we can never go back to what we had for several years, but I'm worried about the fact that our sex life has gone down.

BEV: It really has, and there's no reason. We try to figure out why. The love is there, and we hug each other, we caress. I think a lot of it has to do with my job, because I get up at three-thirty in the morning. So at eight o'clock at night, I'm just about dead and Judy's wide awake.

JUDY: I try to be flexible with my schedule, but it's awful to keep those hours.

BEV: That's probably been the biggest detriment, because we have no bedtime when you get a little cozy. We have to go to bed with the intent of sex, and that's no fun. We've probably gone six months without it. But she lets me vibrate. She gets the biggest kick out of it. I need a release, and so I get my little vibrator out and Judy comes over and kisses me.

JUDY: It just hasn't been like it used to be.

BEV: It's real quick with the vibrator. I have an orgasm in like twenty seconds, and she laughs. I turn it on and I go "Oh, oh, oh," and she starts cackling. But I don't consider that sex. Inserting a finger into each other is sex to me.

JUDY: I miss it, but we've reached that point where it's "Night, night," and you roll over. I still love her when she comes home. She smiles and gives me a kiss hello, so I don't think there's a lack of affection.

BEV: And on the couch when we watch movies, we snuggle and we'll rub each other. There's a lot of snuggle time, but the actual wild and crazy sex isn't there. We hope the sex will come back. But we're still very happy.

Even the couples with sexual conflicts still considered themselves to be happy. I asked Cassandra and Anne about this, because I wanted to know how they reconciled no sex and calling themselves happy.

Cassandra and Anne haven't had sex for a year, and they believe they need to go into therapy. As Cassandra noted, she suspects that her weight gain has led to Anne's lack of interest.

CASSANDRA: I don't think that sex, in and of itself, makes one happy. There are lots of people who are in committed, married relationships who have very active sex lives, but they have miserable relationships. I work with this woman, and she talks about sex all the time. And I think she's got a really messed-up marriage. But they've got a great sex life. I don't think that sex leads to happiness. I think it can enhance it, and I'm sure that we could be happier in some ways if we had a more fulfilling sex life, but what makes me happy with Anne is just being with her. It is a joy to be with her.

ANNE: We're pretty inseparable.

CASSANDRA: Yeah, we are always together. Maybe that's sick. I don't know.

ANNE: When we're in this house together, we're in the same room.

CASSANDRA: You know, we have all these rooms, and for what? Look, we're very physical with each other, even though it may not be sexual. Lots of touching, stroking, kissing, holding hands, grabbing each other. You know, all that kind of stuff. It just doesn't go beyond that.

(In the year since I first spoke with Cassandra and Anne, they've told me, "Things are a lot better in a certain category.")

All the couples, whether they were having lots of sex or no sex, talked about how physically affectionate they are and how important that is in their relationships. And almost everyone made a point of differentiating between having sex that leads to orgasm and having a physically affectionate relationship that may or may not have sexual content. Apparently, there's a lot of snuggling, hugging, cuddling, spooning, patting, groping, and kissing going on behind closed doors. And while many of the people I spoke with said that they could imagine living without sex—or that they already do—no one said they could survive without the physical affection they share with their partner. Amen to that.

I thought Ruth and Zenobia, the former Correction Officers, said it best. Ruth is sixty-three, and Zenobia is fifty-five. They've known each other for thirty years, they've been a couple for the past fifteen years, and they're both grandmothers.

RUTH: I guess I really should say that sex is overrated. Sex, like every-thing else, changes. And, you know, looks are sexual, touch is sexual. So just because you don't get between the sheets or on the floor—or on top of a table—and actually go through the acts, it's not to say that you're not still very sexual with each other. And I think we are. We touch a lot. We're always tapping and patting, but the bed business? Guess what? She aches a lot, and I ache a lot. The hips, and whatever. So we're using massage apparatuses now to encourage us along. You need a little help. I say, Do whatever makes your boat float.

ZENOBIA: Right. Sometimes I say, "Oh, I just need to give you a hug." And I do it.

RUTH: And you can feel the whole passion.

ZENOBIA: Sex always changes in any relationship after a while.

RUTH: We're tired now.

ZENOBIA: Yeah, we done wore it out!

RUTH: We're trying to take in a little hiatus here, right? And we're finding other ways of being joyously sexual.

As an almost forty-year-old guy looking forward to growing old with my significant other, I took comfort in what Ruth and Zenobia had to say about dealing with the changes in their sexual relation-ship. I also found solace in what Jim and Martin had to say.

JIM: Our sex life isn't bad, but sometimes we can go a month without it. It depends on how you feel. It's still good, though.

MARTIN: I don't think it's as important as it was in the beginning, you know. But we still do a lot of kissing in this house.

JIM: And a lot of times, I just have to touch him, put my arm around him. And as you get older, I notice that I like to be in the same room with Marty. He'll be in the bedroom there, typing on his word processor, and it'll be real quiet and I won't hear anything for a while. So I'll get up and sneak a look in to make sure everything's okay. I do that especially since he had the cancer and the stroke, because things go wrong, don't they, Marty? I suppose that's how it is in any house where you get real old.

TWELVE

Family

INTRODUCING a new beloved to one's parents is a nerve-racking experience for anyone. Take that high-anxiety experience and add parents who are deeply religious and a beloved who is the same gender as oneself, and, well, it's enough to make you want to avoid the whole thing. And that's exactly what Stewart did after he arranged for his Orthodox Jewish parents to meet the man with whom he was now sharing his one-bedroom apartment.

STEWART: We decided we were going to do it on a Thursday night, so I invited my parents over for coffee and cake. I didn't tell my mother why, so she had to know something was up, but I'm sure she didn't know exactly what. Well, Thursday night came, and I decide to take my time coming home because I'm a nervous wreck about them coming over.

STANLEY: I don't know if I was really worried, but it was beginning to look like Stewart's parents were going to get there before Stewart did, so I used my noodle. Knowing they were religious, I put a yarmulke on my head and some nice music on the stereo. The doorbell rang, and it was just his mother—his father had gone to park the car. And when she saw who was at the door, her face dropped.

STEWART: She realized why I'd invited them over.

STANLEY: Then I introduced myself, and seeing the yarmulke on my head and hearing the nice music, and also seeing how much things had shaped up around here, she threw her arms around me, hugged me, and said, "Thank God you're Jewish!"

Stanley welcomed the hug, but still, it was a startling beginning to what has become an intensely close and mutually supportive relationship with both of Stewart's parents.

Almost all the couples have significant relationships with one or both partners' families, relationships that have, in general, improved over time as loved ones have grown to accept a same-gender partner. These relationships range from extremely close and rewarding, as with Stanley and Stewart, to complicated and painful. This subject led to more tears—of both joy and sorrow—than any other in my interviews.

The tears came for Stanley when I asked him what he liked best about Stewart.

STANLEY: Don't take this wrong. I love Stewart dearly, but what I like about Stewart most is his family. With Stewart, I have acquired family members that have been so understanding and so warm and so caring, and I couldn't get that from my own family. My mother, yes. She was always there for me. She always knew . . . She passed away three years after I married my ex-wife. But my father . . . Stewart's father has been more of a dad to me than my father was. It's a terrible thing to have to say, but it's true. Whenever I go over to Stewart's parents' house, I'll give a kiss to his dad when I walk in and when I'm leaving. My father's idea of affection was a two-minute phone call every two weeks at ten A.M. on a Thursday.

STEWART: If we weren't home, he'd leave a message on the machine.

STANLEY: But Stewart's father . . . If I need anything . . . I was in the hospital . . .

STEWART: Stanley fell and shattered his elbow a year ago March. He needed surgery. My parents came right away.

Despite how happy Stewart's mother was to see that her son's new friend was Jewish, it took time for a close relationship to develop, just as it took time for Stewart's parents to accept the fact that their son is gay. Like almost all parents, their initial reaction was not positive. "It wasn't great at the time," Stewart explained, "but they were still supportive. They were still going to love me, regardless."

Over time, as Stewart and Stanley and Stewart's parents found their way to the warm relationship they now enjoy, Stewart has sometimes had to help his parents along, and sometimes they've had to push Stewart and Stanley.

STEWART: My mother made a comment that my father felt uncomfortable about walking into the bedroom of our apartment. So after that, for a couple of months, every time they were here, I had something to show them in the bedroom. Now we walk around the house and it's no big deal. And recently, when I was sick, my mother actually told Stanley to give me a kiss. I've never touched him in front of them, and she told Stanley to kiss me.

STANLEY: I had come home from work on a break to check on Stewart.

STEWART: It was a couple of days after I'd come home from surgery, and I was bleeding all over the bathroom.

STANLEY: He's standing naked in the bathtub, and his father is trying to clean him up. After he was all cleaned up, we were all hugging in a pack.

STEWART: My mother said, "It's okay, give him a kiss."

STANLEY: And I did. There's that old saying: "You can pick your friends, but you can't pick your family." Well, I picked Stewart, and the package that I got with him was not to be believed. There isn't a gay man or lesbian person in this city that wouldn't kill to have the family relationship that we have. If I have so much as a hangnail, his mother worries about it.

Nate and Danny discovered quickly that they had to create their own family. They were among the few younger couples I interviewed who couldn't count on the love and support of even one parent during most of the years they've been a couple.

NATE: It reinforced that we were primary for each other. Especially after my father died and Danny's mother died. We had known for some time that we were primary for each other, but to go through those losses when we were still relatively young . . . We just realized that *we* were the family and that whatever family we created had to be of our own doing, because our own families, for different reasons, were not supportive of us and really didn't nurture us and give us what we needed.

It was the hostile reaction of Danny's parents to his homosexuality that encouraged him to move to Boston in the first place, a move that led to his serendipitous meeting with Nate. A year after he and Danny became a couple, Nate decided it was time to make things clear to his parents, and he came out to them in a letter. He thought it might not be news to them.

NATE: My mother and grandmother came to Boston for my cousin's graduation in June 1980.

DANNY: They knew I was a roommate, but they didn't *know*. There were a lot of bedrooms.

NATE: But my mother's not stupid. I mean, her son's a preschool teacher living with three men in Somerville? *Hello.* But my family has always been very heavy into denial.

In his letter to his parents, Nate explained that he was gay and that he was happy. He told them he knew that this knowledge was going to be hard for them to deal with, but he loved them and needed their support. He did not tell them about Danny, deciding to save that for another time.

NATE: I was pretty anxious waiting for them to call. When she called, my mother said, "We got your letter," and she made it pretty clear that she and my father were very devastated by this. I had timed the letter so it was right before a scheduled visit, and I told them in the letter that I wanted to come visit and talk to them, but if they didn't want me to come at this point to let me know. And my mother said something like "Well, your father says you should still come; I wasn't so sure," which was really like a knife in my heart. I'm sure she would deny this if she ever heard it, but that's what she said.

DANNY: I strongly encouraged Nate to hang in there with his parents, because I felt like I had lost my own family.

NATE: Some people would have said, "Screw your family," but he encouraged me to meet them halfway. He didn't exactly say I had to understand their position, but he encouraged me to at least try to deal with it. I had this very dramatic image in my mind that there would never be any way that they could begin to accept this.

So I went down to see my parents, and they were very unhappy about this and wanted me to go to see a therapist about changing. I told them I wasn't willing to do this, so it was a very tense time. And then when I called to tell them I was moving to Philadelphia and Danny was going with me, they said, "Why do you have to hang on to your friends? Why can't you just go and start a new life?" It was all in euphemisms, but I knew what they were saying.

DANNY: His mother was always saying, "Why don't you meet new friends?"

NATE: "Meet new people." It was always "people," always couched in these euphemisms. "You need to meet new people. You're still young." They never really got it. And in fact, my father never did. He died five years later, without ever really accepting it. And I think it's only in the last few years that my mother has really understood.

Two years after he and Danny got to Philadelphia, Nate completed his master's degree. He invited his family to the graduation, but when his parents discovered that Danny would be there too, they refused to attend unless Nate told Danny not to come.

NATE: Danny was the person who had gotten me through the two years of graduate school, and there was no question that he was going to be there. It was as much his event as it was mine. I think my parents were very surprised when I told them Danny would be there whether they liked it or not. I imagine they just assumed that I'd say, "Okay, he'll stay home. You come." It was their loss.

One of my brothers called me and tried to convince me that it was just this one time. He said, "Why don't you let Mom and Dad come?" I refused. So my parents sent him and my little brother with all of this money to take us out to dinner. It was guilt money. But it was a real big thing not to have my parents there.

Nate's parents were benign in comparison to Sherri's. For the first five and a half years of her relationship with Chris, Sherri's parents were openly hostile toward Chris, to the point of trying to destroy her relationship with their daughter. Things got off to a rocky start when Sherri's mother referred to Chris as "an old, fat, poor person."

SHERRI: It was not pretty. My parents slammed Chris for years. I've blocked out most of what they said, because they were so ugly.

CHRIS: Probably the most negative influence on our relationship is Sherri's parents. And they really didn't get better until Taylor was born. They're still not good, but until Taylor, they didn't even say my name. I was just "that woman."

Despite knowing how Sherri's parents felt about her, Chris would reluctantly agree to go with Sherri to visit her parents.

SHERRI: They never came over here. I always went over to their house.

CHRIS: Occasionally I'd go along, if she could force me to go. And once we got there, her mother sits over *there* and her father sits over *there* and Sherri sits over *there,* and they carry on a conversation as if there were no one else in the room. I could torture the dog, and nobody would notice. But I'm not being fair, because sometimes Sherri's mother would talk to me. She'd say things like "When are you going to get a *real* job?"

See, both of us believe that a family is really important, so I couldn't say things back to her parents for fear of jeopardizing her relationship. I could say to Sherri, "I don't like your mother," but I couldn't say to her mother, "I don't like *you.*"

SHERRI: We discuss families, at great length, because our families are seriously dysfunctional.

The real low point—and what turned out to be the turning point—came when Sherri's parents decided to celebrate their daughter's twenty-fifth birthday by taking her on a special trip. Chris wasn't invited. During our interview, I felt guilty pursuing this story, because it was clear as soon as we started talking about the incident that the old feelings of hurt and anger were very close to the surface.

SHERRI: They decided to give me a couple of nights on the town. And I finally relented and said—

CHRIS: No, you didn't relent.

SHERRI: Well, no, I didn't.

CHRIS: Sherri didn't make a commitment to them one way or the other. She kept saying, "Well, I may have to work." Well, her dad worked in the same hospital—he's also a nurse—and he went to Sherri's supervisor and got her the days off that they wanted to take her away for, so she didn't have that excuse. And because she wasn't very good at saying no to them *or* to me, she just kind of left it up in the air. So they planned it, and she ended up going on this trip. I wasn't very happy about it. It was the indecision that upset me. Say to me that you *want* to go, or say to them that you *don't*.

SHERRI: I felt trapped, because if I said no to them, they would be angry, and if I said yes, I wanted to go, Chris would be angry. You know, we were still in what I would consider a really new stage in the—

CHRIS: Even though we were, like, five and a half years into it.

SHERRI: You know, I had a lot of insecurity issues that I was dealing with at that time.

CHRIS: "If she makes me mad, I will leave." That kind of thing. That wasn't true, but that's how she felt. So she went to Vegas with them.

What Chris and Sherri didn't know was that Sherri's parents had planned a little surprise that they hoped would get Sherri to leave Chris.

CHRIS: I told Sherri to call me when she got to Vegas, because I wanted to know that she arrived safely. So she calls to tell me that she's arrived, and she says, "But I can't talk right now. All kinds of things are happening. I'll call you later." And she hangs up. Well, I waited up until three or four in the morning, and she didn't call back. And she didn't call and she didn't call and she didn't call. Well, I thought, Oh my God, I wonder what's happened. I had no way of reaching her, because I didn't know where they were staying. It was all a surprise. I woke up the next morning and she still hadn't called. And I thought, *Be dead, because otherwise you're gonna be dead.* I was a wreck.

So finally she calls at ten o'clock in the morning, and I'm just livid. But I listened to what she had to say. She told me that the surprise was that they had flown her friend Rob, who she had dated in high school, out to Las Vegas, and they had rented a room for him and gotten tickets for him to take Sherri to shows, and all kinds of stuff. In their little warped and distorted minds, I knew they were thinking, Rob and Sherri are going to rekindle that old flame. They're going to get together, and Sherri will move away from Chris, and that will be the end of that. It was their little fantasy. Well, I went wacko, and I'm arguing with Sherri on the phone, and I could hear her dad in the background going, "Well, she doesn't have any right to be mad." Well, excuse me, I do. And I told Sherri, "I've never said anything bad to your parents, and they treat me like crap. They can drop you off at our house, but do not let them come to the front door, because if they do, I'm ripping them apart." And I hung up on her.

Sherri sat silently as Chris continued with the story, explaining that she saw only one way of dealing with the ongoing problem with Sherri's parents.

CHRIS: I felt like if we didn't do something, it was just going to go on and on and on like this with her parents. I told Sherri that she needed to tell her parents that this was the way things were, that we're in a relationship. I said, "You need to take a stand. And if you're not going to take a stand, that's it, because I'm not doing this anymore."

SHERRI: See, I couldn't believe that my parents had an ulterior motive. It wasn't until we talked about this at great length that I began to see what was going on. It was very difficult, because I love my parents on a level. I really do love them. But my way of dealing with things has always been just to run the other way, to avoid conflict. So I never said anything when they would make digs about Chris.

CHRIS: And I'm a confronter. You know, people either really like me or they hate my guts. Because if you do something that annoys me, I will tell you. Sherri's a don't-rock-the-boat kind of person.

SHERRI: It was a real crisis in my life, because I had to make the decision: Do I want to have a relationship with Chris, or do I want to go back to live with my parents? I knew that I wanted my relationship more than I wanted anything else.

CHRIS: It was a real crossroads at that point, a do-or-die kind of thing. So she went and did it. That very same day, she went to her parents' house and said, "Listen, Chris and I are a couple, and we're going to be together. I'm never going to be with anybody like my old boyfriend. Get over it."

SHERRI: "You don't have to like it, but this is how it's going to be. I don't want to hear those things cross your lips, because if you say it to me, I'm going to tell you where to go."

CHRIS: A couple of times after that they said things, and then it would be months between times that we'd see them. So they finally got it.

The battle with Sherri's parents is long since over, but Sherri and Chris's relationship with them is distant at best. Fortunately, from the very beginning, Chris's family has welcomed Sherri with open arms.

CHRIS: They're totally, totally accepting.

SHERRI: But they've had a lot longer to get used to it. They've been through all the ups and downs of finding out Chris was gay and about the different relationships. Of course, I endeared myself to her mother when I took care of Chris's father for the last three months of his life.

CHRIS: When we first got together, my dad was dying. He had a brain tumor. Sherri was wonderful, because she was able to do things for the family that no one else could do, because she was in her last year of nursing school and knew the best things to do.

SHERRI: I knew where to get the equipment to lift him out of bed and move him around.

CHRIS: And she was able to come over and help him bathe when no one else could, because my dad didn't want me to see him. My brothers were useless, and my sister lives too far away to be of any use. So from the very beginning, she endeared herself to my family, and especially my mother, because she was so helpful. And my mother just loved her.

A few of the couples I talked to are involved in caring for sick or elderly relatives. Interestingly, in two instances it was the child-in-law who became the primary caregiver, as with Sherri and Chris's father, and with Jim—of Jim and Lane, the couple with the matching tattoos—who took care of Lane's elderly mother.

When Lane's mother became too frail to care for herself, Jim and Lane moved her into their cramped trailer. They had never explicitly discussed with her the nature of their relationship, but she was the first to defend them against anyone foolish enough to make an antigay remark. And whenever her favorite television evangelist decided to rail against the sin of homosexuality, she changed the channel.

JIM: She stayed with us a couple of nights when she wasn't doing good, and she stayed with us more and more. That was about 1981, and she was with us for twelve years.

LANE: She couldn't take care of herself, and nobody else would help her. She's got all these children—I'm one of nine—and nobody else would help her.

JIM: I guess it was more convenient for them that somebody else was taking care of things.

LANE: I had two brothers living here on the family property, and they wouldn't even come see her.

JIM: They didn't like to see her being old and frail. It was hard for them, just like it was hard for Lane, but they chose to bury their heads in the sand. Both of his brothers have wives at home, but we were the ones who gave Mom her baths and everything. They didn't even come to help with that. It was difficult for us to have to bathe her, and at first it was embarrassing for us and for her, but after a while you just get used to it. But it always astonished me. I would think that at least the women folk could come give a hand with the hygiene care. Our friend Lila was the only one who helped with those things.

LANE: We did all those things, especially Jim. And he knew how to take care of the medical problems.

JIM: I kept close watch over her medicine. Her health had got real bad, and I started taking her to Charlotte to different doctors, because the doctors here didn't know what they were doing. Of course, she didn't have any insurance. She had Medicare, but a lot of the doctors were a lot more expensive than that. They'd fall in love with her, and I'd talk them into treating her for whatever Medicare would pay.

Over the next few years, Lane's mother's health gradually deteriorated. She became increasingly arthritic, her memory receded, and she could no longer be left alone at home when Jim and Lane went out on jobs.

LANE: That's when Mom started going to work with us.

JIM: We couldn't get anyone to stay with her, and we didn't have the money to pay for anybody to stay with her. Everything we did has been out of necessity. You do what you have to do when you ain't got the money to do it. You make the best of it and improvise. So we had a van, which Lane remodeled. He put in captain's chairs, and he put a window in the side and installed an RV bathroom. Every morning we'd walk Mom up the ramp into the back of the van, and she'd go to Charlotte with us to clean carpets. We brought along our dog and our cat, and the cat would sit on her lap all day. We did that for about two years, and Mom loved it. She had her picture window right by her seat, and she'd watch everything going on. And a lot of the people at the apartment complexes got to know her, and they'd come and visit with her out at the truck. When the weather was pretty, we'd take lawn chairs with us, and when we were doing a job, we'd put the lawn chairs out and let Mom sit in the yard. She liked the routine, and it got her out of the house.

Following a series of small strokes, Lane's mother often slept in the same bed as Jim.

JIM: She was getting up during the night and would fall. So a lot of nights I slept in bed with her, or slept in the room, so I could make sure she didn't get hurt.

LANE: I couldn't handle that part, so she was lucky to have Jim.

JIM: It was too hard on Lane. It upset him so bad.

LANE: It bothered me a lot. Her mind was gone, and she'd accuse the kids of stealing stuff, and accuse me, and that would tear me up.

A major stroke and a kidney infection landed Lane's mother in the hospital, and from there she went to a nursing home.

JIM: We couldn't do it anymore. It was to the point where you had to pick her up to do everything. She didn't last long there. Just six weeks.

LANE: We went to the nursing home every day.

For many of the older people I interviewed, who grew up in a time when homosexuality was a forbidden subject, there was never any expectation that such a thing would be discussed with family. But as I learned from Jim and Lane, not coming out to family members didn't preclude being accepted and embraced by a loved one. For others, though, staying hidden contributed to distant family relationships. Their partner was their "friend" or "roommate" who was sometimes, but not always, included in family gatherings. And while the relationship might be obliquely acknowledged, it certainly wasn't celebrated.

Homosexuality was unmentionable when Martin brought Jim home to live with him and his mother. But they've now lived long enough to see the world change, and over the years they've been increasingly open with their relatives, who have warmly embraced them in return.

Jim and Martin have been together longer than any other couple in either of their families. I asked them if over the years they've felt support for their relationship from their family members.

MARTIN: Yes, because they all got to know that we are gay.

JIM: I remember telling my sister. She was talking about a friend of hers whose son was gay. And I asked, "Are you afraid of him?" "Oh," she says, "my goodness, no. He's a wonderful fella." And I said, "You know, Martin and I are gay." And she said, "Oh my dear, I've known it for years." She has six grown kids, and they've all known for years. They always say, "What Uncle Jim and Marty do, that's their business. I love them just the way they are."

But my brother didn't like hearing about it. One time, my sister and brother were at a gathering and she said, "You know, Bob, Jim and Marty are not like you and I are." And he says, "Oh, I think I'm gonna go out and have a cigarette." See, he accepts it wholeheartedly, but he won't talk about it. He calls us up about every two or three months and he says, "I want to talk to my brother Marty."

And he always says to Marty, "I love you, Marty." But he would never discuss it. So that's all right with me. And Martin's nieces, they are very good to us. They always want us to come visit them.

MARTIN: One of them is in Ann Arbor, Michigan, so we don't, but she comes down here quite often. One niece is a psychiatrist, and she knows all about gay people, you know. She says, "I always hold you two up as a model for some of my patients."

JIM: She just loves us. Both of the girls do. And on our fiftieth anniversary, our apartment looked like a funeral parlor.

MARTIN: Oh, there were so many flowers.

JIM: Flowers, and cards, and everything, from our family and friends. It was just outrageous.

Of course, not everyone has had the wonderfully supportive experience that Jim and Martin have. There's never any guarantee that by coming out you'll be embraced by your family. So I wasn't surprised to find that a handful of the relatively younger couples felt compelled to hide their homosexuality and the nature of their relationship for fear of being rejected. Marta and Rita* were one of these couples. Marta, in particular, had good reason to hide, following a shockingly painful experience with her father.

MARTA: I decided early on that I didn't want to lie about being gay, because I didn't want them to think that I was ashamed. But I wasn't going to be very vocal to them, either. My mother died before I had a chance to talk to her. I was seventeen. I put off telling my father until I was twenty-two, but I didn't bring it up. He asked. I tried to get out of answering by asking him, "What are you asking me that for?" He said he wanted to know, and I asked him if he was ready for an answer. He paused, and he finally said, "Yes." And I finally said, "Yes." He said, "Thank God your mother's dead. And I wish I were dead, too." A week later he died of a heart attack. Talk about a nuclear lesbian. You can imagine how I felt. Fortunately I had a straight woman friend tell me, "Who the hell do you think you are to imagine that you're important enough to cause anybody's death?" That was exactly what I needed to hear.

* Not their real names.

Marta and Rita met in 1984, shortly after Marta's father died. They were introduced by mutual friends at a feminist vegetarian restaurant. The friends thought the two should meet because both are Cuban. Marta's parents emigrated from Cuba to the United States before Marta was born, and Rita was born in Cuba and came to the United States when she was nineteen. Marta is thirty-five, and Rita is fifty. They've been a couple since 1987.

Though they're different in many ways, Marta and Rita have cultural bonds that they say make their relationship stronger. Both consider Spanish to be their first language, and they speak it at home; they share the same attitude toward family life; and they are both reluctant to say anything to their relatives about their relationship.

MARTA: Our family bonds are very cultural for us. We always talk about the fact that Americans don't get the way Cubans sometimes are with their families.

RITA: Everybody is family. Not just your immediate family, but your aunts and uncles and cousins and second cousins are family.

MARTA: It's also the way you take care of your family. For me, it's not my parents, because they're gone. But I have my aunt, my father's sister, who is almost like a grandmother to me. She's my godmother, and she raised my dad. And for Rita there's her mother and her nieces. If one of them needs something, there's never a hesitation of whether we're going to pay for it.

RITA: There's no question that if there is any financial or emotional need from our families, we're going to be there.

MARTA: But we're not real out to them, although we're accepted very much as significant others.

RITA: But they don't treat us as a real couple. They accept that we live together, but I've never told my mother anything about being a lesbian. I have a feeling she knows. My mother is a very bright woman. I know she's not very happy about it. She makes a lot of comments about things she sees on television, about what a horror homosexuality is. The only thing I can say is "Mom, times have changed."

MARTA: When we go to Florida, Rita stays at her mother's house and I stay at my aunt's house. It gets more difficult every year, but we can't think of how not to do it.

RITA: We haven't told them, because we don't want to put them through facing something that I know they don't want to face. I'm very happy with the way I am, who I am. I don't know how I can take my mother's rejection. I really don't know that I can take that.

MARTA: If somebody else dies on me . . . after what happened with my dad . . . I had a nightmare about how my aunt was coming here to visit for two weeks. And before she came, we were straightening up the house, putting away tons of books, getting rid of the refrigerator magnet that says, "Sally's Gay with Midol," and getting rid of the mugs that have sayings on them that would give us away. But by mistake, we left one book out that she picked up. She read the cover and keeled over.

Marta and Rita are glad that they're equally anxious and fearful about telling their families that they're gay; otherwise, they're sure there would be tension between them. Each understands what the other is feeling.

MARTA: We're very grateful that one of us isn't more militant about being out, that we both feel the same way towards our families. I think it would be much more difficult if one of us was much further out than the other one.

RITA: Then it would cause friction in the relationship.

MARTA: But I think we're both sort of pissed off and embarrassed at ourselves for how we feel, and supportive with each other, because we know we both feel this way. I mean, talk about internalized homophobia. We're so worried about everybody else that we can't deal with the repercussions from our family. What's so scary about this?

RITA: Deep down I know they're going to love me regardless. But it's always going to be a subject that they cannot touch.

MARTA: I'm afraid it's going to crush my aunt. She's eighty-five. She's going to be so crushed that I'm not going to have kids. I'm an only child. If she asks me point-blank, I'm not going to lie, but I'm not sure that I'm going to say anything until then.

RITA: This is not easy. It's not something that I like to deal with, if I had a choice. I guess I do have a choice, and I don't have a choice.

What makes the conflict all the more hurtful for Marta and Rita is the growing distance they feel from their families. Not being able to share who they are and not being able to be a couple when they go to Miami for visits three times a year makes them feel like staying home and avoiding their families.

MARTA: I think it's hurting our relationship with our families to a certain extent. We are finding ourselves wanting less to go to Miami. I would have gone by now again or be planning to go this summer, but I don't want to go, because it's not right the way things are.

Marta and Rita aren't willing to predict what will happen in the future.

Judy and Bev had every reason to believe that once they were past the rough spots with Judy's mother, their family problems would be over—at least the problems that had to do with homosexuality. Judy's mother had trouble reconciling her religious beliefs with her daughter's homosexuality. As Judy explained, "She told me that the Bible said I was going to hell. But, gosh, talk about a turnaround. She loves Bev like a daughter now, and she knows that we're going to be together forever."

Judy and Bev have enjoyed positive relationships with their families during most of the years they've been together, and they've been especially close to their nieces and nephews. Several months before I met them, Judy and Bev had planned to take their five eldest nieces and nephews for a summer vacation.

BEV: We invited my niece and two nephews, and we invited Judy's oldest niece, who is the same age as my niece, and Judy's nephew who is ten, the same age as my little nephew. We thought they'd have a ball together.

JUDY: So we had this all arranged, and a week before, my sister-in-law called to say that my brother said, "I can't allow them to come down to visit you without supervision. You can't be with them without supervision." I was just so shocked.

BEV: I heard her sobbing.

JUDY: It was an absolute terrible shock.

BEV: We've known that they don't agree with our lifestyle, but we've gone camping with them for eight years.

JUDY: Rented a houseboat with them. They drove from Ohio to help us move.

BEV: Just total acceptance. They've known about me since the beginning. They loved me, accepted me, and then *boom.*

JUDY: They've always said, "We don't approve," but certainly they've never been hostile or wanted to stay separate from us.

BEV: When Judy told me what happened, I said, "I'm going to pick up the phone and call your brother and tell him that he's a sorry son of a bitch." Judy didn't want me to, and instead she called her mom. It was agony, pure hell.

Judy's family is Southern Baptist, and Judy suspects that the Southern Baptists' anti-Disney efforts and her brother's recent involvement in the Promise Keepers men's organization had something to do with his decision.

BEV: The Promise Keepers are a bunch of men who get together and rent a stadium. He's really changed since he got involved in that.

JUDY: Also the Southern Baptists have been strong about Disney. My brother and sister-in-law have given away all their Disney tapes to my mother. She has them all now. They gave away the TVs, except for one thirteen-inch television.

BEV: They got rid of the Nintendo.

A month after the disturbing phone call from her sister-in-law, Judy called her brother.

JUDY: I said, "If I come up to visit, and I want to take the kids to a movie or the Dairy Queen for a milk shake, you mean I have to have somebody go with me?" He said, "Well, we're still working on that." I asked him what he thought I was going to do with them. And I also told him that if he said it was okay for me to be alone with them, then he wasn't being right with God for letting the kids do something that he was opposed to.

BEV: If they let the kids go with Judy, then they would be saying to the kids that being gay is okay.

JUDY: To me it was a total contradiction. You're saying on the one hand I need supervision to be around them, but if I'm visiting you or if you're visiting me with them, just by coming into my home or letting me come into yours, then you're approving it. It's totally biblically related. He's not being a good father if he lets his kids be around a lesbian.

Judy's mother had an idea that she hoped would solve the family dilemma, and she offered it to Judy and Bev over lunch at a local restaurant when the two women were in town to help Judy's youngest sister move into a new apartment.

JUDY: My mother had been no problem up to this point. Her attitude toward me and Bev was "Leave them alone, they're happy." So we're sitting down at lunch with my mother and two of my sisters, and Mom says, "I've got the perfect idea. You guys just continue to be friends, but don't have sex and don't be a couple for the world to see." I couldn't believe what I was hearing. I got up and ran out to the parking lot, and my mother followed. I told her, "Mom, you are killing me here."

Things have settled down in Judy's family since that lunch. After Judy chose not to go home for Christmas that year, for the first time in her life, Judy's brother wrote a note suggesting they find a way to work things out. And Judy's mother has not repeated her suggestion that the two women be just friends. The brightest spot, however, came shortly after the original phone call canceling the camping trip.

JUDY: My sixteen-year-old nephew called. He walked down the block to his grandmother's house—his other grandmother—and called me from there. He said, "I know Mom just told you we can't come, and I'm not supposed to call you. But as soon as I get my driver's license, I'm going to come to see you. None of what they said matters. I love you, and I love Bev."

My gosh, here was this sixteen-year-old reasoning out what his mom's saying and what the church is saying, and it doesn't matter to him. I said, "When did you get to be so grown-up?" I told him that he needed to obey his mom—my sister-in-law—but I also told him that we'd love to have him visit.

BEV: Every time Judy talks to the kids and they ask about coming to visit, she says, "Love to have you come down."

JUDY: "Whenever you can, you're always welcome."

BEV: With every generation, their eyes are more open. So we're hoping that with this generation of kids, they'll be able to see things differently. But they're not going to change their parents, I don't think. Time will tell.

For Dayna and Alison, time has made all the difference with Dayna's dad, a Catholic deacon who was less than pleased that his daughter had chosen a partner who was female and white. Alison's mother, on the other hand, was thrilled with Alison's choice.

ALISON: She's beyond supportive as far as me being gay. She's so thrilled to have a black lesbian daughter-in-law. She lives in Northampton, Massachusetts, and she marched in the Northampton Gay Pride parade before I did.

Alison's parents have been divorced for many years, but Alison remains close to her father, who is also supportive of her relationship with Dayna.

ALISON: My parents are former hippies. Anything goes. Very, very liberal. Three weeks after I met Dayna, I wrote my dad a letter to tell him that I met a woman. In the letter I also said, "I know you won't have a problem with this, but just so you know what she's all about, she's a black woman." I don't remember what I told Mom, but I knew that would never be an issue for either of them.

DAYNA: My father didn't say a thing about Alison. I just knew how he felt, mostly from his behavior.

ALISON: I couldn't tell if he didn't like me because I was a woman, because I was white, or because I wasn't Catholic.

DAYNA: Or if it was all three. My father is the kind of man who is not necessarily thrilled with a lot of things about either me or my two sisters, just because of his religion. His religious beliefs tend to get in the way of his being able to accept his daughters for who they are. There's something about all three of us that goes against his religious beliefs.

When I told my father about the ceremony Alison and I were going to have, we were all together at a restaurant in D.C. having dinner. I was there, my sisters were there, and my dad was there with his second wife. I told them about our plans, and he just went off about it. "That's so unacceptable," and "Two women can't marry. I love you and I love Alison, but I can't condone this."

DAYNA: Well, I screamed and hollered at him. I got very defensive, and was arguing points of what's right versus what's wrong. It was a religious-right-versus-the-liberal-left kind of debate.

ALISON: And Dayna's sisters were chiming in, saying, "Well, what do you want her to do, be alone for the rest of her life?"

DAYNA: My sisters are wonderful, because they got involved and pointed out how he couldn't accept things *they* had done in *their* lives. Pick an issue. We've all experienced it, and he can't deal with it.

Dayna's father did not attend the commitment ceremony, but Dayna's sisters did, as did both of Alison's parents. Over the years, Alison's relationship with Dayna's father remained cool, but recently there has been some noticeable warming up.

ALISON: He's never been really warm. He's not very warm to Dayna, either, so I try not to take it personally. Every Christmas he'll kiss me hello and then not speak to me the rest of the visit. He and his wife will show up very briefly before they go off to church, and he usually writes out a Christmas card to his daughters and grand-daughter. So it's usually very obvious that he's handing out these cards and skipping me. But last Christmas I got a card, and inside it said, "Merry Christmas, Alison—Love, Daddy," which is what Dayna and her sisters call him.

DAYNA: It's a big step.

ALISON: Then he never spoke to me the rest of the visit. But it was a big step, and it took a lot of years to get there.

I'm sure it hardly needs stating, but family relationships, whether you're gay or straight, are never perfect. For plenty of the couples I spoke with, their family problems have nothing to do with homosexuality and everything to do with run-of-the-mill family madness. Still, the addition of homosexuality to the basic lunacy makes for some potentially volatile situations. I've learned from Dayna and Alison, and from many of the other couples, that no matter what the family problem, (1), you can do only so much, and (2), you can do only the best you know how. That's been Stanley and Stewart's tactic when it comes to their relationship with Stanley's father and, especially, his stepmother.

STEWART: At Stanley's son's bar mitzvah, I remember Stanley's step-mother calling me over and saying I'm so much better than the ex-wife. But a couple of years ago they had a combined eightieth birthday party for her and twenty-fifth wedding anniversary in Flor-ida. Stanley was invited and I wasn't—because I might be an em-barrassment down there to their friends. They can deal with me up here, but not in Florida, where someone else would see. And she was stupid enough to tell Stanley.

STANLEY: It's amazing to me that I didn't get on the next plane and go home.

STEWART: I had very little contact with his parents after that, although I did go to the funeral when his father died. I've also been to Stan-ley's nephews' weddings. They put me at the family tables, but when they take the family pictures, I'm not included. And when they write the thank-yous, they write, "To Uncle Stanley and Stew-art." Now, to *my* nephew, he's Uncle Stanley. I'm not happy about it, but we live with it.

STANLEY: I'm not happy, either, but what am I going to do, rant and yell and scream and then have no relationship? It does hurt, but no matter what the family function, we're not sitting at a table in the back with the third cousins or by the kitchen. Table one or table two, whichever is the family table.

Stanley's stepmother is coming up to New York from Florida in the near future for a party celebrating the birth of Stanley's oldest nephew's baby girl. The date has yet to be set, but Stewart has already decided he's not going.

STEWART: Ever since that comment about my being an embarrassment, I don't want to see his stepmother more than I have to. Inevitably, someday, I may open my mouth, so it's safer not to put me in the same room. As quiet as I sometimes am, I can open my mouth, too.

STANLEY: Meanwhile, let her live and be well. When she passes away, he'll go to her funeral, too.

THIRTEEN

Children

THERE WAS NOTHING about Chris and Sherri's windswept, weatherbeaten house that hinted at the wondrous realm I'd find beyond the door of little Taylor's room. Taylor, as I've mentioned, is Chris and Sherri's very self-confident and thoroughly conversational two-year-old son. The afternoon of the interview, Taylor was napping when it came time for me to leave, and Chris asked if I wanted to peek in and have a look at his room.

You know the scene in *The Wizard of Oz* where Dorothy opens the door to her house after crash-landing in Munchkinland, and the movie suddenly bursts into Technicolor? I had something of the same, breathtaking experience when Chris opened the door to Taylor's sanctuary.

As I stepped through the doorway, I was struck first by the cool serenity. The shades were drawn to keep out the bright afternoon sun, so it took a moment for my eyes to adjust to the gentle glow cast by the light of a small fish tank. Quiet music played on the stereo, accompanied by the hypnotic bubbling of the water filter. And when I listened closely, I could hear the steady breaths of little Taylor, who was sound asleep, safely enveloped by his boat-shaped bed. There was a pile of teddy bears in one corner, a rocking horse in another, and the carpeted floor was covered with an enormous, colorful rubber alphabet puzzle. Two walls were decorated with professional-looking cartoon murals, which Chris had painted herself. Everything about the room said that this child is loved by his parents and by all their friends and family who contributed to make it such a special place. I was moved to tears.

Chris and Sherri are one of seven couples I interviewed—five female and two male—who have chosen to have children, either through adoption or artificial insemination. These couples have a total of eight children, ranging in age, at the time I met them, from two weeks to ten years. In ten other couples, one or both partners had a child or children from a prior relationship—twenty-one children in all. And five of these couples have a total of thirteen grandchildren. In addition, one couple has informally adopted a teenage boy, and Amy and Jama mentor a little girl.

There is nothing new about gay people having children. Gay people have always had children. The difference today is that gay couples have an·option that was unthinkable in the days when Anyda and Muriel and Jim and Martin were young couples. Now, if gay couples want children, they can choose to have them themselves. Of course, it's generally not as easy for gay and lesbian couples to have kids as it is for most heterosexuals, but it's not nearly as difficult or uncommon as it once was.

The subject of children first came up for Chris and Sherri during their telephone courtship.

CHRIS: I told Sherri, "Get back to me in ten years," because I figured that if we couldn't be together for at least ten years, then we shouldn't bring a child into the world. I didn't want to bring a child into something that would be torn up within days of him being born. And truthfully, I thought she'd outgrow it. But she didn't, because she got back to me.

None of the couples who chose to have children rushed into it. One couple had their first child five years into their relationship. The rest waited at least nine years before having a child. Nate and Danny started talking seriously about adopting a child in the mid-

1980s. They had been together fifteen years when Danny brought Sophie home from China in 1995.

DANNY: We talked about children early on, but we didn't know any gay couples who had adopted. Then, about twelve years ago, a lesbian couple we knew adopted a girl from Latin America, which made it seem like it was something we could do, that it was actually possible.

NATE: We both love children and have been involved with kids for a long time. We've had a lot of training with nephews and nieces. But even as a child, I was a camp counselor. Danny used to baby-sit. I always thought I'd have a lot of kids, so I was sad when I realized I was gay and that I wouldn't have kids. But then, having met this lesbian couple—that was a very significant thing.

DANNY: We talked about it more and more, and we put it out to our friends that this was something we might want to do someday. Over time, it became much more real to us, not just this fantasy.

Though Nate and Danny were both very clear that they wanted children, being a parent was something Chris never anticipated. She was very happy not to have children, and every once in a while she mentioned to Sherri how lucky they were to be free to do whatever they wanted. Sherri felt pretty much the same way—until she turned twenty-nine.

SHERRI: All of a sudden, I felt like a sledgehammer hit me between the eyes. I had a biological clock slamming away in there, and I started really feeling the need to have a child. It was something I was never able to explain to Chris, but I knew that I needed to have a child, because I felt incomplete.

CHRIS: It wasn't like she was saying, "I want to have a child." It was "I'm going to have a child because I *must* have a child." I wasn't happy about it, and I told Sherri, "Several things are going to happen. One is, I'm never going to have you the way I had you before. We're never going to have time. It's always going to be divided, and I like the way things are now." And I added, "Are you sure you want to have a kid who you're going to have to teach all those living skills that you aren't yet real good at yourself, like the cooking and cleaning?"

SHERRI: So I said, "You can teach them that part."

CHRIS: My fear, in my mind, was that I would then have two children—Sherri and the new baby—and I didn't want that.

Chris and Sherri did a lot of talking before deciding to go ahead and have a child. All seven of the couples did lots of talking and planning, and much of what the couples talked about are the things that I imagine lots of young straight couples discuss, from finances and child care to names and gender preferences. These gay and lesbian couples had a few additional things to talk about, from who would be the one to legally adopt or bear the child to whether they needed to move to a more accepting community.

But before Chris and Sherri could get to the logistics of having a child, they first had to come to an agreement about whether or not to actually have one.

CHRIS: Because I don't make enough money to support us, even in a good year, I knew I'd be home taking care of this child all of the time. And I wasn't sure that this was something I really wanted to do. But then it dawned on me that I didn't have a choice. Because either I would say no, and eventually we'd break up because Sherri resented me for saying no, or we'd break up because she was going to have the child and I didn't want it. Finally, I decided that Sherri was much more important to me than not having a child. If it meant having a child and getting to keep the relationship, we'd just have to have a kid.

The next step for Chris and Sherri was to have a commitment ceremony. As I already noted, Chris didn't believe in having a child out of wedlock, and although, of course, gay people can't marry, they did the next best thing and had a public ceremony. With the relationship as secure as it was going to get, Chris and Sherri began researching artificial insemination.

Nate and Danny's conversations, research, and planning went on for years, beginning, whimsically enough, with what they were going to name their child.

NATE: We talked about it kind of backwards, since the name isn't the most important thing, but we asked ourselves, "Which dead relative will she be named after?"

DANNY: In the great Jewish tradition.

One assumption both Nate and Danny made was that they would adopt a girl.

NATE: We always knew that we really wanted a little girl. We were partial to girls, and we felt like it would be easier for a little girl to grow up with two men.

DANNY: And the peer groups seem to be easier.

NATE: Right. There's less peer pressure, it seems, for girls. But mostly, we just had this image of having a girl.

Nate and Danny also began subscribing to a newsletter for gay and lesbian parents, and they took an adoption class.

NATE: The class was arranged by the Jewish Community Center where we lived in suburban Philadelphia, and the notice included a line in small print that said, "Older individuals and gays and lesbians welcome." The whole class was lesbians and us.

After that class, we began looking at our various options, like adopting from Russia. At the same time, we didn't feel that Philadelphia was the place we wanted to raise our child. There were only one or two other gay families that we knew, and we really wanted to live someplace with a lot of diversity, where two men raising an Asian girl wasn't that big an issue.

Thinking back, we would have done fine raising a child in Philadelphia. We had a big support system, and there are more and more lesbian and gay parents in Philadelphia, but in the late 1980s, we were thinking that it would be better for us in the San Francisco Bay area.

Chris and Sherri described their community as "pretty rednecked," but the couple didn't have any concerns about raising their child there.

SHERRI: We've never been touched by a lot of homophobia, so it's not been a real big issue. Every time we've gone someplace or done something together, it's always been acceptable. Maybe not accepted, but acceptable.

CHRIS: We really believe that whatever you project to people on your comfort level is how comfortable they feel. So if we go someplace to buy a new stove for the kitchen and we're obviously a couple and we're comfortable with being a couple, then they deal with us as a couple and they don't say anything. Consequently, we've never had a problem. So we didn't see Taylor as being a problem.

The next step for Nate and Danny after deciding to move to California was to get tested for HIV. They had been so focused on adopting a baby that it was quite a while before it occurred to them that they ought to verify their health before proceeding.

DANNY: The odds were that we weren't infected, but we had to know, because if we *were* positive, then adoption would not have been a direction we probably would have gone in.

NATE: So we go in to be tested, and they ask us why we wanted to be tested, and we said, "Well, we're here because we want to adopt a baby, and we have to make sure we're not infected." We didn't think anyone had given them that answer before.

It was at this point in our interview that Nate and Danny's daughter, Sophie, awakened from her nap, and Papa Danny went upstairs to get her. Moments later she was tearing through the family room, heading straight for Daddy Nate's lap, giggling all the way. Her grinning dad picked her up and gave her a big hug and a kiss. She was wearing a lavender dress and had one pink Band-Aid on her ankle and another on her elbow, and she was eager to point them out to me. Sophie is a robust, happy two-year-old, with rosy cheeks and a great laugh—the sweetest child (and, I might add, so were all the other children I met in my travels). It took a little while for her to settle in, but once she did, her fathers and I continued with our discussion.

In 1991, Nate and Danny relocated to the West Coast, and they spent the next couple of years putting down roots, making friends, and buying a child-friendly house in a culturally and ethnically diverse neighborhood. By then they had settled on adopting a girl from China, so the next big decision concerned who would be the one to adopt first, as they couldn't adopt as a couple.

NATE: We worked with an adoption agency that we were out to as a couple. It was just with the China connection that we couldn't be out.

DANNY: We had to find an agency where we could go in openly and not have to hide. And the agency we found was great about telling us what you could and couldn't say. We had to work the system a little bit, because our money and the house are in both our names. I remember that the home study said something like "Lives with another adult, due to the high cost of housing."

Initially, the plan was for Nate to be the first adoptive parent. Once that adoption was complete, he and Danny would then execute the second adoption so that Danny could become Sophie's legal parent as well.

NATE: We thought that on paper, as a single father I had more superficial qualifications because of my background of working with children and my degree in social work. I was also able to talk about my extended family in a way that Danny couldn't, because of the limits of his extended family.

DANNY: As it turned out, it was a nonissue, because anyone who can totally support a child, psychologically and economically, can adopt. And Nate's age proved to be a problem. He wasn't yet forty, and for whatever reason, the Chinese weren't permitting adoptions for people under forty. So I wound up being the one.

Among the lesbian couples, all of whom had their children by artificial insemination with a known or anonymous donor, deciding who would bear the child depended on a number of factors. For Jennifer and Brigid, the decision was easy.

BRIGID: I don't ovulate.

JENNIFER: We also figured out that it would be a good balance of power if I had the baby, because Brigid has the maternal instincts and I don't. We thought that by my having the baby, I would have the physical thing. And I think that's bearing out. It's amazing to me how automatic the bonding has been for me.

The decision as to who would bear the child wasn't as obvious for Stephanie and Lilia. Both women were physically capable of bearing a child, and both were willing to be the biological mother. Their jobs proved to be the deciding factor. Stephanie, you'll recall, is a 911 dispatcher, and Lilia is a bus driver. Both enjoy liberal maternity-leave policies, and either could have continued working through the entire pregnancy. But because Lilia's job requires bouncing along Portland's roads all day long, she'd have been forced to transfer to light duty for the last months of the pregnancy.

LILIA: At my job they won't let you drive a bus after you get to a certain point. They don't want to be responsible for anything happening to you or the baby. So they take you off and put you on light duty type of work.

STEPHANIE: Lil knows a couple at work who just had a baby the same way that we did, and it was horrible the last couple of months.

LILIA: Yeah, she ended up staying at home because they put her on light duty. You're so used to going and going all day long. So when they put her on light duty, it's just like a total letdown. So she said, Screw it, and stayed at home. So we decided that Steph would be the one to do it.

For Chris and Sherri, there was no question that Sherri would be the one to bear the child. Chris had no interest in being pregnant. Besides, she was well into her forties, and Sherri was just shy of thirty. There was also no debate over whether they would use a known or an anonymous sperm donor.

SHERRI: We always wanted our child to know who his father was. Being adopted, I don't know who my biological parents are. I didn't want him to be left with the questions that I have, like "Do I look like my mother?" "Do I look like my father?" "What characteristics do I have from them?" "Do I have my mom's personality or my dad's personality?" And being in the medical field, the health issues are important for me. I'd like to know my biological mother's medical history.

CHRIS: It was a big issue for both of us, because if we were going to do this, I wanted him to know what his father looked like. Even though we didn't want the dad to take a very active role in his life, we wanted our child to be able to say, "My daddy lives down the hill."

Stephanie and Lilia decided on an anonymous donor, and with Stephanie serving as the biological mother, the couple decided that Lilia would be the one to choose the donor's characteristics.

STEPHANIE: There's a lesbian mothers group on the Internet, and I've read about gay moms who have had problems with a known donor. And even before that, I had always felt that it could be an issue. This way, there's never an issue about who the parents are.

LILIA: So choosing the donor was my responsibility. It's like going through the Sears catalog without the pictures. The guys are listed with what color eyes, hair, height. There's also education, IQ, all of that. Basically, I was looking for height first, because Stephanie's short. The next thing was whether or not he liked sports. I like sports.

STEPHANIE: I cared about the IQ.

LILIA: Hers was the IQ, mine was the sports. And I wanted someone Hispanic. I'm Irish, Spanish, and French, and Stephanie's a mutt.

STEPHANIE: We only had a choice of one Spanish donor, and he had blond hair and blue eyes. But at least there was some of that ethnicity that Lilia wanted.

After three failed tries with the first donor and two with a second, the third donor, whose background was Irish, did the trick. Nine months and two and a half weeks later, I was sitting in Stephanie and Lilia's living room, interviewing them as their son slept soundly on Lilia's chest.

Chris and Sherri chose a gay friend who liked the idea of being a donor. He consented to Chris and Sherri's request that he provide no financial support, and he also agreed that he would have no role in any decisions regarding the child's upbringing. In addition, he would visit every four to six weeks and spend major holidays with the women and their child.

Utilizing Sherri's background as a nurse and with the encouragement of their physician, who suggested that the artificial insemination would be cheaper if Chris and Sherri did it on their own, the women commenced the process. It turned out to be more complicated than they had thought.

CHRIS: We were stupid. We just thought, Okay, take semen, insert into vagina, have baby. After Taylor was born, I found this "Lesbian Moms On-line" list, and these people know everything about everything, but we were just ignorant about all that.

SHERRI: I knew the technical aspects of it. I knew how to take a donor.

CHRIS: Yeah, so our friend would come over in the evening and do his thing and Sherri would do her thing. But we could never figure out when Sherri ovulated, so we had to do it over and over again.

SHERRI: It was horrible, because after the insemination there would be all this buildup, hoping you were pregnant, and then you'd start your period. It was depressing.

CHRIS: It was so disappointing. And then you'd start all over again.

SHERRI: By the seventh month we were about ready to give up. But we were going to give it another try. So we all sat down and talked about what we needed to do to make it work.

CHRIS: I said that doing it a couple of days in a row was not going to do it. I said, "We're not hitting the day. That's what the problem is." I said to our friend, "You need to come over the minute Sherri finishes her period and go until she starts the next one and do it every day." So they did that for nineteen straight days.

SHERRI: I had also done a little bit more research by this point and learned about alternating morning and night.

The marathon insemination, in combination with the alternating morning and night schedule, worked, and Sherri became pregnant.

SHERRI: When I saw the test, I started hyperventilating. I just about passed out. I was in seventh heaven.

CHRIS: Sherri called me from work to tell me, and I was very excited. The first few months, every time she didn't get pregnant, I was, like, "Thank God." But then I got pulled into it, so by the time she got pregnant, I was really excited—at first.

Danny and Nate didn't have the ordeal of seven months of artificial insemination, but they still had the anxiety of waiting—though what they were waiting for was a phone call. It came sooner than they expected, and Danny had only two weeks to prepare for his trip to China. Nate saw him off at the airport.

DANNY: My company was so nice. They gave me a free business-class ticket, so at the airport we got to wait together in the first-class lounge.

NATE: We had breakfast together. It was so exciting, and it was scary. And then Danny was gone for two weeks. It was such an anxious time for me.

DANNY: We hadn't been apart that long, ever.

NATE: Right. So Danny was in China about four days when he picked up Sophie and was taking care of her. We had talked by phone every night and then *that* night he called, and he said, "She's here! She's here!"

Nate pauses in the recounting for a moment, overwhelmed by the happy memory. His eyes fill with tears, and he apologizes. My eyes fill with tears, too.

NATE: So I said, "What's she like? What's she like? Is she beautiful?" Danny said, "Oh yeah, she's very sweet." And I thought he wasn't telling me something, so I asked him if everything was okay. He seemed so restrained. Danny said, "Yes, she's fine. She's fine. She's very sweet." And so I just kind of left it alone, but of course, for the next ten days, until he brought her home, I worried.

Nate and several of his and Danny's friends went to the airport to meet Danny and Sophie. They staked out a glass-enclosed waiting area overlooking Customs.

NATE: I saw them come through, and I saw that Danny had on a Snugli, and there was this tiny baby asleep inside, with Danny's hat over her head. I'm banging on the glass, and Danny finally looks up. I said, "Show me," and he lifted her up. It was very emotional. So they finally get through Customs, and we meet, and Danny hands Sophie to me, and I said to him, "Why didn't you tell me how beautiful she was?" Of course, to me, she was the most beautiful child I'd ever seen in my whole life. He said, "Well, you're not supposed to say that about your own baby." Which is what a

Jewish grandmother would say. I said, "What do you *mean?* You were talking to *me!*"

Of course, it took a little longer than two weeks for the stork to deliver Chris and Sherri's son. Which was a good thing, because Chris needed that time to deal with her anxiety about the baby's impending arrival.

CHRIS: I was excited, but I was real panicky.

SHERRI: I could tell she was panicky. She said things like "I can't be there when you deliver. I can't do that. I can't be there." So, consequently, we had private Lamaze lessons with several friends so we could be sure I'd have a coach no matter when I went into labor.

CHRIS: It was the two of us and four of our lesbian friends. And we had a really straight woman instructor.

SHERRI: I'm sure she was trying to figure out what the scoop was here.

CHRIS: We didn't bother to tell her. It was pretty funny. But I kept telling Sherri that I wasn't going to be there. Look, Sherri starts her period and *I* get the cramps. She gets the flu and *I* throw up. So, she'd go into labor and they'd have to give *me* the medication.

It turned out that Sherri needed a C-section.

CHRIS: So we were all there at the hospital—our four friends, and Sherri's dad and her mom—and the nurse turned to us and said, "Well, who's going in?" And all of us turned pale. Sherri's dad went in.

SHERRI: I was busting up, because I knew none of them would go in.

Despite the resistance Chris had originally felt about having a baby, she melted at the sight of her new son.

CHRIS: I think I felt the same emotion that Sherri felt.

SHERRI: As soon as you saw him, and he opened his eyes, it was like "Oh my God!"

CHRIS: He had your heart. From that minute until Sherri went back to work, he had your heart. But the first night Sherri left him, he cried for twelve hours straight! And as she walked in the door, I handed Taylor to her and said, "I'm moving. I can't do this."

SHERRI: Here I am, my first night back at work. I'm tired. I'm also emotional because it's my first night away from them in eight weeks, and she hands me this crying baby and says, "I'm leaving," and is very determined about this.

CHRIS: *"Oh, I'm out of here."*

SHERRI: I'm going, "Oh my God!"

CHRIS: Well, she convinced me to stay.

The weeks that followed were no easier. Taylor cried for hours at a time, and Chris thought she would lose her mind.

CHRIS: I kept an extensive journal of my emotions and how angry I was at this small person who had taken possession of this woman who had once been mine. From the time she got home until the time she left for work, Sherri was completely occupied with Taylor.

SHERRI: I didn't see it. And as I've talked to other women and men who have had children about how their wives behaved during that time, I found it was very common. You become totally absorbed in providing for this little person, who becomes the most important thing in your life.

CHRIS: So one of my biggest fears immediately came to reality, which was that I would no longer have the same relationship I had before, because I had no time with Sherri at all.

Most of the things the couples with children told me regarding parenthood were the kinds of things you would expect any parents to convey about the challenges of taking care of a newborn and adjusting to a life with very different rhythms and responsibilities. But some of what they talked about was unique to same-gender couples, from the complexities of drawing up legal papers with the known donor to the expense of doing a second-parent adoption. Even the fact that both parents were of the same gender was a subject of concern.

Nate and Danny, for example, acknowledge their mixed feelings about Sophie's not having a mother, though this was obviously not something that prevented them from proceeding with the adoption.

NATE: As much as I complain about my mother, I was very close to her when I was growing up, and I feel sad about that for Sophie. But I also know that we're there for Sophie in ways that our parents, male or female, were not there for us. Inevitably, it will be hard that she doesn't have that role model in her life, but we'll talk about it.

DANNY: It's certainly significant that, yes, she doesn't have a mother, but she has two parents who love her.

NATE: She has two parents who love her very much, who will do their best.

DANNY: She will have issues. I mean, she's being raised by two men. She's of Chinese heritage; we're not. On the other hand, in this part of the country, it's so much easier to be different. I was more concerned before we met all of these families that are transracial. And we've met a number of lesbian couples with kids, and there aren't any dads in those families, so it's been a nice exchange. She gets a lot of women wanting to hug her and hold her.

NATE: She won't be wanting for women in her life, but it's not the same as having a mother. It's just different.

I could easily go on for several chapters about these couples and how they've divided up child-rearing responsibilities, their experiences with their families, how they're treated by their neighbors, the attitudes of their employers, their plans for more children, how their relationships have changed, et cetera, et cetera. But that's a different book. However, I can tell one more anecdote.

One of the male couples has a ten-year-old daughter. She was asked by a family friend to explain the different things her two daddies do for her, and in a moment of divine inspiration, she said that one of her fathers was "the mommy daddy" and the other was "the daddy daddy." In other words, one of her fathers did the more typically motherly things, and the other did the more fatherly things. I'm no expert on this, but from what I saw and from everything I've read, kids seem to adjust to their gay parents without batting an eye. If only it were so easy for the rest of society.

Not every couple who talked about wanting a child decided to have one. Amy and Jama, for instance, are just beginning to explore the possibility; others have weighed the issue and decided against children. Some knew more or less from the start that they didn't really want children.

I asked Marjorie and Marian, who speak of their cows almost as if they were their children, if they had ever thought of having kids. The answer was an emphatic no, although Marjorie added that they had talked about it "here and there."

MARJORIE: I probably would have wanted to more than Marian would have. But I think you can have a totally fulfilling relationship without children.

MARIAN: My aunt reminded me that when I was four years old, some little kid came over to visit and I said that I didn't like children. I never had any inkling that I wanted kids.

MARJORIE: And it's a lifestyle change. We wouldn't have the life we have now if we'd had children.

MARIAN: We couldn't have kept farming.

MARJORIE: One of us would have had to get a job, because we couldn't have lived at the level of poverty that we were living in when we started out. Although plenty of poor people have kids.

MARIAN: I would have felt like I needed to make money for the kid's education and stuff like that, and we never had any money. It also seems to me that people that we've known who have had kids devote their entire life to it, so they stop being what they were and become somebody else. Then the kids get out on their own and shit on you. I know what I did to my parents.

MARJORIE: My brother has two children, and I have three first cousins who each have kids. And we have friends who have kids. Our best friends are farmers who have a little boy. So we've watched him grow. And all these kids can come over, and we love them and we do things with them, and then we say goodbye. Life is full of decisions, and if we had made the decision to have kids, we would not have the life we have now. It would still be a good life, but it wouldn't be this one.

Cassandra and Anne got as far as talking with adoption counselors, but they were told that the best they could hope for would be a special-needs baby. Other issues ultimately derailed any notion of children.

ANNE: We responded to an ad in the local paper where they were looking for adoptive parents for minority children. Cassandra explained that we were interested, but that they had to understand that we came as a package. We went in and were told, "We're willing to put you through the system with all the other people, but if you get anything, it will be the worst-case scenario."

CASSANDRA: That would mean putting a child with severe disabilities into an interracial lesbian household.

A severely disabled child was more than Cassandra and Anne thought they could handle. The adoption posed further problems. Because the two women aren't a legally married couple, they would have had to go through the adoption process twice, once for each of them, and in their state, at the time they were contemplating adoption, this kind of adoption had never been done by a lesbian couple.

I asked Cassandra and Anne why they didn't then have a biological child. Cassandra had been through a hysterectomy, but Anne "still had the gear."

ANNE: But I had a bad back. I bend over the wrong way to pick up a piece of paper, and I can't walk for a month. What am I gonna do with something hanging on the front of me? And then we'd be short an income, because I'm self-employed. Besides, I've never had a job with decent benefits.

CASSANDRA: If I had the baby, everything would have been covered through my benefits at work. But I can't have a baby, and Anne's not covered by my benefits.

Then, as we started getting older, we grew disinterested in the whole scene.

At one point, Cassandra and Anne talked to a therapist about their baby debate. The therapist suggested they go home and pretend for a week that they actually had a baby.

ANNE: We were supposed to set the alarms for all these different times in the night—

CASSANDRA: And get up and pretend I was taking care of this baby, and then go and drive the kid to day care.

ANNE: We didn't do stitch one on that.

Given nature and the current laws that make adoption difficult, if not impossible, for gay people and gay couples, it seemed to me that the couples I interviewed who had children were the ones who had really, really wanted them. They did whatever it took to have them, and the reward has been the joy I was privileged to witness during my brief visits with these families. Those couples who were at all ambivalent, like Cassandra and Anne, ultimately chose not to have children. I think it would benefit all couples to do the kind of thinking and talking these gay couples did before making a decision to have children.

None of the ten couples I interviewed who had children from a prior marriage still had their children living at home. (Although one male couple had just said goodbye to an adult daughter, her husband, and their four young children, all of whom had been living for a year with them in their small house. The two men were giddy with relief, to say the least.) Of the ten couples, only Pam and Lindsy had had young children at home full-time when they first started living together. Others had teenagers who split their time between the homes of their divorced parents or who came home from school on vacations. Other children lived full-time with their heterosexual mothers and visited their gay fathers on weekends or holidays.

The issues that came up for these couples were little different from the joys and heartbreak experienced by all couples who have children from prior marriages—with the added complication, of course, of homosexuality. And from what most people told me, the gay part proved relatively insignificant.

For example, when Lucy broke up with Dixie to be with Patsy, Lucy's nineteen-year-old daughter, Carol, who had already left home for college, was furious. Her anger had nothing to do with her mother's being gay and everything to do with her mother's breaking up the most stable family life that Carol had known. For some time, Carol barely spoke with Patsy, blaming her for wrecking her mother's relationship with Dixie. It wasn't until 1984, when Lucy was mistakenly diagnosed with ovarian cancer, that Patsy and Carol developed a relationship.

PATSY: That's when Carol and I bonded, because all of a sudden I had a double role, which was to take care of Lucy *and* Carol. We really got to trust each other over that experience.

Patsy and Carol were in the recovery room following Lucy's surgery to deliver the good news that Lucy's doctor had been wrong: She didn't have cancer. The trauma of that experience brought all three women much closer and marked the beginning of a strong relationship between Patsy and Carol. It's a relationship in which Lucy takes comfort, or at least tries to.

LUCY: If anything happened to me, and I wasn't here anymore, I want to believe that Carol and Patsy would have a really loving relationship that would be wonderful for them both, and that Carol wouldn't be left absolutely motherless.

PATSY: Trust that, won't you?

LUCY: I do. I do.

Carol is now married and has two young children of her own, who bring much joy to both Lucy and Patsy—as well as new tension to their relationship. Lucy doesn't think Patsy is a good enough grandmother.

LUCY: Patsy is their grandmother as much as I am. They know us on equal terms. It's Grandma Patsy and Grandma Lucy. They're wonderful, but Patsy has a problem, because when Carol and the kids come, the house is turned into chaos. So Patsy pretty much locks herself away.

PATSY: It's my way of getting along, because when I walk into my own living room and cannot walk across the room for the junk on the floor, it makes me crazy! So I just try to stay out of the way and hang out in my studio. I'm not unavailable. I don't lock the door. But there isn't room for me.

LUCY: There isn't room for me, either, but I'm so thrilled that they're here. They're more important in my life than they are in Patsy's life. They're my children. Biologically, these are my lifeline.

PATSY: So even though we're both a grandma, you're number one grandma. No, you're number one and number two grandma, and I'm number three grandma.

LUCY: Well, you see, this is not a perfectly comfortable place with us, and we're still working on it, because I think Patsy is not coming through all the way with Carol and the kids.

PATSY: I'm only able to come through monetarily.

LUCY: Well, that to me is really bullshit, because that's not what we care about. What we care about are the relationships. And if we fight or if we disagree, or if I have feelings of disappointment and she has feelings of anger or being put out, this is the place we wind up. Before the children came, I think it's fair to say that Patsy was already very jealous of the very close relationship that Carol and I have.

This was clearly a very live issue for Lucy and Patsy, one they were not going to resolve in an afternoon. But before we finished discussing their current tensions over being grandmothers, both were emphatic that while this is the most difficult problem they've faced during their nearly two decades together, it's not a relationship-breaker.

PATSY: No one's separating over this, but it's a difficult area. Lucy thinks that I can turn on and off how I behave. And it's not like that. I feel the way I feel. I don't feel the way that Lucy wants me to feel.

LUCY: That's very true. The way I want Patsy to feel is not the way she feels, and that's why we have to keep talking about it.

PATSY: I feel that I'm very generous, and I do my part, and I do more than I have to do, and that's the only way I can do it.

LUCY: It can't only be money. You don't want money to be at the center of your relationships.

PATSY: Do you want me to stop paying my share?

LUCY: If you want to.

PATSY: I don't want to.

LUCY: You do it out of love, I hope, and concern. But that's not a substitute for relating.

PATSY: I didn't say it's a substitute. I said that's how I can do it. And at the moment, that's how I can do it best.

LUCY: So all I can say is: To Be Continued. This has not been resolved.

A final story, one that I think says a lot about familial resilience and the potential for ongoing love and respect between parents and children. Stanley—of Stewart and Stanley—wasn't a full-time dad to his son, Andrew, but from the time Stanley separated from his wife, he spent every Sunday with Andrew until Andrew was twenty. Stanley came out to his son when Andrew was seven years old.

STANLEY: I figured I better tell him before he hears it from somebody else at school or from his mother. So one Sunday we were on our way back to his mother's apartment, and there are some benches on the way into the complex where she lives, and we sat down. I explained to Andrew how there's all kinds of special love. "There's love that a child has for his parents; there's a love I'll always have for your mother, even though we're not still married; there's a special love that I have for you, Andrew; and there's also a special love for someone very special in my life."

STEWART: That wasn't me at the time.

STANLEY: This was the man I was involved with before Stewart. I said to Andrew, "It's a man, and we love each other and we're living together." This next part was a lie, but I said, "He's making me happy, and I have a good life with him." We had this long conversation, and at the end I said, "Andrew, do you have any questions?" And he said, "Daddy, whatever makes you happy makes me happy." He never said a word after that.

Stewart has known Andrew virtually since he met Stanley, and they've had a good relationship from the start. The relationship grew closer when Stewart volunteered to be Andrew's bar mitzvah teacher.

STEWART: And since his family didn't go to a synagogue, we actually had the bar mitzvah in my family's synagogue. On a Sunday of Chanukah. And we had a catered brunch. His ex-wife's family, my family, and his family all sat together.

STANLEY: I could barely talk that day, I was so nervous. Her family, my family, and his family under one roof in a synagogue.

STEWART: Her parents refused to talk to me.

STANLEY: Both grandparents were called up during the ceremony, and my brother-in-law, who is the dearest person you'd ever want to know, videotaped the whole thing for me.

STEWART: My father was the emcee of the candle-lighting ceremony for the cake.

STANLEY: It was just a beautiful day, and if I didn't have it on film, I would not believe it.

Andrew is now in his early twenties, and he recently introduced to his father and Stewart a young woman he's been dating.

STANLEY: Andrew made it a point of bringing her over. We had a lovely dinner. And after dinner, I'm walking them back to the subway. So she turns to me and says, "What should I call you? Mr. ——?" I said, "If you call me Mr. ——, I'm going to feel very old." I said, "By all means, call me Stanley, and call Stewart, Stewart."

Just before she went down the stairs to the subway, she said something that floored me. She said, "At least you were lucky the second time around."

FOURTEEN

Crisis

BEING A HAPPY COUPLE is no insurance against crises. It just means, ideally, that you're better equipped to handle one when it comes. Most of the couples I spoke with have faced one or more crises, ranging from a serious illness or the death of a loved one to a lost job or a broken trust. But only some of the couples have experienced the kind of crisis that jolts the foundation of a relationship and sends shock waves that reverberate for months or years to come.

The major crises I heard about were of two basic types: the kind that come from outside the relationship, like an illness or a death, and the kind that come from inside the relationship, like the collapse of communication or an infidelity.

Some of the couples faced crises from the outside very early on, crises that tested them individually and as a couple. Brian and Curt were confronted with Curt's HIV diagnosis, and Amy and Jama faced a breast-cancer nightmare that began well before they were finished with the honeymoon period of their relationship.

AMY: We were robbed! We didn't think about it that way at the time, but looking back, that's what happened. And no one can believe it when we tell them the story. People always say, "And you're still together?"

Amy never had a doubt that she and Jama would stay together, but Jama did. Their odyssey began just six months into the relationship, right after they moved in together. It was Amy who discovered the lump.

AMY: We were in the shower, making love. We made love in the shower a lot. And I touched the side of Jama's breast with my hand and felt a lump. I said, "Oh my God, what is that?"

JAMA: And I said, "Oh my God, I don't know."

AMY: It went through me like a lightning bolt. I just knew immediately that it was cancer. Jama had not felt the lump before, didn't know it was there, and it was a fairly good-sized lump, about the size of a quarter under the skin. But Jama was very large-breasted, and the tumor was on the side, heading toward the lymph nodes and under the arm, so it would have been easy for her to miss.

JAMA: I was only twenty-eight, but I'd always checked my breasts, and I'd never found it.

AMY: This was the weekend, so we decided that we'd go to the doctor on Monday. Then we made love. That's what we were doing, so we made love.

Unfortunately, Amy was right. It took three tests to confirm, but the lump was cancerous.

AMY: You know, when Jama was first diagnosed, I took it a lot harder than she did. I'm thinking, I'm gonna lose this woman I have fallen in love with. This is not fair. This is not right. I have finally found the one, and she's gonna die. It was overwhelming. It permeated every cell of my being, every waking moment of my day. I was terrified and angry, and I felt so hopeless and helpless. Somebody that you love is in danger, or is suffering, and you always think there's gonna be something that you can do to help. And there wasn't anything that I could do in any way, shape, or form. Jama's reaction to getting sick kind of made it more difficult. She was in denial. Well, she was in shock.

JAMA: Actually, I was.

AMY: We sat in the room with the X rays, and the doctor said, "You have cancer." And he started pointing out things, and Jama's mother and I became hysterical. Jama sat there like a stone.

JAMA: My reaction to this was "Give me a good doctor. I have a piece of my body that doesn't belong there anymore. Get rid of it, and I'm gonna be fine." I probably cried two or three times—twice with friends, and once with Amy. But I was feeling, like, Who the hell are they to be upset and carrying on? This is happening to me. Why am I standing up, being the strong one? After five or six years of therapy, thank you very kindly, I find out they're the ones that acted just fine, and I had bottled all of this up inside me.

Jama's surgeon recommended either a lumpectomy or a modified radical mastectomy.

AMY: The doctor says, "We can do this, or we can do that." She gave us the options, but I said, "What would you do if it was your breast?" I mean, that's specifically why we went to a female surgeon in the first place.

JAMA: She said, "If it were me, I would do the mastectomy." And she said, "I work with this plastic surgeon, and he'll be right beside me to put the breast back for you."

Within a month of discovering the lump, Jama was scheduled for surgery. She and Amy spent their last night before the operation at home, alone.

AMY: We stayed up and made love. It was very difficult. It was very difficult.

JAMA: I kept crying.

AMY: We were both crying, because we knew that something was gonna change. You don't know what it's gonna change to, but we knew that what we had was lost, and it was gonna be different than those first six months. When we were first getting together and moving in, we felt so safe, and this was a rude awakening.

JAMA: Before this happened, Amy and I had shared this belief system that as long as you get up and do the next appropriate thing in life, God, whoever He or She is, is gonna make us safe and secure. And me getting cancer shattered that for her. That made me sad, because she didn't have that anymore. I would say, "Come on, Amy, let's pray." And Amy would say, "I don't want to." And I would say, "Well, then I'll pray for you." And Amy would say, "I don't believe in this anymore." And I would say, "Then I'll believe for you." That was really hard.

So we made love that night, and I remember the sadness and thinking that I will never be this way for her again. My love for Amy wasn't going to change, but I knew my sense of self was about to change, and what I could give Amy physically was going to change.

Amy was the first person in my life that I felt totally and utterly comfortable and secure with, especially in our sex life. I was comfortable with how I looked and the way my body was. I was a size fourteen. I was a little chunky, and I liked it that way. I had large breasts, and I liked it that way.

I asked Amy and Jama if they had had any doubts about getting through the crisis as a couple.

AMY: Never, not for a moment.

JAMA: I had doubts. I didn't think she'd stay. It's an awful lot to put on somebody in a new relationship, don't you think? I just got diagnosed with cancer. They might take my breast and find a lump somewhere else next month.

AMY: I never gave her a chance to say any of that. I told her, "I don't love you for your breasts. I love you for you."

JAMA: All the time. All the time. Very supportive. "It doesn't matter."

AMY: It didn't matter. It just didn't. It never mattered. I knew it was not ever gonna matter. It wasn't the body that I fell in love with. It was the soul inside the body.

The next day, Jama was wheeled into the operating room.

AMY: I was afraid for what would happen, but I can honestly tell you that deep down I knew she was gonna make it. And I think everybody around Jama understood that she's a battler, that she would make it—not saying it's gonna be easy, but she's not gonna die from this. No way! Not with as many people as we had supporting us. There was just no way.

JAMA: I didn't read any kind of fear from Amy until I went into the operating room.

AMY: *The anesthesiologist is gonna screw up! She's gonna come out a vegetable! She's not gonna live!* I mean, that's the fear I went through.

JAMA: She looked at me with tears in her eyes, and I'm like, "Don't worry, I'll be okay." Of course, by this time, with the sedative, I'm feeling no pain. And my mother was saying, "I love you. I'll be right here."

AMY: I was terrified.

JAMA: I wasn't worried until they moved my butt off that stretcher onto the cold stainless-steel operating table. I looked down at myself and realized, "I am never gonna look like this again."

Three days after surgery, Jama decided to remove the bandage to see what the surgeons had done.

JAMA: I made certain nobody was there. I moved the bandage, and I didn't scream or anything, but my face got so beet-red, and I couldn't catch my breath. I tried not to cry or hyperventilate, because I knew that if I got too upset I'd end up being in pain or popping the stitches. But I couldn't help it, so I pulled the pillow over my face and burst into tears.

One of my first thoughts was, I was right about what I'd thought when I looked down at myself right after they put me on the operating table. And look what they've done to me! *Look what they've done to me!*

Five days after Jama went home, Amy asked if she could have a look underneath the bandage.

AMY: I was, like, "I want to see it." I'm like a little kid wanting to see something gross. "Can I see it?"

JAMA: So I showed it to Amy, and it was okay.

AMY: Yeah, I was fine.

JAMA: As soon as Amy left the room, I got hysterical.

AMY: I told her, "Jama, it's not so bad. It's gonna be better." But it wasn't my body.

During the next eight months, Jama went through chemotherapy, additional plastic surgery, and a breast-reduction operation. Most of that time, she was too exhausted to work, and she spent much of each day in bed.

AMY: She'd get up with me in the morning when I went to work.

JAMA: I'd eat something, and then I'd get back in bed by about eleven and wouldn't get up until six or seven that night. That's how I managed to put on a hundred and twenty pounds.

AMY: The only time she felt good was when her stomach was full, and that was all I cared about, so we always made sure there was enough food in the house for her to eat. But basically, I was on automatic pilot. You just don't know what you're gonna do until it comes up, and then you realize, *I'm just gonna do whatever I need to do to get it all done.* I had work, I had school, and I had worries. Constant worries about money.

JAMA: I would get upset, because I wasn't contributing. So four months into the chemotherapy, I started to feel better, and I got dressed and took Amy to work and then went to the United Way. I said, "I'm an educated person. I work. I've worked all my life. I'm not a bum, looking for money. I'm a cancer survivor. I'm going through chemo and"—this is where I lied—"I'm about to be evicted from my apartment. I have somebody who's helping me, but I have no job, my checking account is empty, and I'm about to be evicted from my apartment. And I will be happy to do whatever volunteer work I can when I'm through with this, but I need help."

AMY: She didn't tell me she was doing this before she went, but I understood that she needed to do it to feel okay about herself. I thought going to the Food Stamp office was a little bit extreme, though, and I drew the line at that.

JAMA: "You're never going back there again!" She wasn't going to get an argument from me. The Food Stamp office was horrible! But I was glad I went to United Way, because they paid our rent for three months.

AMY: It made all the difference in the world for us. We were already behind in our rent.

JAMA: I work for the county now, and with every check I make a donation to the United Way Campaign, because they were there for me.

Amy and Jama know that their relationship was ultimately strengthened by this experience, but the shock waves resounded for years. As I noted earlier, Jama's illness shifted the balance in their relationship in ways she and Amy didn't recognize for years. Amy became the parent, and Jama became the child.

AMY: I don't think there's any problem in a relationship if you're acting like you're a parent, but when you become somebody's bad step-mother, and you're not really sure how you got there and you don't know how to get out of it, then you have a problem. I know we were both unhappy, but I think Jama was unhappier, because I can be a bitch on wheels. But I have to point out, I was never unhappy with Jama *as a person*. I was unhappy with the way we were inter-acting.

For a long time, Amy and Jama blamed each other.

AMY: Before we understood the dynamic that was going on between us, we each assumed that it was the other person who was at fault.
JAMA: It was your stuff, or it was my stuff.
AMY: And what would happen was, someone would get really un-happy and say, "You either go to therapy or we're not gonna make it." And I would go off to therapy and I would get better, and then I would say, "You're a lunatic. You need to go to therapy." And she would go off and see a therapist. Eventually we figured out that we both needed to go together.

Brian and Curt knew from the start of their relationship that Curt might very well be HIV-positive, so Curt's test results weren't the unexpected shock that Jama's cancer diagnosis was. But until the diagnosis was a reality, Brian and Curt were able to keep the threat of illness from disrupting their lives. That was in 1988, and they had been together for one year.

BRIAN: Once we knew for sure about Curt, I got panic-stricken. I went over in my mind what we'd done and what I'd done with everyone

I'd been with before Curt. It was terror, terror. But I kept most of that terror from Curt.

CURT: That was going on quietly within Brian. I might know it now, but then I did not know the depth of what Brian was experiencing. I assumed he was concerned, but I didn't know how terrified he was.

Within days of Curt's diagnosis, Brian got tested at a public testing site, which meant waiting three weeks for results. This was the time for Curt to worry.

CURT: I assumed Brian would be negative, but I was afraid that there had been some slipup or something we weren't aware of. I was nervous that it would be my fault, even though we hadn't done anything unsafe.

BRIAN: I was concerned, but by this time I'd gotten over my panic. I knew I was negative, because I knew enough about HIV and I knew what I had done, so I couldn't imagine I was positive.

Brian's test indeed came back negative. Now that each of them knew where he stood, they found themselves wrestling with an army of conflicting feelings, including intense anger. Both men were angry—but for different reasons.

BRIAN: I was angry that Curt was positive.

CURT: I was angry at Brian because I felt like I was being blamed and judged. Like: "If you'd read the papers like I did in 1981, then you wouldn't have had sex and you wouldn't have gotten infected."

BRIAN: I remember we talked about when he thought he got infected, and I didn't understand how someone could actually get infected knowing that the possibility existed. Like, why would you possibly have unsafe sex if you had the information?

CURT: I wasn't alone. But anyway, any bad feelings I already had about myself, all the low self-esteem, were just magnified a hundred times. It made me feel awful. So there was this really horrible dynamic, and I wanted out of it. I felt like a bad person most of the time, so on that level I wanted out. It would have been so much easier being with someone who was HIV-positive.

BRIAN: I thought about leaving, too. We were only together a year, and I could get out of this now, but then I'd be a heel. But this person was going to die on me. I'm a fool to be with someone who is HIV-positive. I was also angry at myself for picking this person who was HIV-positive. I kept saying to myself, I should have picked that other guy who I really liked, who was cute and really smart. I hadn't even been on a date with this other guy, but we'd flirted and I'd been to a party at his house, and I thought, He was the one I should have picked. I should dump Curt and go to him. Then I happened to be on a plane on the way to Boston to meet Curt at an AIDS conference, and I was reading *The New York Times,* and this guy who I thought I should have picked is written up in an article, and he's identified as a big guy with ACT-UP and he's HIV-positive. What that did was enable me to see that I wouldn't know who was HIV-positive and who wasn't. So this is just chance, and Curt and I already have a year under our belts, and it's worth staying. But it was so scary. It was terrifying.

CURT: Very scary.

BRIAN: Because I thought I was going to put all this energy into this relationship, and he's going to be dead. He's going to die. You know, I would stare at him—

CURT: Like I was some kind of specimen.

BRIAN: Curt would be lying in bed sleeping, and I would just look at him to see if he was dead. He was going to drop dead. I'd comb his body with my eyes, looking for lesions.

CURT: I had no symptoms. I was fine. I *am* fine. And my doctor wasn't an alarmist, *ever.* He was very reassuring. What was scary was this support group I was in. People were getting sick, so for me it created a sense of urgency that we better get on with our lives, not wait.

BRIAN: We needed to live life. I remember wanting to go to Europe, and a year later we went, and I thought, *We made it to Europe and now Curt can die.*

CURT: Everything was *Now I can die.*

BRIAN: *We bought the carpet, now he can die.* When I found out I was negative, it was the opposite. *I bought a bookcase, because now I can live.* With Curt, it was *Now he can die.*

Curt didn't die. He and Brian moved in together. They went to Europe. Brian stopped blaming Curt for being HIV-positive. Brian stopped thinking about leaving Curt for someone who was HIV-negative, and Curt stopped thinking about leaving Brian for someone who was HIV-positive. Around them, people they knew continued to die, including everyone in Curt's support group except him and one other person. But Curt didn't die. He didn't even get sick, although he continues to take prophylactic medications.

Only in the last couple of years has Curt acknowledged to himself that he's probably not going to die anytime soon. I asked Curt and Brian what it was like living with the expectation that Curt might not be around in a year, in two years, in three years, and what impact that had had on their relationship.

BRIAN: There was the urgency, an urgency to move in and an urgency to connect on a very spiritual level.

CURT: I think it increased the intensity of our connection to each other. We really worked on things. We went to therapy together, just a couple of times, to work on things.

BRIAN: And it was over a whole range of things, not just the HIV stuff, but me clinging and Curt pulling away, money issues, things like that.

Brian and Curt's commitment to working things out and living life intensely has made for a very passionate relationship, with plenty of ups and downs over the years. The shock waves of the initial crisis have long since receded, but the impact of Curt's diagnosis changed their relationship in fundamental ways, and HIV remains a shadow on their lives.

Lee and Catherine were lucky enough to have nine years together before they were faced with crises that affected each individually and disrupted their life as a couple. In 1991, Lee and Catherine got hit from both sides, and hit hard. Lee's mother had a stroke and was left completely paralyzed, and Catherine's beloved baby brother, Matt—the one who was holding Lee's cut-glass vase hostage—was in the final stages of AIDS. "We were walking zombies," Lee told me.

At the time, Lee and Catherine were living in an apartment in Pacifica, a small coastal city a short drive from San Francisco. That proved to be too far for Lee to drive every day to take care of her mother, who was in a nursing home in Palo Alto, so Lee quit her job and took on contract work that left her free to move close by her mother. Catherine stayed behind, working full-time as a vocational counselor, seeing clients and resolving their problems all day, then taking care of her brother through the night.

CATHERINE: I spent the majority of my time living with Matt and his lover. I don't know when I slept. Fortunately, my sister came out to California to help, so I would get a free weekend every now and then. I would call Lee in Palo Alto and say, "Lee, I've got free time this weekend. You want to do something together?" And I would drive down to Palo Alto.

LEE: And sometimes I could get up to San Francisco. We'd be so shell-shocked.

CATHERINE: It was just a chance to connect. We were so emotionally and physically exhausted from being pulled in so many directions. So when we managed to get together, I'd crawl into bed and we'd cuddle and go to sleep. It was just having someone that you cared about, who you could hold on to and feel comfortable enough to go to sleep and say, "Okay, I can relax for a while."

We'd sleep through the two days we were together, except for maybe a walk and a cup of coffee. And then we'd part again. We tried to talk by phone, but between our work schedules and the care-giving, it was difficult.

When Matt first became ill, Lee and Catherine joined a local support group for people caring for loved ones dying of AIDS. They had already endured the deaths of many of their friends, and they needed to talk to other people who knew what they were experiencing.

LEE: We were wiped out. We didn't know how to deal with all of it. All of our male friends had died. And now her favorite brother, the person she was closest to in the world, was dying.

CATHERINE: Exactly. Everybody that we associated with was gone.

LEE: I'll give you an example. George, Matt's lover, was Irish, so he and Matt had this enormous St. Patrick's Day party at their place in Noe Valley. They had bought a beautiful house with a couple of three-bedroom, two-bath apartments. They lived upstairs, and we lived downstairs. So we opened up all the doors to the whole place, and people could just wander in and out. The first party was packed with maybe a hundred people. And over the years it got smaller and smaller. The last year we did it, in 1990, Matt, George, his mom, and Catherine and I and maybe two other people sat around the fireplace talking. That was the last of the St. Patrick's Day parties.

CATHERINE: We had so many friends who passed away, one right after the other. We were numb. We didn't want to make any new male friends, because they could die.

LEE: It was just a very horrendous thing for us. And on top of that, we have very close family relationships. For instance, her mother and grandmother love me. I and my children are their family. Her sister and I and her sister's lover are close, and my family loves Catherine. So she became part of my family. I became part of her family. Now here I was losing my mother and she was losing her brother and we were all close. Everybody was in need, so it was a very, very difficult situation for us.

In March 1991, Lee's mother died, but Lee remained in Palo Alto at her mother's apartment, visiting Catherine on weekends. A few months later, she took a consulting job in Atlanta. Catherine stayed behind to continue caring for her brother. I asked Catherine if she was at all resentful that Lee went off on her own in the last months of Matt's life.

CATHERINE: No, because I was close to her mom, and I knew how painful it was for her. I told her to go.

LEE: I needed to take off. My way of healing is to drive and write.

Matt died on December 8, 1991. Lee returned in time for the memorial service and to help spread Matt's ashes. With both Lee's mother and Matt gone, Lee and Catherine had time to focus on themselves and their relationship.

CATHERINE: It took us about a year to get back together—1992 was the healing year. Between the counseling and Lee closing up her mother's apartment, it was a year before Lee moved back in with me in Pacifica.

LEE: I came home. And we took long walks.

CATHERINE: On the beach.

LEE: On the beach.

CATHERINE: A lot of walks.

LEE: A lot of walks.

As Lee and Catherine echo each other, I can hear the weight of that time in their voices and see it in the way they've collapsed into the sofa. Through much of the interview they've been full of energy and very expressive, but revisiting that difficult time in their lives has sapped them of their strength. I ask if they felt at any time in 1991 and 1992 that their relationship was in trouble.

LEE: We were in trouble. We, *individually*.

CATHERINE: Right, but not the relationship.

LEE: We, the couple, were in trouble because there was so little of us left for each other or for anyone. While Catherine was still the most important person in my life and I was still the most important person in her life, it wasn't in the way that we had lived it prior to the trauma.

CATHERINE: The relationship suffered in terms of the physical closeness, but I think it gained a lot more, because we came back into our relationship as a much stronger emotional support for each other. We had been through so much that anything else is a piece of cake.

LEE: But while we were in counseling, we found out that we had some stuff in our own relationship to deal with. For one thing, we never argued. We were so proud that we weren't bickerers, or naggers, that we never argued. She took a walk. I took a walk. We parted. It didn't mean we were never mad or angry or resentful.

CATHERINE: We just buried that anger.

Another big issue that came up was how each had worked so hard to accommodate the other that, more often than not, *both* were resentful.

CATHERINE: During counseling, it dawned on us that we really, truly cared for each other, loved each other, and wanted our relationship to work, but we didn't want the relationship going in the same direction it had been going. It had to go off track in order to get better.

Lee and Catherine feel that their crises and the subsequent counseling have benefited their relationship by making it stronger and more flexible. Over time, they've overcome their fear of arguing and have become more aggressive about expressing their needs. And by dealing with issues that they believe would have caused problems down the line, they've likely avoided a crisis within the relationship later on. They feel well-equipped for the next crisis that threatens from without, if and when it comes.

As sapped as Catherine and Lee were by their individual responsibilities, they were still able to offer each other some comfort, however limited. That's the couple's advantage when a crisis strikes from outside the relationship: You still have each other. But when the relationship itself is in crisis, you can't turn to the one person you're most likely to want to turn to for the comfort and support you need.

Marta and Rita, the two Cuban women who have kept their relationship a secret from their families, have been through the kind of crisis that comes from within a relationship. Their crisis did not come out of left field but arose from an issue they had been dealing with for years.

RITA: Marta belittled me. She would call me stupid.

MARTA: I grew up with that sort of talk, and I realize how horrible it is, but calling someone stupid had different implications for me.

RITA: If you know somebody, you don't belittle the person. I remember talking to Marta about this many times.

MARTA: And I shouldn't have.

RITA: Well, about four years ago, we had a big, big blowup over this. And it wasn't just the belittling. It was three or four things, and I can't remember exactly what it was, but it was cumulative, and the belittling was the trigger.

Marta called Rita "stupid" one too many times. Rita told Marta that the relationship was over.

RITA: I was serious. I said, "I've reached my limit. No matter how much I love you, I cannot deal with this anymore." I was really pissed. I said, "How could this happen again after all we had talked about this, after all we had gone through talking about the things that we should not do to each other, like trying to tell the other person that she's not worth anything." At that moment I just couldn't see going further into the relationship. I was too hurt. I told her that I didn't want to be hurt like this again. "I'm through with this."

MARTA: I thought it was over. Now, I'm not a crier, but all I did was cry.

RITA: I had to leave on business the next day. We slept together in the same bed that night, but we didn't talk.

MARTA: We didn't get near each other.

RITA: We talked only briefly the next morning.

MARTA: This was September, and I was supposed to deal with getting our new boat out of the water for the winter.

RITA: Marta said, "What are we going to do about this?" I said not to worry, that we'd sell it.

MARTA: Rita came back from her trip a week later, and I didn't know if everything was still over. I couldn't tell what was going on, and I was still walking on eggshells. Then she handed me an insulated bag that she'd bought on her trip, and she said, "Oh look, I got this for the boat next year."

RITA: That was my way of saying to her, "I'm over it."

MARTA: Rita wasn't over it, but we didn't really have a chance to discuss things, because we left that day for a women's weekend in Provincetown with all these other people.

RITA: We talked that night.

MARTA: She said that we were going to be okay, but she wasn't saying that our relationship was going to last. She made me think that it was just part of the process of breaking up. She did.

RITA: I did?

At this moment in the interview, I recognized that we were touching sore points, and that Rita and Marta each had her own recollection of what had happened.

MARTA: Yes, you did. Rita's really good at mixed signals.

RITA: I was still mad.

MARTA: I think you had begun to forgive me, but you didn't want me to know that.

RITA: I was still mad. It was a very hurtful experience. I knew that I was not going to leave this, that I wasn't going to quit. But I wasn't going to have a patching-up conversation.

MARTA: So I still thought she wanted to quit, but at least once she gave me the bag I thought there was a hope or a prayer.

RITA: Marta gets over things very quickly. More quickly than I do. I cannot let go of some things when they are very hurtful from the person that I know loves me. And then when that person really hurts me, I'm left wondering, Does she really love me? This is something we talk about a lot. I tend to look for a lot of signals as far as somebody caring for me. I look for the endearments, the hugging, the making you feel better when you don't feel okay. Some of the times I complain to Marta that I don't see it back from her. To me it's a very important thing that the other person treats me well. I'm seeing it more and more now, but in the beginning, Marta was not that kind of nurturing person at all.

Obviously, Marta and Rita continued in their relationship after their big blowup. And things have improved, although Marta's first instinct is still to deliver a put-down when she gets mad.

MARTA: I will not say that I don't do it at all anymore, but I think that the incidents are greatly diminished. It's my nature, and I know that's not acceptable and that's not an excuse. Being in a relationship, I've had to learn that no matter how natural and how justified I can feel in saying it, it's still inappropriate for me to say it. I also think that part of it is for her to realize that when something like that slips out, she can say "You're not allowed to say that" rather than "It's over."

It's funny, because I'm the marrying kind. I'm in for the long haul. It doesn't matter how pissed off I am. It doesn't cross my mind that this is over. It just doesn't. I don't think I've ever implied or said that this is over. It doesn't mean that I haven't been pissed as hell at her, too. She's no angel. She just yelled at me the other day when I put my foot through the attic floor. Rita yelled at me *right away*. I didn't let her live that one down for a while.

RITA: I wasn't belittling her. I thought she was going through the ceiling.

MARTA: Rita can get an attitude to die for. She gets self-righteous. And then she'll find the one thing that I say that's inappropriate and turn the whole world around on me. She thinks I don't know that.

With this, Rita leaned forward in her chair, smiled, and turned red.

After eighteen years together, Clarence and Ric had drifted apart in ways that neither of them recognized until a full-scale crisis erupted during a 1994 trip to England. Ric is now forty-eight and works as an AIDS educator. Clarence is sixty-two and teaches hairdressing at a school in the Midwest, where he and Ric live in a sunny, rambling turn-of-the-century apartment.

CLARENCE: My school sent me to a black school in England to teach them hairdressing techniques that we do here in the States. And they videotaped me doing demonstrations. That was the whole idea of the trip, and then we stayed for pleasure. We saw London, and we went to Oxford. My daughter was over there, too, at the time. So we were going to make this a fun trip.

One night midway through the trip, after a day of shopping, Ric asked Clarence if he wanted to go out to the bars.

CLARENCE: I was really tired, and I was also getting myself organized for a taping that was coming up in a couple of days. Ric really wanted to go. We had a slight argument. "I'm here in England, why can't we go out?" I told Ric that I didn't feel like it, and told him to go on his own.

Ric went out and didn't return until three-thirty that morning. Clarence knew the London bars closed at eleven and figured that with travel time Ric should have been home by twelve-thirty at the latest. Clarence woke up when Ric returned.

CLARENCE: I saw what time it was, and I saw that Ric was feeling no pain when he came in. Now, I have very good intuition.
RIC: He does have excellent intuition.
CLARENCE: I can call my kids up and I know just what's happening. So I got up the next morning, and Ric had left on top of the dresser what had been in his pocket. And there was a matchbook from a gay bar, and I opened it up and there was a phone number written inside. Now my mind is working overtime. I know the bars close at eleven

o'clock, so where could he be until three in the morning? We didn't have a phone in the apartment where we were staying, so I went around the corner to the store and used the telephone there to call the number. This guy answered the phone, and I hung up. I went back to the apartment, and Ric was in the kitchen fixing something to eat. I didn't pay any mind to Ric at that time. I was pissed, though.

Ric could tell that Clarence was angry, but he just assumed it was because he'd come in so late. This was not something he ever did when they were home. If Ric stayed out late, he did it with Clarence.

Later that day, Clarence and Ric took the train into London and spent the afternoon shopping. Ric was looking at a display surrounded by flashing lights when Clarence noticed something on Ric's neck.

CLARENCE: At first, I thought it was shadows. I said, "Oh, those lights are throwing a funny shadow."

Clarence walked up to Ric and looked closely at his neck. As Clarence described this scene to me, Ric was cringing.

CLARENCE: It was hickeys, serious hickeys. I asked what happened, and he said, "Oh, he took advantage of me." I was freaking out. I thought to myself, I'm in Harrod's. I cannot tear this store up. I don't have that kind of money.

Ric had seen this rage once before, years earlier, following an argument Clarence had with their then landlord.

RIC: He was so angry when he came into the house that he walked into the bedroom and picked the dresser straight off the floor and slammed it back down. And this dresser was full of clothes! I said right then and there that I am never, ever going to get him as angry as he is today. And I was pretty successful, up to that point.

Clarence was furious that Ric had been with someone else. He had no idea what the extent of the involvement was, but he knew that something had happened that wasn't supposed to happen.

CLARENCE: I'm from the old school. If you're going to go ahead and do anything like that, don't bring it home. Don't let me know about it. I'll be all right. But if you flaunt it in front of me, or in front of my friends and it gets back to me, that's another story. It's a respect thing, and it's a matter of trust.

So we had to get back on the Tube to ride back to where we were staying, which was about a forty-five-minute trip. And Ric is sitting across from me on this crowded train. I could not do anything. I couldn't say shit. I was just, like, Okay, wait until we get off this fucker. So when we got off, we had to walk about a half mile to where we were staying. But we stopped in this little park, and I just had to sit down and talk to Ric, because I was freaking out. He was saying that they didn't do this, they didn't do that. The whole bit. I said, "Well, how'd you get these marks and everything? You didn't just shake hands and exchange recipes! I know this."

In their eighteen years together, Clarence had never questioned Ric about anything having to do with other men, and now he was left wondering what Ric might have done in the past.

CLARENCE: I just assumed that he had not done anything. He was just my person. That's the way I looked at it. And when this took place, all that went out the window, because I'm thinking that maybe this has happened before. It was a real big, big, big thing. So I was really getting ready to go ahead and do a big job on him, physically, but I thought, No, I can't do this. I have a taping tomorrow. The show must go on.

RIC: He didn't have to do anything for me to know how mad he was, because I could feel how mad he was. I guess that really scared me, because all of the trust that I had tried to build throughout the whole relationship, I could feel it slipping, slipping away. And it was my fault, because I let something like that happen. I felt like the kid getting caught with his hand in the cookie jar. I knew that Clarence was real pissed, real pissed. And it never ended. We could talk a little bit about it, and it would be all right, and then a little while later it would blow up again and it would be thrown back in my face. This went on throughout the trip, and then after that. We had to go to a counselor.

I was impressed that Ric and Clarence, like many of the couples I spoke with, were willing to talk to a professional counselor when they were unable to get through a crisis on their own. More than a third of the couples have sought the help of a professional therapist—for a one-time problem-solving session or for more extended therapy. And many of the individuals have sought counseling on their own. Ric and Clarence went for six months' of couples counseling.

CLARENCE: I was explaining to one of my clients what had happened to me in England with Ric, and she recommended her therapist. So this incident happened in July, and we started seeing the counselor two months later. In between, I had called the person up again and I talked to him. I asked him what happened, and he told me that Ric initiated the first kiss. That one really threw me. So I really got on Ric's case after that.

I asked Ric and Clarence what they had hoped to gain from seeing a counselor.

CLARENCE: We had to find out how to communicate again and how to rebuild trust. The counselor explained how this was like a garment being torn. You can mend it back together, but it's not going to be that strong at the mending point. You have to work with it, and we have. All of this has actually made our relationship much better.

FIFTEEN

Intimacy

I DON'T THINK most people have any idea what they're asking for when they say they want an intimate relationship. No. Maybe it's not fair to project my own thoughts on all of humanity. I don't think *I* knew what I was asking for when I told myself I wanted an intimate relationship. Looking back, I realize that I confused romance with intimacy. I thought of intimacy as a moment that involved candles, no clothes, and the man of my dreams. And while such a moment can certainly be intimate, intimacy doesn't necessarily have anything to do with sex.

As I've thought about this subject, what has repeatedly come to mind is what Bev and Judy told me when I asked them, "What's the best thing about being together for as long as you two have been a couple?" What they said had nothing to do with my romantic notion of intimacy, but it struck me as intensely intimate. Bev answered first, with one word: "Comfort."

JUDY: You can burp and not have to leave the room.
BEV: Farting. I can remember tooting in front of Judy once, and I thought I was going to die. And now we do it to see who can be the loudest.

When I mentioned to a couple of my gay friends that I planned to include Bev's comment about farting, they were horrified over how it might reflect on gay relationships in general. "You can't write that! What will people think?" As if gay people are the only ones who pass gas. But I knew that almost anyone who had ever been in a couple relationship would understand the point I was trying to make by including Bev's comment. In general, most of us toot only in front of those people we know will still love us after the fact. (Of course, there are people who wouldn't dream of tooting unless they were certain they were alone.)

Bev and Judy had more to say about what they like best about being a long-lasting couple.

BEV: Walking around not worrying if you've got a little pudgy tummy. We love each other for what's in the heart, not for what the body looks like anymore. Bad breath in the morning—who cares? I can remember early on, Judy would chew gum all night so she could have fresh breath in the morning.

That's intimacy: letting your beloved see your imperfect belly, inflicting morning breath on each other, tooting, burping. Intimacy is revealing those things you're not likely to reveal to anyone who *isn't* an intimate, whether it's bad breath or a bad mood. Intimacy is bearing witness to each other's imperfections. It's allowing yourself to be emotionally and physically vulnerable in ways that you don't allow yourself to be with other people. It's knowing someone as well as anyone knows him, perhaps even better than he knows himself. It's inviting someone into your private realm, and creating a private realm *with* her. Intimacy can be wonderful, agonizing, earthshaking, and eminently practical.

I'm reminded of a little ritual my grandparents had. When Grandma May served chicken, my grandfather, who had a keen mind for most of his life, always asked, "May, do I take the top or the bottom?" In other words, did he like the dark meat or the light meat? When I was young, I couldn't understand why Grandpa couldn't remember what part of the chicken he liked. Of course he knew, but, in a way, my grandmother knew *better,* and he trusted her to choose for him.

Just the other day, dining out with my partner, I ordered a steak.

The waiter asked me how I liked it done, and I found myself asking my partner how I wanted my steak. At first I wasn't aware of what I was doing, but when I thought about it I realized that I asked because I knew he knew better than I how I really liked it prepared. We'd been together long enough to have experienced several occasions where I'd ordered steak that I found overdone and he'd said, "You should have ordered it medium-rare instead." I remember getting mad the first time he did that. Didn't I know better than he what I liked? But I didn't. So on this occasion, without thinking, I asked him what he thought I would like, and he indeed knew better than I. That's intimacy.

Although I was a relative stranger in the homes of the couples I interviewed, I heard about some of the intimate details of their relationships and occasionally saw them being intimate, whether that intimacy was an arm draped around a beloved's shoulder in a way that might never be done in public, a knowing glance, a stream of tears, or flashes of anger that the partners—I imagine—usually save just for each other. Pam and Lindsy come to mind. They have a deeply intimate and passionate way of relating, and sometimes I felt as if I shouldn't be there to witness it.

I also took photographs of most of the couples—originally for my own use in bolstering my feeble memory when it came time to write about them. Some of these photographs are wonderfully intimate in the ways the partners chose to share a touch or a look.

Some of the couples told me about the intimate things they do, from clipping each other's stray ear hairs to setting out a partner's medication. Marjorie and Marion did a nonverbal check with each other before telling me about their nightly kissing ritual.

MARJORIE: I go to bed earlier than Marian. She goes down to the barn every night and feeds the cows one more bale of hay and says good night to everyone. And then, when she gets into bed, she kisses me all over.

MARIAN: Often Marjorie will be asleep when I come to bed, and then in the morning she'll say, "I had this feeling that you didn't kiss me all over last night." But I always do.

In turn, Marjorie always puts the toothpaste on Marian's toothbrush. It's something she started doing when Marian had trouble with her hands from a repetitive-motion injury.

MARIAN: I couldn't squeeze the toothpaste tube.
MARJORIE: Now I do it without thinking about it. In fact, we had somebody staying with us one night who had the same color toothbrush as Marian. I didn't realize it wasn't Marian's, and our guest couldn't believe that I put the toothpaste on for her.
MARIAN: In summer, when it's really hot, sometimes the toothpaste melts off the toothbrush by the time I get back from the barn.

Lucy and Patsy revealed to me a particularly charming intimate daily ritual. I had asked if they had special names for each other. (Anyda and Muriel had felt that this question was too intimate to answer. And when they told me that in their forty-eight years together they had never told anyone what names they called each other, I could understand why they weren't about to reveal them to me.) Lucy and Patsy didn't hesitate in answering my question.

PATSY: "Miss Honey."
LUCY: One of our cats was named "Mr. Honey," and somewhere along the line we turned that into "Miss Honey." Very often, at the start of the day—
PATSY: Wait until you hear what's coming next!

Lucy shot Patsy a glance that said, "Hush, I'm telling a story," and then she started over:

LUCY: Very often, at the start of the day, we ask each other, "Would you be my honey today?" or "Would you like to be my honey today?" or "Would you be my sweetheart today?" It just comes up. And very often it's when we're having a soft moment in the day or in our travels. It could be in the supermarket, and she or I will look at the other and say, "Are you my honey today?" It's just a way of saying "I love you, and I'm feeling very close to you." Isn't that true?
PATSY: It's nice.
LUCY: It's very sweet.

Andy and Matthew, the couple whose nonmonogamous relationship evolved as Andy pushed Matthew into increasingly adventurous
sexual exploits, have a nonverbal but intimate way of expressing
their love when they're in public. But unless you're watching care-
fully, you're not likely to see it.

MATTHEW: When you're together a long time, you develop certain
    secret little signals that don't mean a whole lot to anybody else, but
    a glance across the room and a slight hand motion might mean *I
    love you.*

I ask Matthew to demonstrate, and he looks at Andy, cocks his head
to one side, and rests his cheek on his closed fist. There's a look that
goes along with the head on the hand, just a very faint smile and a
slight furrowing of the brow. Andy does the same in response, and I
can't help but melt at the sight of such a tender gesture.

MATTHEW: It's very subtle, but we can see it even from across the
    room. And why would we do that? Just for the same reasons that we
    would say "I love you." And we say it a lot to each other. I don't
    know of a day that we don't say "I love you."

Andy and Matthew's publicly expressed intimate gestures are subtle
and easy for outsiders to miss. Other couples choose or feel compelled to consciously censor themselves in public, which is what Bev
and Judy do, except when they forget themselves and call each other
"honey." But however much couples may think they're keeping
intimacy under wraps, many, if not most, of the couples interact in
the public realm in ways that suggest a relationship more intimate
than that of just good friends. I'm taking a bit of a leap here,
because I didn't explore this subject with the couples thoroughly
enough to feel completely confident in what I'm suggesting. But I
think it's worth taking the leap.

My evidence? Many of the couples said they've been mistaken for
siblings. Part of this confusion may come from the fact that many
people who are coupled for a long time begin to look alike. For
example, they may go to the same hairstylist and wear similar
clothes. I saw this kind of similarity, to greater and lesser degrees,
with most of the couples.

Jim and Martin, for example, are often mistaken for brothers, even twins. Not only do they dress similarly, but they're both approximately the same height and weight, and they both have white hair.

JIM: They always think we're brothers. And twins. I don't think we look like twins.

MARTIN: When you get to be our age, all old people look alike, I think.

But it's more than just looking and dressing alike. There's something about the way that two people in a long-term relationship interact that betrays their intimacy. And as it doesn't occur to most heterosexual observers that this intimacy is taking place in the context of a couple relationship, the only kind of relationship they can imagine between two similar-looking and similar-acting people of the same gender who are relatively close in age is that of brother and brother or sister and sister.

What do I mean by the way two people in a long-term relationship interact? What comes to my mind just now is the checkout line at the grocery store. The simple fact of two men or two women shopping together suggests a close relationship. Then there's the act of unloading the grocery cart and preparing to pay the bill. It's something you've done over and over, so there's a familiar ritual to it—a dance, even—as each of you reaches into the cart and removes an item and places it on the conveyor belt. Maybe as you do the unloading, you're physically close in a way that only intimates would be. Perhaps one of you gets annoyed with the other about something you've forgotten to buy, or you come across high-fat cookies in the cart that you can't believe your partner has decided he can't live without. You throw him a look of exasperation, he says something in shorthand, you say something back, and the moment passes. In the meantime, the check-out clerk, who it never occurred to you is taking in the whole scene, is keeping mental notes and growing increasingly perplexed. And as one of you is paying the bill, she adds up all the clues and lets her curiosity get the best of her and asks, "Are you two brothers?"

Intimate grocery-store rituals—or any other intimacies, for that matter—aren't instantaneous. As was made clear in my conversations with the couples, an intimate relationship is one that develops over time—more quickly for some than for others, but never from the very moment a couple begins a relationship. Over the months and years of the relationship, you begin to trust each other enough to reveal things about yourself that you're not likely to reveal on a first date. For example, when Chris and Sherri met, Sherri didn't know that Chris suffered from anxiety attacks that left her so shaky that even going to the mailbox was difficult. But as they courted by phone, Chris decided to risk telling Sherri, because she knew it would come up sooner rather than later.

CHRIS: It's kind of difficult to hide. It's classic anxiety. I'm sure I'm going to die right then. I feel like I'm going to throw up. I sweat. My blood pressure goes up. So we talked about it a great length. I said, "You know, there will be times when you want to do something, but if you wait until I go with you, you're never going to get to go, and this will be an issue. So, if you want to go do something, you need to do it without me."

SHERRI: I didn't know the night I met Chris what a big event it was for her to be out at a bar. But I've dealt with it. You also have to understand that as a nurse, I'm a caretaker, so I didn't see it as a problem.

CHRIS: I saw it as a huge problem, because most of my relationships ended because they didn't feel that I was able to go and do. So it was something that we discussed, and she has been very good about it. If she wants to go do something, she just goes and does it.

SHERRI: So that's taken a lot of stress off the relationship.

CHRIS: And she knows now—didn't at first, but knows now—that if you go and have a good time, you're not going to come home to bitterness. I would say, "Did you have a good time? Tell me who was there." So she realized she could go and have a good time and not be punished for it when she got home.

SHERRI: And by not putting a lot of stress on her to go, it has enabled her to feel less anxious about going places.

CHRIS: So consequently I have enlarged my world slowly, and now I can pretty much do whatever I want, within reason.

Chris trusts that Sherri will never use what she knows about Chris's anxiety problem against her. In an intimate relationship, you learn lots of things about your partner that leave her or him quite vulnerable. You know exactly where the soft spots are—which means you can wound a beloved in ways that almost no one else can. Armed with what they know about each other, the challenge then for all of these couples has been to avoid using this intimate knowledge as a weapon, even at those times when it's awfully tempting.

SIXTEEN

Change

M Y BEST BUDDY and I have a saying: "Nothing changes, everything stays the same." And we always use it at those moments when the ground shifts beneath us so fast that we can hardly stay on our feet. So if I call him up and ask him how he's doing, and he says, "You know: Nothing changes, everything stays the same," I know I'm in for a good story.

In long-lasting couple relationships, as in every other aspect of life, virtually everything changes, and nothing stays exactly the same. Most of the couples I talked to know that change—both incremental and dramatic—is a given. They also know that it's an essential, if sometimes painful, ingredient in keeping a relationship interesting over the long haul. As the couples told me, and as I hope has become obvious by now, change is a part of every aspect of couple life. You will change, your partner will change, your relationship will change, and everything around you will change in ways that are both predictable and unimaginable.

Despite the fact of constant change, one thing you can't change is the person your partner is. People may change in subtle ways, but fundamentally, people are who they are. Danny now dresses far better than when he first met Nate, but nice clothes and good restaurants will never be as important to him as they are to Nate, although these things are now less important to Nate after nearly two decades of Danny's influence. Alison will always need more time to make travel plans than Dayna, but after nine years together, Dayna knows this, and she tries to be understanding of Alison's need to plan ahead and, more often than not, tries not to leave off making plans until the last minute. Pam and Lindsy are both volatile people, and while they've learned to rein in potentially destructive tendencies, they are still fierce arguers.

Lucy and Patsy have had different feelings about money from the very beginning, and while that hasn't changed, Patsy is more generous now than when the two women first got together.

PATSY: Lucy is extremely generous. I've learned to be more generous.

LUCY: Yeah, Patsy was kind of tight. I used to have to take her out to dinner all the time.

PATSY: It was my training. I was trained to be tight.

LUCY: Here she was, the rich WASP, and I was taking her out to dinner.

PATSY: I was brought up feeling like I had to be very careful. And I also didn't want to use my father's money. I only wanted to use the money I earned, and I never made that much. I think when you're nineteen, twenty, twenty-one, it's very important to feel like you're on your own and not on your daddy's coattails.

LUCY: Well, by the time I was taking you out to dinner, you were in your forties.

PATSY: When I finally figured out that I had plenty of money, I started being more generous with it.

LUCY: Patsy really is more generous than she used to be.

Given Patsy's history with money and the fact she came from a more formal background than Lucy, who is the more gregarious of the two, I might have guessed that when it came to affection, Patsy would have something to learn from Lucy. But it was Lucy who had to make the changes in that department. "Patsy had to teach me how to cuddle, how to be more affectionate," Lucy told me. "I was always affectionate with my daughter, but that's as far as it went until I met Patsy."

A very recent change has been Patsy's new interest in early music and the recorder. Given that it was their shared interest in music that brought them together in the first place, I was startled to learn that their now divergent musical tastes are the source of enormous discontent for Lucy.

LUCY: I don't like the recorder, and I don't particularly like early music. I've never been able to sing it, because I don't have a feel for it. I'm very much more a contemporary and romantic music person. I also love jazz, country and western music, some rock, and folk rock. So it kind of serves me right that Patsy has taken up with the one area of music that I really don't like. She's obsessed with the recorder, and with work.

PATSY: I love what I do, so it's not a chore to me to be doing it all the time.

LUCY: The recorder has taken over her life.

PATSY: Lucy says, "Oh, the goddamned recorder!" Or, "Those goddamned recorder people!"

LUCY: They're all nerds! So now when Patsy's occupied with her recorder groups, I go and do my own thing. I go out with other friends. I teach in the city, where I get to see a lot of my gay men friends. I go to movies by myself. I just make a separate life.

In addition to changes the individual partners experience, the relationship itself changes over time. From talking to the couples I learned that after many years together there is generally a greater sense of commitment and security, better communication, more intimacy, and less sex. And, as I've mentioned earlier, the balance of power also shifted for many of the couples: One partner may have had greater success in his or her work, or been sidelined by an illness, or perhaps the older of the two partners retired and/or faced physical limitations brought on by age.

One of the key changes the couples talked about was the understanding that came from getting to know each other. That meant, for example, that they learned to anticipate how a partner would react to a given circumstance or how to respond to an angry outburst. In the early years of her relationship with Lucy, Patsy had difficulty dealing with Lucy's temper.

PATSY: Lucy has an extremely fierce temper, but she explodes and then it's finished. I explode with more difficulty—which is to say, less often—but then I tend to pout. I've learned to be better about that from Lucy.

LUCY: Patsy has learned to stand up to me and my temper. She's no pushover.

PATSY: Well, I had pretty good training, because my mother was a yeller and had a fierce temper, so although I find Lucy's temper very scary, I have learned by experience with her that it doesn't mean she hates me. It just means there's a temporary explosion.

I asked what kinds of things Lucy blew up over, and Lucy was off and running about something that hasn't changed over the years of her relationship with Patsy. She doesn't think that Patsy is tidy enough.

LUCY: She's a slob. Capital *S,* capital *L,* capital *O,* capital *B.*

PATSY: I'm not a slob. I'm just a pack rat. I never throw anything away.

LUCY: That's the way it is. I really become infuriated by things like, we can't clear the mud room out. She keeps promising to get rid of things, like canceled checks from 1968. When we built Patsy's new music studio, I got her old one, and it's still full of her things, which she's never cleared out. So after being pissed off enough, I finally have to let go, because it doesn't do any good. I could die, and it wouldn't help. Yet with other things, she's great.

Some of the changes in the relationships of the forty couples have come in response to shifting circumstances beyond the relationship—like the illness of loved ones, which caused enormous upheaval for Lee and Catherine, or the arrival of a new child, which dramatically changed Chris and Sherri's lives. Judy faced months of depression after she left both a job and friends she loved in order to accommodate Bev's advancing career. But now that she's gotten used to changing cities every few years, she's looking forward to packing up and moving on to the next place.

JUDY: I tell Bev to listen to her voicemail all the time in the hope that she's gotten a call about a transfer. I have this desire to ramble on, to see more. I don't know where it comes from, but now I don't want to settle down.

When I was young, I imagined that when you reached adulthood, you were done with all the upheaval and constant change that made childhood such a challenge. Once you were a grown-up, you simply lived until you died. And when I was old enough to think about having a relationship, I assumed it was the same for couple life.

When I told Lucy and Patsy that I assumed most young people believe that you reach a plateau in a relationship where things stop changing, they had a good laugh.

PATSY: Forget it, young people!

LUCY: Young people should assume that it never stays the same. It's never the same.

PATSY: And that's what makes it possible to go on for twenty, thirty years. If it stays the same, who the fuck needs it? I mean, it gets boring!

Speaking of change, I suspect that Patsy never used the F-word before she met Lucy.

Although a few of the couples I met would have preferred a little less change than they've had to endure, not one of the couples I met told me that their lives together had been anything close to boring.

SEVENTEEN

Out in the World

O N A FLIGHT from Salt Lake City to St. Louis, I was reminded what an adventure it can be for a gay person traveling beyond the safe precincts of home. We were seated three across, and I was sandwiched between two women, both about my age. The woman to my left was on her way to her twentieth high school reunion. She was a nurse and the mother of five. This was her first trip on her own in thirteen years, and she was eager to talk.

The conversation moved from children to work to why I was on this particular flight—I was heading from one interview for this book to another—to my other books to gay civil rights to AIDS. It wasn't until shortly before landing that the woman to my right, who had been reading a book throughout the trip, interrupted our conversation to ask me what my books were about. I was flattered by her interest, and I mentioned a couple of the titles and explained that I wrote primarily on gay and lesbian issues.

The woman paused for a moment before asking if I'd ever heard of Focus on the Family. My heart sank. The Focus on the Family program that I'd listened to while driving through Utah was very fresh in my memory. Cautiously, I said that yes, I had heard of the organization. Then my seatmate told me that Focus on the Family had classes for people like me. I could only imagine. "It doesn't work for everybody," she said, "but some people have been helped to turn away from homosexuality." I thought to myself, Of course! Why wouldn't I want to give up my happy relationship and my successful career for a life of loneliness and misery? I wondered if I'd have to forsake my Jewish heritage as well.

I'm normally polite when confronted by the kind of ignorance displayed by this woman. Anger doesn't usually do any good in a moment like this, but I was deeply offended by her presumptuous-ness and the stupidity of her suggestion. So in the iciest tones I could muster, I said that I had no interest in changing and no interest in talking to her any further. She then said, "But I care about you." Now my heart was pounding with rage. I told her that she had no idea who I was and that it was a good thing our plane was landing because I couldn't stand sitting next to her for another minute. I left the plane feeling both angry and guilty—angry that someone would have the chutzpah to presume that she knew what was best for me, and guilty because I'd been so rude.

For the couples I interviewed, the experience of being a same-gen-der couple in an overwhelmingly heterosexual world comes with its own set of challenges, even for those who are comfortably out of the closet in all aspects of their lives. For example, introductions alone can be a minefield, because there's no one word that works as well as "husband" or "wife" to describe one's beloved. So the couples most often wind up using different words depending on the circumstance. That's what Brian and Curt do.

BRIAN: In a formal setting I use the word "partner" to introduce Curt. I hate it, because it suggests that I'm in business with Curt, but I use it anyway. There was a period when we were introducing each other as "significant other."

CURT: I never said "significant other." Maybe, "my domestic partner." But I'm back to "boyfriend." I kind of like that the most.

BRIAN: I say "lover" sometimes, but I'm always uncomfortable using it because of the sexual connotations. But if I'm talking to another gay man, I'm perfectly comfortable using it, because he'll understand exactly what I'm talking about.

Of all the words people told me they have used to introduce each other—"friend," "spouse," "significant other," "companion," "lover," "husband," "wife," "the little woman"—"partner" seems to be the choice of the moment. Kevin, of Kevin and Paul, reserves the word "partner" for "straight people we've not met before." I tend to use "partner" in those circumstances, as well. It's a relatively neutral word that lets people think what they like and leaves me feeling the least exposed—although, like Brian, I don't like it, because it always makes me feel as if I'm not being entirely truthful or that I'm somehow devaluing the significance of my relationship with a man who is far more than my "partner."

For the handful of older couples I interviewed, who started their relationships in a world very different from the one in which we now live, introducing a significant other as one's partner, in all but the most private settings, was unthinkable, no matter what word was used. And great effort was made to keep one's homosexuality and the relationship hidden.

John and Dick met in New York City in 1954, outside a gay bar next door to the St. Regis Hotel. John was thirty-one, and no stranger to gay life. Dick, a thirty-nine-year-old executive with a multinational company, was in town on business; he had had virtually no experience with homosexuality. They've been together ever since.

During the first year and a half of their relationship, John and Dick enjoyed a comfortable and relatively open life in New York City—although, as Dick explained to me, they maintained separate bedrooms, "so there wouldn't be a question." But after Dick was transferred to Brazil, he and John found their new life to be very different. They knew no one gay in Brazil and felt compelled to bring female dates to social functions to make certain that no one found them out. They also double-dated, never sharing with their dates the nature of their relationship.

For most of the twenty-two years John and Dick spent in South America, they managed quite well to keep their public and private lives separate. They did their best to cope with the isolation they often felt, and they even survived an accusation by one of Dick's colleagues that Dick was gay and in a relationship with John. John remembers one incident as perhaps the worst of their time abroad. One night, John found himself at home alone with a date who decided she was going to stay over.

JOHN: I told her that I had syphilis, and that there was nothing else I could do. She was furious with me, and wanted to know who gave it to me. I told her that I didn't know, and that seemed to satisfy her. And luckily she didn't persist, but still, she stayed all night. I remember lying there in bed with this girl and thinking, If Dick walks through the door and finds me with this girl, this is going to be the end of our relationship. I won't have the chance to explain to him that I told her that I had syphilis.

Fortunately, Dick was in Argentina, and stayed a day longer than expected. By the time Dick came home the next afternoon, John's date was long gone.

Gordon and Jay also remember a time when bringing female dates to social occasions was standard operating procedure.

GORDON: I was a set designer for the Baltimore Opera, and I was invited to one of the big openings. So there was a huge party, and we would not have thought of going to that party together without bringing dates. It would not have occurred to us. We had very dear friends, Angela and Ann, who came to Baltimore to go with us to this fabulous party. The girls were called "arm pieces," "window dressing." And of course, they knew we were gay.
JAY: This is how things were done. You didn't question it.

For the past twenty years, Gordon and Jay have gone to social gatherings, as well as family events and weddings, as a couple. But there are still limits to what they feel comfortable doing.

GORDON: We go together and we sit together, but we don't dance together, unless it's a gay ball.

For Anyda and Muriel, despite their travels together on World Bank trips, keeping their homosexuality secret was a given.

ANYDA: It wasn't something that you thought you could acknowledge. It was something to be ashamed of. You might feel personally that it was the right thing for you to do, but you couldn't explain it publicly to somebody else. You had to defend yourself, as a matter of fact, if anybody accused you of something.

Up until ten years ago, whenever Muriel and Anyda entertained friends on their screened-in front porch, Muriel would remind a particularly boisterous friend to keep her voice down.

MURIEL: She had a voice that carried, and whenever she said the word "lesbian," I told her, "Shush." I was always reluctant for the word "lesbian" to be used in public, so we developed this business of using "shush" instead of "lesbian," like, "Do you think she's a shush?"

In my travels, I've heard a lot of odd words used in place of "gay" or "lesbian," everything from "tribal" to "dixie." But I had never heard of a "shush" before.

In 1993, Anyda and Muriel went well beyond using the word "lesbian" in public. Anyda was profiled in Delaware's main newspaper, the *News Journal*. The article featured a large photograph of Anyda on the front page of the second section and discussed her books as well as her relationship with Muriel.

ANYDA: If you're in the *News Journal,* everybody knows it. It's not made any difference. The senior warden at our church said, "How are your books selling?" And one of the women from church met me in the aisle of the supermarket and said, "I saw your picture in the paper." I was not surprised, but Muriel was very uneasy. She didn't know how these churchgoing people were going to react. These are conservative people, but they're not unsophisticated. They just accept it. After all, we're the same people as we were.

MURIEL: It was no different at all. As a matter of fact, the couple who were the official greeters outside the church the first Sunday after the article appeared were very cordial. They had to greet us because they were the official greeters, but I was expecting coolness.

ANYDA: Since then, life has been as perfectly calm as it always is. As a matter of fact, one of the members of our church was here last Saturday. This time of year, on Saturday afternoons at five o'clock, we have happy hour and an open house. We've got ten or twelve people on the porch here. They are a mix of gay and straight. Some of them are the oldest and most respectable people in town. And this woman from the church was there, too. She lives just down the street. She knows all about us.

MURIEL: I still don't like to hear the word "lesbian." Basically, I don't like to be labeled anything.

Chris, of Chris and Sherri, never had to wonder whether people were going to label her, because they always did.

CHRIS: I look just like my dad, so people automatically assume that I'm gay. People won't look you in the eye, and they won't talk to you. They act like you're invisible.

With her son, Taylor, in tow, Chris finds that people treat her very differently, and she and Sherri never have to question whether people can tell they're a couple, because Taylor takes care of that.

CHRIS: With Taylor, it's totally different. Same clerk at the grocery store: "Hi, how are you doing? How is he? Look how big he's getting!" It's pretty amazing but a little depressing that people have such preconceived ideas of what you're like. Then you add a child, stir twice, and you're totally different. So we're actually more accepted now. We go places, and Taylor helps us all the time, because he calls us "Mommy-Momma," as if it were one word. So, you'll be sitting in the children's section of Burger King and he'll totally out you, because he goes, "Mommy-Momma, come look! Mommy-Momma, come look!"

SHERRI: Every once in a while you get an odd glance, but for the most part no one seems to care.

Most of the couples I talked to censor themselves in public in some way. For example, Jim and Martin are not affectionate in public, and kiss only in their own house. Judy and Bev hate that they're not able to be physical in ways that feel natural.

BEV: It's a miserable life in that you can't walk hand in hand as you stroll, window-shopping. And I can't put my arm around Judy in a movie theater. And I can't reach out and touch her when she's cute when we're eating at a restaurant. That's what's sad. But that's the only disadvantage of being a gay couple. Otherwise I think that two women together are perfect.

When Keith and Kenneth,* who live in a leafy suburban neighborhood outside Hartford, Connecticut, leave their house for work, they don't hesitate to kiss each other goodbye while standing in their driveway, but they didn't start out being that public. Keith is thirty-four, and Kenneth is thirty-nine. Both have corporate jobs, and they've been a couple for twelve years.

KENNETH: We started at the top of the driveway, and we've moved progressively down the driveway toward the sidewalk.

KEITH: And we don't care who's coming by or who's seen us. So that's kind of a milestone for us.

KENNETH: Pretty soon, we're gonna be making out at Starbucks in the center of town.

To Keith and Kenneth, it's important that people know they're gay and in a relationship, but when the issue comes up, they don't always explain the way things are. Kenneth was at the hospital where he's a baby-holding volunteer, when a nurse he'd never met before asked, "So, are you married?"

KENNETH: I said, "No, not technically, but I've been in a relationship with a man for twelve years, so I feel very married." And she said, "Oh, okay," and then went on with a conversation she was having with someone else. This wasn't someone I knew and not anyone who was important to me. You always have to choose: Do I have the energy to come out to people I don't care about, or don't know, just to educate them? Or do I just want to eliminate the potential for an uncomfortable moment and answer, "No, I'm not married." I remember in grad school, I was giving a presentation with a group of people, and the woman next to me said, "Why is your ring on your right hand?" And I wanted to say, "Because I'm gay and in a relationship." But I just didn't have the energy or the courage to deal with it right then, and I said, "Well, it's a family heirloom." The older I get, the more likely I am to say, "I'm gay. Get it, okay?"

* Not their real names.

KEITH: We feel that we're constantly put in positions where we have to make choices.

KENNETH: I keep assuming that some people are gonna be smart enough to think, Oh, a man with a wedding ring on the right hand. That must mean he's gay. It's a burden. You know, straight people never have to explain the way they are. So you're always faced with choosing whether to open this potential can of worms. How will they feel? And are they fundamentalist Christians? When I was younger, I didn't have the courage. Now I have the courage and I just don't have the energy.

KEITH: There are certain days when it's great to be an educator, and there are certain days when you want to be left alone.

Keith and Kenneth recently went to Keith's family reunion, and when it came time for family pictures, the photographer couldn't quite figure out the family relationships.

KEITH: Basically he told us to "put yourselves however you go together." And we did, but then he didn't like it. And he was trying to move us all around, because he couldn't get it through his head that we were a couple. So he asked me, "Who's your wife?"

KENNETH: And Keith patted me on the shoulder and said, "He is."

KEITH: With my father and mother standing right there!

Even if you say nothing to anyone about your relationship, don't wear rings, never kiss while standing in the driveway, avoid all newspaper interviews, act straight (whatever that's supposed to mean), and even take opposite-gender dates to public events, there's no guarantee that while shopping at the grocery or sitting at a restaurant someone won't mistake you and your partner for brothers or sisters, which could easily lead to a coming-out conversation. As I noted earlier, being mistaken for siblings is something that's happened to a lot of the couples I interviewed, even those who look nothing alike.

Kevin and Paul, who could scarcely pass for distant cousins, have often been mistaken for brothers, especially when they're in Ohio visiting Paul's mother. Sometimes the confusion is understandable, since Paul's mother usually introduces them as "her boys." But for whatever reason they're asked, "Are you two brothers?," their response depends on the circumstances.

PAUL: Sometimes we say yes.
KEVIN: It's not always worth it.
PAUL: Depends on whether you're caught off guard or not.
KEVIN: We are always aware of our environment and of who we're with. We're certainly not going to embarrass Mom back in Ohio. If somebody thinks we're brothers, fine. It's no skin off our backs. We're not that type of an activist that's got to be in front of somebody's face all the time.

Cassandra and Anne never get "the sister thing." Cassandra is black and Anne is white, and they've found that it's sometimes hard to get people to recognize that they're even together, let alone a couple.

CASSANDRA: It happens all the time. For example, we go into a store, and we're obviously shopping together. We go up to pay for something, and I might have something and Anne might have something.
ANNE: We put it all down on the counter and then they'll look at us—
CASSANDRA: And they'll separate our things. Then we'll have to say, "This is together." They refuse to see the relationship, like we're two separate entities. And that, I think, is the racial part. It used to make me angry, but I'm just kind of used to it, so it doesn't make me angry anymore.

Race also figures into how Cassandra and Anne are treated at restaurants where they're not regulars.

ANNE: If we go out to dinner and we have a white waiter or waitress who doesn't know us, they talk to me and don't even look at Cassandra. And they'll always give me the check.
CASSANDRA: Then I make a point of being the one to hand the check back to the waitress.
ANNE: You know, you try to do a little educating.

Many of the couples have tried to do a little educating. Their one-on-one efforts have ranged from explaining that they're not in fact brothers to setting an example in their community by being out.

Part of the reason Keith and Kenneth chose to live in their suburban neighborhood was to set an example.

KENNETH: We consciously said to each other, "We would like to be role models." We feel, because of how we've chosen to live, that the children who live across the street from us will have grown up seeing that it is perfectly normal for two men who are in a relationship to live together. And when I was a kid, there was nothing even close to that.

Many of the people I interviewed have been involved in the gay-rights effort. Keith started a gay employee group at the company where he works. Cassandra recently testified at public hearings regarding a statewide anti–gay marriage bill, which led to a major newspaper article in which she and Anne were featured. Gordon and Jay, who consider themselves "shirt-and-tie activists," also testified at public hearings regarding a statewide gay-rights bill, and they are consistent fund-raisers for local and national gay organizations. Kevin and Paul founded a gay Republican group in their community in 1977. John and Dick are major contributors to gay-rights organizations. Irene, of Irene and Molly, is president of her local support group for Mormon parents of gays and lesbians. And until recently, Lee and Catherine were very involved in an organization for gay and lesbian veterans.

For Stewart and Stanley, their volunteer work for gay groups and AIDS organizations has been a central and binding force in their relationship, occupying vast amounts of time and energy. It all started in 1983, when Stewart signed up to volunteer with a new organization called Gay Friends and Neighbors in Queens.

STEWART: Basically, it was a social group. Then we were invited to come to the membership meeting. Then I went to their steering committee. And then the communication committee chair was vacant. Then we created a chair of the steering committee, and guess who got elected to that position? Me.

Three years later, Stewart became a founding director of a countywide AIDS center, and he's been a very active board member since. Stanley was a volunteer at the same organization, helping to take care of people with AIDS. But these examples only scratch the surface of Stewart and Stanley's extensive volunteer work, work that's earned Stanley a nickname.

STANLEY: I'm known as "the Raffle Queen."
STEWART: When you want to sell raffles, give them to Stanley.

I asked Stewart and Stanley what impact their volunteer work has had on their relationship.

STEWART: I think it's helped.
STANLEY: One thing I have to say about this: If I didn't belong to the same groups as Stewart did, I'd never see him. As it is, I have to plan meals to make sure he can have a quick dinner before running to a meeting.

Although Stewart and Stanley are perfectly comfortable having very public roles in the local gay community, Stewart's mother is uneasy with her son's increasingly high profile.

STEWART: She always tells me she doesn't want me to be in *The New York Times.*

EIGHTEEN

Aging

GROWING OLDER can be wonderfully liberating, as well as alarming and terrifying. I've seen this firsthand with loved ones, and it was confirmed for me in my conversations with the couples who are well into middle age and beyond. Fifteen of the eighty people I interviewed are sixty or older. Of these fifteen, three are in their seventies and three are in their eighties. Their experiences of growing older have probably been much the same as for any heterosexual person, but some things were unique.

For four of the oldest people, Anyda and Muriel and John and Dick, retirement certainly brought freedom from the responsibilities of their jobs, but it also meant never having to worry again about being fired because they were gay. Anyda chose to write the novels she'd always dreamed of, and she and Muriel embarked on a new joint venture, distributing Anyda's novels through their own publishing company.

John supported Dick in taking early retirement, in large part so that they could be free from the pressure of having to hide their relationship. John's limited role in a large family business had always given him the freedom to go wherever Dick went, and once Dick retired, the two men divided their time between an apartment in

San Francisco and a rental house on eastern Long Island. In 1990, when Dick was seventy, and John sixty-two, they built their dream house on the edge of a Long Island potato field, just a few blocks from the ocean. They've lived there full-time ever since.

In addition to the usual financial and health concerns all couples face as they grow older, the gay and lesbian couples I interviewed have had to plan for their remaining years without the legal and financial protections that heterosexual married couples take for granted. For Jim and Martin, as I've mentioned, that's meant having to create a special nest egg for when one of them dies, because they can't inherit each other's pensions and they depend on both their pensions to cover costs.

All the older couples I interviewed have filed the legal documents that can best protect them in the absence of legal marriage, including wills and durable powers of attorney. But as Muriel noted, she worries about her and Anyda's not having the force of a marriage license when it comes to gaining access to each other in a medical emergency.

Age brings with it all the expected physical changes, from a decline in sex drive to a decrease in energy. The age-related change mentioned most frequently in my interviews was menopause. And unlike in an opposite-gender couple, in a same-gender relationship, menopause—or prostate trouble, for the men—is something a partner can relate to all too well.

Many of the women told me how being in a same-gender relationship made the experience of menopause easier for them than they imagined it was for heterosexual married women, because their partners could better understand what they were going through. Rita, of Marta and Rita, the two Cuban women who met at a feminist vegetarian restaurant—"a place we would avoid like the plague now"—had just returned from the gynecologist when I arrived to interview her and Marta. Rita is fifty and perimenopausal, and Marta, who is thirty-five, is "going through sympathy menopause." Rita has heard plenty at work from her male colleagues about their menopausal wives. I asked Rita if having a woman as a partner would make it easier for her.

RITA: I hope to God, yes. I see the guys at work and how they joke about their wives. In this age of enlightenment, it's still amazing how some of the guys are unsympathetic. And then some of them are surprisingly supportive. I think it should be a lot easier with Marta. She's going to go through it, too.

MARTA: It's not like I'm going to give her a hard time about it or anything. I can't imagine it.

For Ruth and Zenobia, menopause has led to unexpected upheaval in their relationship. Ruth now has her own bedroom in what used to be the couple's library.

RUTH: We moved to separate bedrooms for physical reasons. As Zenobia began to go through the change of life, she was just hot, sweating, all the time.

ZENOBIA: I understood why Ruthie wanted separate beds. I get real wet sometimes and I want to pull up all the covers, and she can't take that.

RUTH: I'm a real warm-blooded person to start with. I sleep totally in the nude—winter, summer, spring, or fall—and I never use a blanket, just a sheet. There may be a quilt on my bed, but that's for decoration. And Zee is forever freezing. You see her sitting here? Look at her! In a jogging suit and a sweater!

Clearly the issue of hot versus cold had come up for Ruth and Zenobia before Zenobia began menopause, but the night sweats brought things to a head. And there was another reason behind Ruth's desire for separate beds. She has an arthritic hip, which has grown increasingly painful in recent years.

RUTH: When you're really, really in pain, you don't want folks up against your butt all the time. Because even being gentle, you just roll over and accidentally touch that hip, and I could see stars!

ZENOBIA: But Ruthie still sleeps with me a lot. Sometimes she'll just come in, or I'll say, "You're welcome to spend the night."

Many of the older people have begun facing age-related health problems, from high blood pressure and diabetes to osteoporosis and severe arthritis. During our interview, Muriel had two canes at her side, without which she's unable to go anywhere. A disintegrating hip makes walking even short distances extremely painful, and emphysema precludes hip replacement surgery. Two of the men—Martin, of Jim and Martin, and Dick, of John and Dick—have had surgery for prostate cancer. Dick had his surgery in 1990, and the cancer recently returned, spreading to his bones. He's no longer able to work in the luxuriant gardens he planted on the land surrounding his and John's house, but he still takes pleasure in telling the gardener what to do.

The limitations brought on by age and ill health were not restricted to the oldest of the couples. Marjorie and Marian are only in their forties, but their work is labor-intensive, and they have had to adjust their plans as they've faced the toll that nearly two decades of dairy farming has taken on their bodies.

MARIAN: We had decided we would keep our herd of dairy cows until I was fifty-five. Then at one point we decided that maybe fifty would be a better age. And then, when we were looking at a little less than three more years until my fiftieth birthday, we figured out how many more milkings we would have to do, and it came out to 950 more. And then multiply that by fifty cows at four-thirty in the morning.

MARJORIE: We thought, Oh my God! That's when we decided to sell the herd.

By this point, Marian had already had a serious back injury from falling off a truck while moving bales of hay.

MARIAN: When you first get up from an injury like that, you don't think much of it. You think you'll keep going. But in the days that followed, I could tell it was really bad. When we were milking the cows, I can remember kneeling in between them to milk them, and having to grab on to them to pull myself up. I actually took a couple of milkings off after that, but then Marjorie's back started hurting because she was doing so much. And I'd hurt myself other times, falling off things. My back is the weak link here. So I was getting nervous because I was getting older. And we were just exhausted all the time. We thought if we had just a few cows, we could make cheese and stop shipping milk.

MARJORIE: So we kept only our favorites.

MARIAN: We had one family that was a favorite of ours.

MARJORIE: We kept Orbit and Lollipop from that family. And Lassie from another family.

MARIAN: Now we just milk four cows, and we have a bunch of young ones. It's taken a lot of the physical trauma out of living.

MARJORIE: Our long-range view of the farm had been to make milk and cheese in the winter and to garden in the summer. That's what we have now. We just got there a little sooner than we'd planned.

Aside from the not insignificant disadvantages the older couples told me about, including the lack of the legal and financial protections that heterosexual marriage provides, the gay couples' experiences of growing old turned out to be much the same as straight couples'. For example, Jim and Martin were just as scared by Martin's prostate cancer diagnosis as any other couple would be. Fortunately for them, because their doctor knows them as a couple, Jim had no fear of being prevented from seeing Martin at the hospital. He was given the same access and respect as any other lifelong spouse of a patient.

MARTIN: Our doctor is just great, but you feel real funny when you get that kind of news, because you don't want to break down like a fool when he's telling you all this stuff, you know. So, when I got out to the car and told Jimmy . . .

JIM: We both cried.

MARTIN: We both cried.

JIM: I'd be walking around the house and I'd start crying, you know. I couldn't believe that this could happen to us.

MARTIN: And then, when we thought it was all gone, it came back two years ago. I had radiation to treat it.

Last year, Martin had a mild stroke and was hospitalized for a week. Happily, he recovered completely in a matter of days.

MARTIN: But now I have to go to the doctor once or twice a month for him to draw blood and check my medications and make sure everything's going all right. It's hell getting old, you know!

One thing Martin is grateful for is having had Jim there with him through his recent illnesses.

MARTIN: It's nice to have someone with you when you're sick. Jimmy didn't cook any better than he ever did, but he managed very well. He helped me get better, fast. I don't know what the hell I'd do without him. I'd be lost. I think all people who have been together a long time feel that way. Jimmy's just wonderful. He's always kind, never nasty, always loving. He'd do anything for me.

NINETEEN

Loss

I HAD NO IDEA what tender territory I'd strayed into when I asked Muriel how she knows that Anyda loves her. It was a question that I asked all the couples, but this time I unintentionally struck a terribly painful nerve. Muriel stared at me wide-eyed, and her face flushed. She struggled to get off the sofa and out of the presence of a virtual stranger before the tears came. Both Muriel and Anyda are very private about their emotions, in the way that people of their generation and background often are. But Muriel's bad hip prevented any quick getaway, and after a brief struggle she sank back into the sofa. Her already rheumy eyes, which were magnified behind thick glasses, welled up, and as the tears spilled down her cheeks she buried her head in her hands. She sobbed silently, her heaving shoulders the only evidence of the painful emotions I'd inadvertently unleashed.

There was no way I could have known that just the week before, Anyda had been hospitalized for a flare-up of a serious heart problem, an episode that Muriel feared would leave her without the most important person in her life, the woman she not only loved but on whom she now depended so heavily.

As Muriel regained her composure, I offered her a tissue. I asked if I could get her a glass of water, but she shook her head no and tried again to get up. Anyda turned to Muriel, placed her hand on her leg, and spoke with great tenderness.

ANYDA: Sweetie, you want some help?

Muriel again shook her head no, and settled back into the sofa. Anyda turned to face me. She spoke slowly, with just a hint of emotion in her voice.

ANYDA: There's so much that goes on in fifty years. Asking this question . . . So much goes on that you can't possibly convey.

I ask Anyda what it means to her to have been with Muriel for nearly a half century.

ANYDA: Maybe I can say it negatively. I can't understand people who have been together for a large number of years suddenly breaking up. This I can't understand, unless it's a question of two bodies in one house without real communication. If there's real communication, you become part of each other. This goes for heterosexuals as well as homosexuals. And the loss of one means the loss of life for the other.

We have talked about this in the context of the fact that we both have very serious physical problems, and we're faced with the idea that one of us is going to presumably be a survivor, unless we both get killed in a car wreck or something. We have a very good doctor who understands this situation, so she's trying to keep us both alive.

Muriel listens attentively but is still unable to speak. I ask Anyda if they've ever imagined life without each other.

ANYDA: It's really not comprehensible. You can stop and think, Well, if Muriel wasn't here, I wouldn't be doing this. Something like that. But it's just something that's got to come about. There's nothing we can do about it. I know there would be many things that I would not bother to do if there wasn't Muriel, such as taking care of myself. I don't know that I'd make sure to take my medicine. I have a temperament that tends to let things take their course.

By this point, I feel that I've asked Muriel and Anyda more than enough about what is obviously a very painful subject, and we move on.

For John and Dick, the prospect of loss has become very real since the recent return of Dick's prostate cancer. At the time I met him and John, Dick was undergoing radiation treatments, and while he had no trouble getting around, and even drove us all to lunch, he depends on John to handle all the day-to-day responsibilities. John is well aware that Dick would not be able to live on his own.

JOHN: I worry about the fact that if I were to die first, I wouldn't be here to take care of Dick. I want security for him, so I've made arrangements with our lawyer to make certain Dick would have help here at the house. Everything would be taken care of.

All the older couples have talked about the future and the inevitability of one partner eventually being left behind. For Ruth and Zenobia, the conversation has been oblique. Zenobia doesn't like talking about a future that doesn't include Ruth, but since Ruth is sixty-three—eight years older than Zenobia—Ruth has brought it up from time to time.

ZENOBIA: Ruthie has told me that she wanted me to get somebody else after she's gone.
RUTH: Because she doesn't do well by herself. She's not a loner. I think I'd be fine. I think I'd be okay.

Zenobia is shocked by Ruth's comment that she'd be fine on her own. Ruth quickly reassures Zenobia that she would miss her, that life would not be the same without her. Zenobia looks a little skeptical.

Jim and Martin have made certain that whichever of them lives longer will have enough money to live on, and they've decided to be cremated.

MARTIN: We look at death realistically. We talk about it more often now than we did before, because we worry about the one that's left behind. But the practical things are arranged. There's not gonna be a funeral or any of that stuff. It's cremation, and scatter the ashes out in the ocean.

JIM: My sister lives in Arizona, and Martin and I are both close to her. I told her, "You know, if anything happens to me, I've given Marty instructions to call you after I've been cremated." "Oh," she says, "I don't know if I can handle that. I want to see you lying there at the funeral." I said, "Well, you'll never see me lying there. You would probably look at me and say, 'I saw you when you looked better.' " But she understands. And I also told her, "If anything happens to me, everything goes to Marty. Everything. Nothing goes to you or the kids or anybody." And she said, "Well, I expect that. That's the way it should be." My sister's a wonderful person.

Jim and Martin know that the practical arrangements are the easy part. They struggle with the rest.

MARTIN: It's almost frightening.

JIM: Oh yeah. We worry about if something is going to happen. It's *gonna* happen.

MARTIN: It's inevitable, but we worry about how it's going to be.

JIM: So we just say, "Let's have a martini and cry a little." So we do. We have to face it, just like anybody else does. Everybody else does. We just try to take good care of ourselves, and keep ourselves healthy. Go to the doctor all the time. Martin sees that we eat good—that we have the right foods. And we don't overdrink.

Clarence and Ric have also discussed the prospect of losing each other. For many years, Ric has talked about his fear of being left behind by Clarence, who is fourteen years older than Ric. Clarence, who is a remarkably youthful and robust-looking sixty-three, had always assumed that he would be the first to go. Until recently, he had never even considered the possibility of being the one left behind. He and Ric have been a couple for twenty-one years.

CLARENCE: I've always heard Ric say, "Clarence, if anything happens to you, I don't know how I'm going to go on." But until we talked the other day, I had never shared with him that my feelings were almost identical, that I couldn't imagine how I'd go on without him.

And when I shared it, I couldn't hold back. I just broke down and started crying. It came out like a dam was bursting.

RIC: I had never heard him say it, and I felt overwhelmed. I was full. I didn't cry, but I comforted him and told him that he never had to worry about being alone as long as we're together.

It's not just the older couples who have had to face the prospect of losing a partner. Some of the younger couples, including Brian and Curt, Amy and Jama, and Kevin and Paul, have also had to consider the possibility of a beloved's death.

It was just in the last year, when Stanley had emergency surgery to repair a shattered arm, that Stewart considered the possibility of life without his partner. The surgery wasn't life-threatening, but for Stewart, it raised the possibility for the first time that Stanley could die.

STEWART: It was the only time I thought I would lose him. Even though I knew the surgery itself was not life-threatening, I know how some patients don't come out of the anesthesia. So, it was like, My God, I might lose him, and he's not even worth that much.

STANLEY: Monetarily.

STEWART: It felt like, My God, I don't know how I would go on without him. If anything were to ever happen to him, I'd have to put up a billboard in town to announce that we're not together, because the assumption is that we *have* to be together. If people see one of us, they automatically think, Where is the other one?

Fortunately, the surgery was uneventful, and Stewart's fear of losing Stanley remains abstract, as such fears do even for those couples who know they are likely to experience such a loss sooner rather than later. Nancy and Penny were the exception.

I first met Nancy and Penny in December 1989 at their long-neglected—verging on decrepit—Victorian house in Jamaica Plain, Massachusetts. It was like something out of an old black-and-white movie, with turrets, dimly lit hallways, once-elegant wood floors desperately in need of restoration, beautiful decorative woodwork darkened almost to black by age, and a faded grand staircase that called out for Norma Desmond to descend it. From the dining room where we sat during the interview, I could see into a kitchen that looked as if it had been hit by a hurricane and never rebuilt.

Nancy's wicked wit, Penny's warm and gracious hospitality, and both women's enormous good spirits, brightened the gloomy atmosphere considerably. The house quickly faded into the background as Nancy regaled me with stories of their lives together and her work as a comparatively conservative columnist for the decidedly liberal *Gay Community News*—the newspaper in which Nate and Danny's roommate-wanted ads once appeared. It was Nancy's work as a columnist that first brought her to my attention for a book I was writing on the gay and lesbian civil rights movement. Nancy was then fifty-three; Penny was forty-four.

Well before she met Penny, Nancy was a headstrong tomboy who bucked both her parents and convention.

NANCY: Growing up, I really felt at odds with the world, but I didn't know why. I always felt peculiar. For one thing, I was at odds with my family. I wasn't what they wanted. My mother was a perfect lady. When she had a little girl, she thought, Oh, a little me! Well, I wasn't at all like her. She wanted to dress me in pretty little pink dresses. But I wanted to climb trees. I would put worms in my pockets. I was going to do what I wanted, so there was a lot of fighting. I would defy my parents, and they would beat the shit out of me. I always remained who I was and never felt guilty for anything. I didn't even feel guilty for telling my mother I hated her.

By the time Nancy was in high school, in the early 1950s, she had a growing sense of what made her different. She decided to do a little research as part of a senior-year high school term paper.

NANCY: I narrowed my choices to three topics. I only remember two of them: homosexuality and rabbits. The teacher said, "Rabbits!" So I learned a lot about rabbits. I went to the library and looked up homosexuals anyway. What I found was just horrifying.

At college, Nancy met and married a fellow student. A short time later, in 1954, she fell in love with Valerie, a young woman she met at a convention in New York City of the National Conference of Christians and Jews. The crush was never consummated, and the young woman later married and moved to California. Nancy was heartbroken. Eight years later she met Penny at Hofstra College, on Long Island, where both women attended classes and where Nancy's husband was by then the assistant technical director of the Hofstra Playhouse. Penny was a first-year drama student.

PENNY: I walked into the design room at the drama school with my friend Bill, who was taking me on a tour. He was telling me about how this was where they designed sets for the shows, and suddenly there's this woman who comes in. She and Bill started talking as old friends. She sort of ignored me, and I listened to their conversation. Nancy had come back to Hofstra to study Latin, and she got all involved in explaining to Bill that she'd been reading the textbook in the Advanced Latin class and could not understand why things were pronounced the way they were. And I was standing there thinking, What kind of nut is this?

At some point in the conversation, Nancy noticed Penny, turned toward her, and said, "Who are you?"

NANCY: It was like déjà vu, although Penny and Valerie are totally different physically. Penny was tall and had black hair. She had this dreadful haircut, and she was gawky. She was still a kid. All her clothes were wrong. But like Valerie, she had an extraordinary speaking voice, and she would say the same damned things Valerie said. We fell in love. Oh God, did we ever!

PENNY: While we were standing there in the studio talking, I asked Nancy if she wanted to have a cup of coffee. Well, I tried to have a cup of coffee with her that day, but every time I tried to take a drink of the coffee she'd say something funny, and I'd wind up spitting it everywhere. So that was the beginning.

Nancy and Penny began seeing a lot of each other, and their unspoken courtship was under way. Three years passed before a word was said about the relationship that was developing between them. Then one night at dinner in Nancy's house, Penny asked a question.

PENNY: All I said to Nancy was "What do you want of me?" By this point I had realized that Nancy wanted more of me and I wanted more of her, but I didn't have the lingo for it. Now, Nancy, being

Nancy, gave me a long answer. In our conversation, we began making sense of what was going on, and that's when I told Nancy that I loved her.

NANCY: And I said, "You're crazy! You don't know what you're talking about! This is not what your mother had in mind." She kept looking at me, smiling, and saying, "I love you." I told her, "I don't believe it. It's puppy love. You'll get over it."

PENNY: She thought I would change my mind, and she tried to keep me at arm's length. But we still met constantly and talked, and she read poetry to me and we'd talk about it. And she introduced me to Edna St. Vincent Millay. We were both English majors, so we had all of that world of things to think and talk about. We really enjoyed hours and hours of that.

By today's standards, Nancy and Penny's physical relationship progressed at a snail's pace. Then one night, more than three years after Nancy and Penny met (by this time, Nancy and her husband had agreed to be friends and roommates), the two women were sitting at Nancy's kitchen table, talking, and Nancy got up to go into another room. Before she left, she kissed Penny's forehead.

PENNY: That was like a bolt of electricity. I think people live in an age that is so sexually explicit and almost without differentiation of moments of courtship that they lose so much because everything is so fast. It's not savored.

Obviously at some point we made love, which was very lovely. And Nan, being Nan and very much a person of ceremony, afterwards read the Song of Solomon to me. It was a way of bringing it from a moment of personal time into a context of saying, We are part of this very long tradition of what love means. So it was very beautiful.

From then on, Nancy and Penny were as committed as two people could be. Penny's career as an academic supported them both; Nancy did personal writing and in 1971 became involved in the gay-rights movement in Toronto, where Penny was working on her Ph.D. They both joined the Community Homophile Association of Toronto (CHAT). Penny became the program chairman and Nancy was the vice president, but the experience proved frustrating for them both.

NANCY: CHAT was politically correct, and Penny and I weren't, which really made us the radicals—we were so different from what we were surrounded by. I remember the women didn't want anybody to be a hostess, and Penny would always try to round up a tray of cookies when there was a meeting. They thought that was terrible. But if no one is supposed to do that, who's going to pass the god-damned cookies? Another time, at a meeting, we had broken up into small discussion groups of ten or twelve people. We were talking, and somebody said to me, "You can't talk! You can't use proper English, because that's part of the Establishment!" I said, "What should we do, sit here and grunt?"

Despite their frustrations, Nancy and Penny remained involved with CHAT until 1975, when they moved to Boston, where Penny had landed a job teaching at Northeastern University. A year later, Nancy began volunteering at the *Gay Community News*. It was also then that she was diagnosed with breast cancer. She had gone to her doctor for a regular visit, and the doctor found a lump on Nancy's breast. A modified radical mastectomy followed, but the prognosis was not promising.

PENNY: I never told Nancy that I had talked to the surgeon. And he said, "Well, given where we found the cells, it could be five years. But in my clinical experience, I would say she has a better chance than that." I never told her that. It wasn't important for Nan to know that. It wasn't important for us to think about anything but the second part of that sentence—"In my clinical experience, she has a better chance than that." That's all that was really important. I was not about to lose her, not in my opinion.

I asked Penny what it was about the relationship that made losing Nancy so unimaginable.

PENNY: Well, it's hard to imagine not breathing, and that's what it would be. She was that critical to everything. What can I tell you? I can't talk about Nancy as if she was something outside of me.

Three major surgeries followed over the next several years as the cancer spread to Nancy's bones. And because Nan was Nan, she named her first two scars. One was Oscar—"because it was 'our scar' "—and the scar from when she had her ovaries removed was Emmy, Penny explains, "because it was a girl kind of scar, as opposed to the Oscar."

Nancy and Penny both lived with the expectation that every medical crisis could be overcome, and for twenty-three years after Nancy's initial diagnosis, despite setbacks and increasingly poor health, Nancy hung on and lived life with great enthusiasm. Penny said she never once felt limited by Nancy's illness.

PENNY: Well, you see, we were very, very odd people. What was a delight all through our years was sitting and talking to each other. I didn't need to do anything else. She didn't need to do anything else. We often joked that we were two girls living one life. We were happy that way. It wasn't a denial of anything. I loved to talk to her, and she loved to talk to me. And don't think that Nancy was just passionate in her opinions. Let her not be underestimated in any regard. We were so content just being ourselves together. Not that Nancy didn't love having other people around. She loved an audience.

That Nancy loved an audience I knew from my afternoon with her and Penny at their dining room table. Nancy wasn't visibly ill when I met her, though she was alarmingly pale. But I had no idea at the time that she had already been battling cancer for a dozen years.

Beginning in 1994, the cancer could no longer be controlled, and Nancy became increasingly ill. Stairs became impossible for her, so Penny made a bedroom for her on the first floor of their house. When Nancy couldn't walk anymore, they bought a wheelchair. But Penny refused to give in to the thought that Nancy might die, even when the cancer spread to the lining of her brain. The doctor told Penny that Nancy had only a few months.

PENNY: Of course, I didn't tell anyone that. I did not want people looking at Nancy that way. I did not want them thinking she was dying. And I was not convinced that the doctors were any more right this time than they had been before. I said, "Tough tamales.

That's your diagnosis. What do you know about Nancy? You know bloody little about her. She's got too much fight in her." But she was in a lot of pain. And this attack on the brain was pretty stinky.

Penny and Nancy never talked explicitly about the possibility of death. Penny found out later that Nancy had confided in one of their friends; she had expressed how worried she was about Penny and how hard it would be for her to deal with Nancy's death.

Penny brought Nancy home from the hospital, and Nancy's health continued to decline. Only in the last week of Nancy's life did Penny begin to acknowledge that the end was near. Penny was convinced by Nancy's doctor to allow a person from the local hospice organization to visit with her beloved.

PENNY: The hospice people were told they could come into the house so long as not one of them said "hospice." I said, "Don't you dare walk in here thinking this woman is dying. She's living. Don't you do that, and don't you say 'hospice' in front of her." Well, I put the fear of God in most of them. But one of them, a jackass nurse, comes in and sits down and starts reading Nancy this list of things that were likely to happen, like losing blood or losing control of your bowels. I was so angry, because it upset Nancy.

Despite Penny's disdain for the hospice nurses, she allowed them to come by each day.

PENNY: They had sort of put it in my head that I might not be able to do something if, at the last minute, Nancy needed something and there wasn't someone here who knew more than I about these things.

On Nancy's last night, a hospice nurse came by the house, assuming she was there to relieve Penny's bedside vigil. She had no way of knowing that she'd be spending the night in the kitchen.

PENNY: The hospice nurse thought she was going to sit at Nan's bedside. I took a comfortable chair, put it in the kitchen, and said, "Please stay in here. If I need you, I will call you." I didn't want anyone near Nan. They were looking at her as a patient. This was the treasure of my life. I knew that I knew how to talk to her and be with her. And I couldn't trust these people. So I sat with her and I read to her. I read the Psalms to her. I read various portions of the

Bible to her, and I read her the Song of Solomon, as she had read it to me that first night after we made love.

Earlier in the day Nancy had said very quietly, "Let me go." And I said what I always said: "Yes, honey, whatever you want." So I guess she was saying that it's okay, we have to do this. This was not what I wanted to hear. She was quiet the rest of the day, and that night I just kept talking to her. I had Christopher Robin, our dog, sit with her, and I held Nancy's hand. And she was very peaceful. She had been quiet for a long time. Her breathing got labored, and then she just stopped breathing. So after all those years of struggle, it was very, very quiet.

It's the summer of 1997, more than a year since Nancy's death, and Penny and I are sitting in the dining room of a stunningly renovated grand Victorian home. I had to double-check the address as I stood in front of the place, because I was looking for the ruin I knew, not a perfectly restored nineteenth-century gem.

My knock at the door was met with the excited barking of Nancy and Penny's now very old and blind thirty-pound mutt, Christopher Robin, and a new toy poodle, Cricket, that Nancy had insisted Penny buy just months before her death. Cricket weighs all of three and a half pounds, and she has a tiny pink bow on her head.

Penny opened the door, and other than a head of unruly hair that was now more gray than black, she looked much the same as she had in 1989. We greeted each other with warm hugs, and Penny walked me into the front hall. It was astonishing. Every wood surface had been stripped and refinished. The staircase sparkled. The intricately patterned floor shone like glass, and the walls were painted in vibrant colors, all selected by Penny after much agonizing.

As Penny gave me the tour, she explained that renovating the house has kept her going during the fourteen months since Nancy's death.

PENNY: I was crying a lot, a lot, a lot, and walking around and shaking my head and just wondering how I was going to go on without the person on whom I spent all of my emotional and physical energy. It was unreal. I had my friends there for me when I needed them, but nothing helped. Then I realized that a number of things were going to have to happen. Nancy and I had talked about renovating the house. She was never strong enough to do it, and we were not going to waste time doing stuff when there was life to live and other things that were more important. So *now* I would renovate the house. I also decided to begin doing volunteer work. I said to myself, I am no longer a married person. I'm Nancy's widow, but I have been given so much. I have been loved as a child and as a woman. I have been so very, very lucky. So I started working at a home for the homeless. I can't help people on a one-on-one basis yet, but I chop vegetables.

We make our way up to the second floor, to Nancy and Penny's bedroom. The dresser mirror is decorated with pictures of Nancy, and there's a bronze container adorned with swimming dolphins. I ask Penny what this is.

PENNY: Fifteen or twenty years ago, Nancy started saying that she didn't want to be buried, that she wanted to have her ashes stay with me. She thought it was disgusting to be buried. I was really uncomfortable with the whole idea, but I followed Nancy's instructions and had her cremated.

Nancy's ashes are in the bronze container, and next to the container is a little glass filled with water and freshly cut pansies, Nancy's favorite flower. We head down the back staircase into the gleaming sunshine-yellow kitchen. The back wall of the house has been moved, and a huge bay window now looks out onto the yard. The hurricane of Nancy's death has passed through Penny's life, and left this lovingly restored house in its wake.

Making choices about the renovation was difficult for Penny, who had never made major decisions without discussing them first with Nancy. It's the thing Penny misses most, talking to Nancy. She tried keeping a journal and writing to Nancy there, but it didn't work.

PENNY: I said some of the things I wanted to say to her, but ain't no one who can say the one-liners that she could say. That humor, that ability to make something funny. And the worse things got, the funnier she was. It brought out the best in her humor. And God knows we had a lot of times when things were pretty bleak in terms of her health. When the doctor told her that the cancer had spread to the lining of her brain—which we had hoped was just a terrible case of sinusitis—she said, despite the pain she was in, "Well, I guess what he just said to us is 'The good news is you're not going to die, the bad news is you're not going to die.'" That girl was in a lot of pain, but she always managed to find something funny.

Penny remains in mourning for the woman she loved, and will grieve for a long time to come. Nancy's place is still set at the dining room table, as if she's just stepped away for a moment. But enough time has passed for Penny to begin reflecting with a little distance on her splendid life with Nancy.

PENNY: I can't imagine anyone growing up the way I did. And to have had only one person that you ever loved, and for that to be the first person you ever loved, and to have that person love you back . . . It doesn't happen. I was very, very lucky.

Penny smiles broadly at the memory of her lifetime with Nancy. She holds Cricket tightly in her arms, and Cricket hungrily licks at the tears streaming down Penny's face.

TWENTY

What Is a Happy Relationship?

WHEN I INTERVIEWED the forty gay and lesbian couples, I saved two questions for last: "What is a happy relationship?" and "What is the secret to a happy relationship?" I didn't really think there was an adequate answer for either question, but as this book is about happy relationships, I thought these two questions were questions that I couldn't not ask.

In answering these questions, no one said that you had to have a lot of money to be a happy couple, although Patsy, of Lucy and Patsy, said that it helps if you don't have money problems. And no one said that a happy relationship had anything to do with how beautiful a partner was; as Bev, of Judy and Bev, said, "I'm sure there's somebody out there with a better body than Judy, but I'm never going to find someone with Judy's heart."

So what is a happy relationship? It's looking forward to your beloved getting home from work. It's loving and caring for each other. It's a relationship in which you're still individuals, as Alison and Dayna told me.

ALISON: To me it's one where each person can still be themselves. Dayna's not threatened by my outside interests. I can completely be myself with her, and she's herself with me.

Being oneself means not being afraid of being laughed at or judged by one's partner. It means being free enough to do the things you like doing, even though you may not like doing the same things. It's being able to say what's on your mind and to share things, which is important to Irene.

IRENE: A happy relationship to me is being comfortable in what you say and do. You don't have to hide anything, because you're not embarrassed by anything.

"Comfortable" is a word that came up many times. As one woman said, "A happy relationship is being comfortable to be yourself and not feel like you always have to prove something." It's also being comfortable enough in the relationship that you can relax and put your feet up. As Irene told me, "It's like you're home and there's no reason to leave." It's also the comfort of enjoying each other's company, as Jim and Martin have during their fifty years together.

JIM: Marty and I enjoy each other's company. That's very important. Some of the gay kids, they have to have crowds around them all the time. We don't have to have that.

MARTIN: Sometimes we don't see friends for days, and I'm just as happy. As long as we have each other, we do what we like to do, and just enjoy each other.

It's the comfort of knowing that you're not alone, that you have someone you love who loves you, someone with whom you can share the joys and sorrows of life and celebrate the milestones. That's how Ruth and Zenobia feel.

ZENOBIA: A happy relationship is a relationship without worry, just knowing that your partner is there for you no matter what. There's nothing and nobody in the world that I would trade Ruthie for, because she's there for me, a thousand percent. We've been through marriages, deaths, births, everything together. And I know that I'm gonna come home, and no matter what happened to me outside I can say, "Ruthie, you know what I did?" And she's gonna say, "It's all right."

RUTH: I'm gonna say, "You jerk!"

Ruth can't contain herself. She starts giggling, then laughing hard. I just know that if she ever in her life called Zenobia a jerk, it was probably wrapped in love and said with a smile. And Zenobia knows that, too.

ZENOBIA: You know she means, "You jerk, but I still love you." And a happy relationship is just knowing that we could do things together, or we could do them separate, and still be committed to one another.

RUTH: For me it's basically the same. Comfort, peace of mind, and we're on the same journey, but on different paths.

ZENOBIA: You never feel like you're by yourself. You don't have to go through anything by yourself. And that's the best feeling in the world, just knowing that she's there no matter what I go through. No matter how bad things are, I know that I have Ruthie, and I can talk to her.

Besides sharing their journey through life, most of the couples mentioned the importance of shared interests—like basketball for Jennifer and Brigid, volunteer work for Stewart and Stanley, and being fathers for Nate and Danny. Then there's the importance of shared thoughts and values, being with someone who really understands you. Pam and Lindsy know they'll generally have the same reactions to something someone said or something they've read.

PAM: After a party, if someone's said something that I think is outrageous, I know the instant we get into the car, we'll just look at each other and go, "Can you believe that?" We have the same reaction to it. Or if I read something in the newspaper that I think is absolutely outrageous, I know Lindsy will never be on the opposite side of the question.

Sharing values doesn't mean you're the same person. A happy relationship, many of the couples told me, means accepting that each of you is different. But acceptance is not easy. Lindsy still wishes Pam would do things that Pam isn't going to do.

LINDSY: I wish she would let her hair go gray. And I know she has many things that she wishes I would do.

PAM: Yeah, I wish she'd get off my back about my hair.

A happy relationship means giving your partner room to be himself or herself, something many of the couples continue to struggle with. It's also giving each other enough room to change and grow. Alison knows that change is inevitable.

ALISON: Dayna and I recognize that people grow and change. That's the big thing with a long-term relationship. I'm such a different person now at thirty-two than I was at twenty-three. Dayna's been able to be with me through all these changes. And Dayna's different than she used to be. We know that everything's not going to be exactly the same.

A happy relationship is also one in which the partners respect each other.

ANNE: I think a happy relationship is where there is a lot of respect, admiration, trust. There's nothing that confuses me more than to be sitting around with somebody who starts ragging on their spouse. Obviously, Cassandra could sit there and bitch about me for a little while.

CASSANDRA: But I don't. I wouldn't. I mean, if I'm sitting around with a close friend, I might say, "Anne really got on my nerves this morning." But to think about having enough grievances that I would criticize Anne to other people—to me, that's not a happy relationship.

A happy relationship also means understanding each other's strengths and weaknesses, and not using knowledge of those weaknesses as a weapon. It's a relationship in which the partners appreciate each other, communicate, and serve as each other's sounding boards. But communication doesn't necessarily mean *saying* something, as Kenneth sometimes has to point out to Keith.

KENNETH: Sometimes I have to remind him: "Right now I don't need you to say anything. I don't need you to judge. I don't need you to give advice. I need you to listen to me." And sometimes I have to bite my tongue and let him vent and rage, and just say, "Yeah, that must be hard," instead of saying, "Well what you ought to do . . ."

A happy relationship is also a matter of trust, something that is important for Dick, as he's grown increasingly dependent on John in recent years.

DICK: What is a happy relationship? I think it's the tranquillity that comes with the complete trustworthiness of the other person, so there are no surprising changes in behavior. A happy relationship is also helped by good manners and a respect for family.

It's family that has been the source of much happiness—as well as heartache—for Jim and Lane. They've raised Lane's son and cared for his elderly mother. And now there are Jim and Lane's two grandchildren.

JIM: I think having children has something to do with why we have a happy and strong relationship, and the fact that we've been through so damn much together. We're not ashamed to say that we're proud of ourselves for making it through what we've been through. We know that we've made good, honorable decisions regarding our family and our kids, our community, and our neighbors. We run an honest business that we're proud of, and we don't have to worry about it. I think all of those things together keep us going and keep us happy.

Jim and Lane also have fun together, as do all the couples in one way or another. Many of them mentioned the importance of humor as a part of their happy relationship. And humor certainly was in evidence during many of the interviews. Several couples wrote or called after the interview to tell me that in discussing all the challenges of their relationship, they'd forgotten to tell me how much *fun* they have, how they laugh together, and what an important part of their happy relationship this is. "Anybody without a sense of humor would be doomed," one person said.

Humor is one of the not-so-secret secrets of a happy relationship. And as Pam and Lindsy told me, none of the secrets is really so secret. Their younger lesbian friends are always asking them what the secret is to their happy, long-lasting relationship. "I get so angry," Lindsy said, "because people are always looking for easy answers. There are no true secrets, because we already know what it takes."

And what it takes are all the things—all the "secrets"—we've heard before, with a few very personal additions. For Andy and Matthew it's the six C words.

MATTHEW: Care, compromise, communication, commitment, compliments—

ANDY: And chocolate.

MATTHEW: Absolutely. But I think you also have to say "I love you" a lot to each other, to let each other know that whatever else might be hard or wrong doesn't get in the way of the most important thing, which is loving each other. I'm not saying you should say it if you don't believe it, but if you believe it, and you reinforce it by telling each other a lot, you let the other person constantly know that whatever else is a hassle in our lives, it's underneath and not on top of that basic element, which is loving each other.

Some of the other "secrets" of having a happy relationship are patience, tolerance, respect for and acceptance of each other's differences, allowing one's partner to be his or her own person, the flexibility to compromise and to ride the inevitable ups and downs, loyalty, trust, honesty, mutual admiration, being happy with yourself individually, and realistic expectations.

Realistic expectations is a tough one, but as many people told me, you have to accept that your partner is a real person, not a knight or a princess on a white horse. And you have to accept that your partner will inevitably grow and change, that not every moment will be happy, and that one person can never fulfill all of your needs, which is why having good friends is crucial.

For Jim and Martin, two of the secrets are spending time together and avoiding temptation.

JIM: I would never live with somebody that always wanted to take vacations alone. Because when you go out alone all the time—we've seen it—first thing you know, they're split up. Such a big temptation.

MARTIN: When you're happy with somebody, keep it that way. Why rock the boat? Straight people have so many restrictions on themselves. For gay people, it's so easy to have sex with a stranger or somebody you just met. I don't think it's that easy with straight people, so it's easier for them to stay together.

Cassandra and Anne's secrets include shared values and interests, but there's another essential ingredient.

CASSANDRA: There has to be joy. You know, just joy. And if there's no joy in a relationship, then how can it work? I look at Anne, I smile. Not all the time. Sometimes she calls me at work, and it's like, "I'm in the middle of something. Get off the phone and leave me alone."

ANNE: She's a very busy exec.

Two of Chris and Sherri's secrets are friendship and shared goals.

CHRIS: You have to be really good friends. You have to really like the person, who they are and what they stand for. You can't just love them. Love is a totally different thing. That's that gut emotion that you have, but the liking is extremely important.

SHERRI: Somebody who complements the things you do by the things they do. But you have to have the same basic moral sense, the same basic likes and dislikes, and the same goals in life. We have basically the same goal in life.

CHRIS: To be rich and famous.

SHERRI: No, it's not. Our goal is to provide the best we can for our son.

Many of the couples said that you have to appreciate each other, never take each other for granted, and don't assume it's just about sex. As Clarence told me, "You've got to remember that it's more than just a bedroom—it's more than that. And I think a lot of people forget that. They think that if I don't have sex, sex, sex, sex, sex, sex, then the relationship won't last. Well, that's not true."

Other secrets include taking pride in your partner, trying to be as gentle with your partner as you are with your friends, having a strong physical relationship—hugging, touching, kissing, et cetera—knowing how to enjoy the relationship, learning how to put up with each other's families, and never going to sleep angry—although some couples went to bed angry and woke up angry and lived to tell me about it.

Lucy and Patsy have been a couple for nearly twenty years, and Patsy offered the secret of shared history.

PATSY: By the time you've lived with somebody for a lot of years, you have developed a history. So we also have our own history as a cement, and I think that's a very important thing for young people to realize.

Another couple of secrets, which I think are perhaps two of the most important, are "Don't sweat the small stuff" and "You don't always have to be right." Stephanie knows there are times when it's better to say nothing.

STEPHANIE: Even when you know you're right, sometimes you have to let the other person be right if they have to be right. You have to learn to accept those kinds of things. If I were to argue with Lil every time she thought she was right even though she was wrong, we would never have made it this far.

Lilia said she didn't think she was ever wrong, but she didn't argue much with Stephanie's comment. Instead, she offered her own secret, which is being attentive.

LILIA: Always be on the watch for what your loved one needs. It might just be a small affectionate touch on the hand to say, "Hey, everything's okay." Or a good strong kiss, a real good, strong hug. But always be looking out to see how their day went. The little things mean more than the big stuff does.

One of the secrets several couples mentioned was luck, having the good fortune to meet one's partner in the first place. And one secret that almost everyone mentioned was work: A happy relationship takes work, and every relationship requires the effort and energy of both partners and a willingness to stick with it, even when it's a struggle. As Bev said, "I look at all these people that keep breaking up, and I don't know what it is. I think people are always looking for something better, instead of working with what they have."

Perhaps the single most important secret, the one I try to remind myself of every day, is to recognize that a relationship is about two people, not just yourself. That's what Stewart and Stanley told me is the secret of their relationship.

STANLEY: I feel that it's the same secret between a gay couple or a lesbian couple as a heterosexual couple. It's sharing. It's giving a little, taking a little. Because if everything is going to be all give and no take, if it's going to be only about me, me, me, it's not going to be a good relationship.

STEWART: I put my extra food on his plate to make sure he's had enough. Or he'll make a bigger lunch just to be sure I have enough to eat.

STANLEY: It's called caring. And as Stewart's mother has said many times, the basic thing in any relationship, besides caring, is loving each other.

Illustrations

Photographs taken by Eric Marcus at the homes of the subjects in 1997, except where noted.

CHAPTER ONE: Muriel and Anyda in the front yard of their summer home, 1996. *Photo by Lila Line.*

CHAPTER TWO: Jim and Martin.

CHAPTER THREE: Stanley and Stewart, 1997. *Photo by Casaso Productions.*

CHAPTER FOUR: Lee and Catherine.

CHAPTER FIVE: Alison and Dayna.

CHAPTER SIX: Jay and Gordon on the steps of their house, "Marion Castle," 1992. *Photo by Beth Bischoff.*

CHAPTER SEVEN: Bill and Stevie.

CHAPTER EIGHT: Chris and Sherri, with Taylor, 1997. *Photo by Sears Photo Studio.*

CHAPTER NINE: Stephanie and Lilia, with Noah, at the hospital on the day of his birth, 1997. *Photo from their collection.*

CHAPTER TEN: Pam and Lindsy, 1995. *Photo by Sigrid Estrada.*

CHAPTER ELEVEN: Jama and Amy, with Winston, 1997. *Photo by Gerlinde Hopkins.*

CHAPTER TWELVE: Lane and Jim.

CHAPTER THIRTEEN: Danny and Nate, with Sophie.

CHAPTER FOURTEEN: Ric and Clarence.

CHAPTER FIFTEEN: Marjorie and Marian.

CHAPTER SIXTEEN: Lucy and Patsy.

CHAPTER SEVENTEEN: Paul and Kevin.

CHAPTER EIGHTEEN: Dick and John, 1956. *Photo from their collection.* Dick and John in their garden, 1997. *Photo by Chuck Baker.*

CHAPTER NINETEEN: Penny and Nancy, 1987. *Photo taken by Cecilia at her party in Fall River, Massachusetts.* Penny, with Cricket.

CHAPTER TWENTY: Zenobia and Ruth.